Turning It On

Turning It On
A Reader in Women and Media

Edited by
Helen Baehr and Ann Gray

A member of the Hodder Headline Group
LONDON • NEW YORK • SYDNEY • AUCKLAND

First published in Great Britain 1996 by
Arnold, a member of the Hodder Headline Group
338 Euston Road, London NW1 3BH
175 Fifth Avenue, New York, NY 10010

Third impression 1997

Distributed exclusively in the USA by
St Martin's Press Inc.
175 Fifth Avenue, New York, NY 10010

British Library Cataloguing in Publication Data
A catalogue record for this book is available from the British Library

Library of Congress Cataloging-in-Publication Data
Turning it on : a reader in women and the media / [selection and
    editorial matter, Helen Baehr and Ann Gray].
        p.   cm.
    Includes bibliographical references and index.
    ISBN 0–340–63220–8. — ISBN 0–340–61396–3 (pbk.)
    1. Mass media and women.   I. Baehr, Helen.   II. Gray, Ann, 1946-.

    P94.5.W65T78   1996   95–37773
    302.23´082—dc20   CIP

ISBN 0 340 61396 3

Typeset by Anneset, Weston-super-Mare, Somerset
Printed and bound in Great Britain by J W Arrowsmith Ltd, Bristol

Especially for our students,
and for Paul Baehr and Nick Gray.

Contents

Acknowledgements

Compiling this reader has been an interesting and pleasurable exercise. Working collaboratively certainly relieves the isolation of much academic work and we have enjoyed discovering, and rediscovering, writings by women on the media. The selection under this cover is by no means definitive, but we believe it is representative of work in the area. We are indebted to the authors for giving permission to include their writing and apologise to them for the necessity to edit their work. This has been done for reasons of space and cuts are marked by the convention [. . .]. We would like to thank Ann Martin, Marie Kirwin, Lesley Riddle and our respective universities for their help and support. We also extend our heartfelt thanks to our female colleagues and to our friends in the industry and wish you well in making the changes which echo through this book.

We are grateful to the following for permission to reproduce copyright material: The American Film Institute for the extract from 'The rhythms of reception' by Tania Modleski, from *Regarding television: critical approaches*, edited by E. Ann Kaplan; Blackwell Publishers for the extract from *Women and soap opera* by Christine Geraghty; *Critical Sociology* for the extract from 'Research on sex roles in the mass media: toward a critical approach' by Noreene Z. Janus from *The Insurgent Sociologist* vol. 3, no. 7 (1977); Carfax Publishing Company, PO Box 25, Abingdon, Oxfordshire, OX14 3UE for 'Ideology, gender and popular radio' by Rosalind Gill, *Innovation* vol. 6, no. 3 (1993); HarperCollins Publishers for the extracts 'When a woman reads the news' by Patricia Holland, 'Behind closed doors: video recorders in the home' by Ann Gray and 'Firing a broadside' by Helen Baehr and Angela Spindler-Brown, from *Boxed in*, edited by Helen Baehr and Gillian Dyer (© Pandora 1987); Indiana University Press for the extract from 'Woman is an island: femininity and colonisation' by Judith Williamson from *Studies in entertainment* (pp. 99–118), edited by Tania Modleski; John Libby & Company Ltd for the extract 'Women on the air: community radio as a tool for feminist messages' by Birgitte Jallov taken from *The people's voice: local radio and television in Europe* (Academia Research Monograph 6, 1992) edited by Jankowski, Prehn and Stappers; Macmillan Press Limited for the extract 'A critical analysis of women's magazines' by Ros Ballaster, Margaret Beetham, Elizabeth Frazer and Sandra Hebron from *Women's worlds: ideology, femininity and the woman's magazine* and Macmillan Press Limited and St Martin's Press Incorporated for the extract from 'The cover: window to the future self' by Ellen McCracken from *Decoding women's mag-*

azines *from Mademoiselle to Ms. media, culture and society* for the extracts
'Identity in feminist television criticism' by Charlotte Brunsdon taken from
vol. 15 (1993) and 'Teenage girls reading *Jackie*' by Elizabeth Frazer taken
from vol. 9 (1987); Oxford University Press for the extracts 'Black feminist
and media criticism . . . ' by Jacqueline Bobo and Ellen Seiter, taken from
Screen vol. 32, No. 3 (Autumn 1991), 'Fruitful investigations: the case of the
successful lesbian text' by Hilary Hinds, from *Women: a cultural review* vol.
2, no. 2 (1991), 'Roseanne: unruly woman as domestic goddess' by Kathleen
K. Rowe, taken from *Screen* vol. 31, No. 4 (winter 1990); 'Viewdata: the television viewing habits of a young black woman in London' by Evelyn
Cauleta Reid, taken from *Screen* vol. 30, No. 1/2 (winter/spring 1989);
'What do people do all day? Class and gender in images of women' by Jo
Spence, taken from *Screen Education* vol. 29 (1978/9), 'Women's genres' by
Annette Kuhn, taken from *Screen* vol. 25, No. 1 (1984); Routledge for the
extracts from 'Don't treat us like we're so stupid and naive – towards an
ethnography of soap opera viewers' by Ellen Seiter *et al.*, in *Remote control:
television, audiences and cultural power*; from 'Housewives and the mass
media' by Dorothy Hobson, in *Culture, media, language*, edited by Stuart
Hall *et al.* (Unwin Hyman © 1980); and from 'Rethinking Stereotypes' by
T.E. Perkins in *Ideology and cultural production*, edited by M. Barrett, P.
Corrigan, A. Kuhn and J. Wolff; University of California Press for the
extract from *Unbearable weight: feminism, western culture, and the body* by
Susan Bordo, Copyright © 1993 The Regents of the University of California;
The University of Chicago Press for 'Women's depiction by the mass
media' by Gaye Tuchman, taken from *Signs* 4.3 (1979); Verso/New Left
Books for the extract from 'Feminism/Oedipus/postmodernism: the case
of MTV' by E. Ann Kaplan, taken from *Postmodernism and its discontents* by
E. Ann Kaplan.

Essence Magazine and Chaz Chiba for Fig. 3 in Chapter 7, copyright ©
1992 by *Essence* Communications, Inc.; Hulton Deutsch Collection for three
illustrations from *Picture Post* in Chapter 3; The Mary Boone Gallery for
Fig. 1 in Chapter 7, reprinted from *Love for sale: the words and pictures of
Barbara Kruger*.

Whilst every effort has been made to trace the owners of copyright material, in a few cases this has proved impossible and we take this opportunity to offer our apologies to any copyright-holders whose rights we may
have unwittingly infringed.

H.B and A.G.
February 1995

Introduction

Since the notorious media coverage of the bra-burning incident at the 1968 Miss America Pageant in Atlantic City, USA, a critique of the media has been central to the women's liberation movement. It is no coincidence that the development of a field of study which focuses on the media has paralleled the history of the women's movement. Just as feminism has developed from a politics based on a notion of a shared female experience into a recognition of difference and diversity, the terrain of feminist media studies has broadened out to produce more complex accounts of media representations and practices.

The title of this collection has an obvious meaning in relation to the electronic media. However, it is also intended to indicate our view of the impact of feminism on media and cultural studies. If there can be one single achievement of feminist media studies over the last two decades, it is that it is now impossible to make any sense of the mass media without paying attention to gender. The development of feminism within the academy has crossed disciplinary boundaries, such as communication and media studies, women's studies and cultural studies, and this has made available a variety of theoretical frameworks and approaches. It is the richness of this range that we aim to reflect in our selection of readings.

The idea for this book came from our own experience of teaching on media, communication and cultural studies courses. We observed that many of the texts we regularly recommend to students are published across a wide number of books, journals and periodicals. We hope that, by putting these essays under a single cover, we are accessing a range of texts which will be useful to both teachers and students. In making our selection, we decided not to include a whole body of important work on film and film theory which is readily available in other publications and collections. Nor are we attempting to provide an overview of the field of feminist media studies which is covered elsewhere (Baehr and Dyer, 1987; Steeves, 1987; Gallagher, 1992; Rakow, 1992; Creedon, 1993; van Zoonen, 1994).

As editors, we have chosen texts which reflect a plurality of approaches in order to show the richness and range of women's writing on the media. The reader encompasses a diversity of theoretical and methodological perspectives which aim to bring the question of women and media into sharper focus. Each piece has its own references and bibliography and we would recommend these to students for further reading. The book is organised into four sections: **I Representation**: image, sign, difference; **II**

Genre: textuality, femininity, feminism; **III Audience**: texts, subjects, contexts; and **IV Interventions**: industry, organisation, working practices.

Section I covers two decades of work on 'women and media', focusing on key shifts in feminist approaches to representation. It takes as its starting point some of the premises and limitations around studies of 'images' and 'stereotypes', highlighting the problematic of an assumed male/female opposition. It includes work which examines the relationship between women's economic subordination and the representation of this relation in the ideological domain.

Drawing on the theoretical framework of semiotics and structural linguistics, this section goes on to examine the feminist contribution to the debate on the ideological role of the mass media. The emphasis on language, as a socially produced system providing the rules and constraints within which all signification has to work, sees masculinity/femininity not as positional but as relatively unstable categories produced in relations of difference.

Section I ends by focusing on 'difference' and questions the notion of fixed or essential gender identities by emphasising the role of representation in the construction of feminine and masculine identities. It recognises the new developments in media and communication technologies as a major feature of postmodern society. Here the concept of identity itself is fragmented, fluid and open to change. There is a warning against a theoretical approach in which gender becomes one aspect of a matrix of subjectivity and is no longer a dimension of power.

Section II brings together issues raised by the concept 'women's genres' and the contribution made to its development by feminist work from different disciplinary areas. Feminist work on film, television, magazines and popular fiction has brought attention to genres which appeal to a female audience and readership. The growing interest in women's genres challenged much existing work which had overlooked, and even denigrated, 'female' forms such as soap opera and melodrama. Feminists analysed these forms in terms of their particular conventions and characteristics. The central concern with femininity and female identity draws attention to pleasure in the consumption of popular forms.

Section III introduces readers to feminist writing on viewing and consumption of media output, particularly in relation to meaning and pleasure. This work insists on the specificity of women's experience, especially in relation to the domestic, and explores the significance of popular forms in women's lives. Each of the pieces raises questions about methods of research and the need to look at the diversity within the female audience. They contribute greatly to the ongoing development of new feminist methodological frameworks.

Section IV looks at ways in which feminist praxis has challenged media representations of women. The essays describe a number of feminist interventions, some made within the media industry itself. The crucial question underlying all the pieces is how, or even whether, women's cultural practice can change media content. In analysing this, the essays address women's position in the media workforce; the pressures of 'professional' values and working practices; and the economic and institutional constraints on women working in media organisations. As feminists, we recognise that there is an urgent need to continue negotiating changes to the representations of women in the mainstream mass media. This section provides an insight into the important relationship between feminist producers and content and highlights the complex debate about what constitutes a specific women's perspective or aesthetic.

We are sure that those who are already interested in the development of work on 'women and media' will find this book useful. However, we also hope that by focusing on women's contribution to studies of the media, we will attract new readers to this rich seam of work.

References and further reading

BAEHR, H. and DYER, G. 1987: *Boxed in: women and television*. London: Pandora.

CREEDON, P. 1993: *Women in mass communication*. London: Sage.

GALLAGHER, M. 1992: Women and men in the media. *Communication Research Trends* 12 (1).

RAKOW, L. (ed.) 1992: *Women making meaning: new feminist directions in communication*. New York/London: Routledge.

STEEVES, H. 1987: Feminist theories and media studies. *Critical Studies in Mass Communication* 4, 95–135.

VAN ZOONEN, L. 1994: *Feminist media studies*. London: Sage.

Section I

Representation: image, sign, difference

This section comprises a diverse selection of essays broadly shaped by feminist writing on representation. This has not been an even or unified body of work, making it difficult to chart a direct route across its terrain (for detailed critiques see Steeves, 1987; Creedon, 1993; van Zoonen, 1994).

Feminist work on the study of representation has its roots in the women's movement of the 1960s and 1970s. It was this political impetus which in large measure shaped the academic agenda of a feminist critique of the media. The mass media were held to be deeply implicated in the patterns of discrimination operating against women in society (Friedan, 1963; Greer, 1971). Feminists involved in the study of media recognised the urgent need to specify a new area of enquiry – the representation of women.

Much of the early American evidence cited on 'images of women' in the mass media originated from a strain of American empirical social science which organised mass communications research around the concepts of 'effect' and 'function' (McQuail, 1987). This 'dominant paradigm' (Gitlin, 1978) looked at the short-term behavioural effects of the media, seeking 'hard data' and measuring content and effect through experiments and surveys. This research and its methodology has since come under severe attack because, it is argued, it deflects attention away from questions of media organisations and structures and the media's role in constructing, mediating and distributing 'social knowledge', i.e. their ideological role (Hall, 1977; Gitlin, 1978).

Many of the American studies published in the mid- to late 1970s on images and sex-role stereotyping were based on the mass communications tradition of quantitative and qualitative content analysis, which was designed to measure certain aspects of a media message. This body of research examined the different roles and stereotypes portrayed by men and women in media content. Regardless of the medium under examination, the conclusions drawn were very similar. In summary, they revealed that males dominated media content and that: 'roles of males in the mass media have been shown to be dominant, active and authoritative, while females have been shown to be submissive, passive and completely contented to subjugate their wills to the wills of media males' (Busby, 1975).

The early work on media images of women has been severely critiqued in recent accounts (Rakow, 1986; Ang and Hermes, 1991; van Zoonen, 1994). However, as Margaret Gallagher (1992) points out: 'Evaluated in historical context, its contribution is clear. Its disclosure and condemnation of sexism in media content provided a first, essential spring-board.'

The first two authors in this section, published in America in the late 1970s, were themselves beginning to question and criticise the dominant themes of images and stereotypes and some of the conventions and inbuilt assumptions of media sociology. They challenge a view of the media as simply a passive 'reflection' of society and propose a more complex view of the media, suggesting that the concept of representation is different from reflection.

Noreene Janus in 'Research on sex roles in the mass media: toward a critical approach' accuses certain studies of women's representation in the media of being consistent with a 'liberal feminist perspective' which sets up Male versus Female categories. The implication is that media content might be less sexist if women characters were shown to have the same occupational distribution as male characters. In her view, this perspective only leads to 'cosmetic' changes in the representation of women because it defines 'maleness' as the goal for women in media images.

She argues that traditional content analysis places its emphasis on the manifest content of the media at the expense of analysing media industries or content in terms of their 'latent ideological meanings'. Although recognising that quantitative content analysis can provide a useful tool in researching sex roles in the media, Janus warns that its uses are limited and its results should be interpreted with great care. Images of women and men are 'related to the fundamental structures of society' and the tendency of content analysis is to be 'ahistorical and apolitical' (for similar criticisms see Baehr, 1981; Mattelart, 1981).

The recognition of the problems of isolating media content from context is taken up by **Gaye Tuchman** in 'Women's depiction by the mass media', in which she examines the relationship between media images and of women and women's role in American society. She posits that women are under-represented, trivialised and condemned, in her phrase 'symbolically annihilated', by the media because of their lack of power. Addressing those feminists who complain about 'sexist images in the media', she replies that images of women cannot be assessed or judged in terms of how they 'reflect' or 'distort' reality. To argue that the media distort images of women assumes that the media should somehow reflect 'reality' as if they were a mirror on the world. To expect media to provide accurate representations of women is to oversimplify women's complex relationship with the media and the symbolic processes involved in representation.

Jo Spence, the British photographer, in her essay 'What do people do all day? Class and gender in images of women', looks at the visual representation of women in *Picture Post* during World War II. She argues that representations of women have to be understood within the context of their lack of economic power, and that the binary opposition male/female favoured in some studies of portrayal fails to take account of the equally important opposition of 'labour/capital'. By taking examples from the illustrated news magazine, Spence traces the 'ideological shifts' adopted by the media to accommodate the changing economic position of women during the war. Photographs of the time indicated that women had 'two jobs', that of paid worker and unpaid wife and mother. It is, however, the question of gender that is addressed by the images at the expense of the question of social class.

All the previous essays show sexual stereotyping is an organising principle in much of the work on representation. **Tessa Perkins** in 'Rethinking stereotypes' asks how certain female stereotypes come to be formed and how we come to recognise them. By analysing the material conditions of women's work in the home, the job of the housewife, she traces the 'ideological' meanings constructed around these everyday domestic tasks. Since society places a negative evaluation on housework, the skills women employ in the domestic sphere are characterised and evaluated negatively to form the basis for the stereotype of the 'irrational, illogical, inconsistent' woman. For Perkins, the strength of stereotypes lies in their combination of validity and distortion.

Judith Williamson's piece 'Woman is an island: femininity and colonisation' pursues the concept of ideology in terms of its major function within signification. Drawing on linguistics and semiotics, she argues that the categories 'masculinity' and 'femininity' operate on axes of 'difference' and are historically locatable. The main function of a dominant ideology is to contain contradiction and the most effective way of achieving this is by setting up difference. Mass culture, in her view, manifests dominant or hegemonic ideologies and, therefore, questions of power and class are always present. Williamson looks at the ways in which advertisement imagery, within a culture 'rooted in imperialism', represents difference and otherness with 'woman' as their main vehicle.

The next two pieces make a theoretical move into postmodern theories and explore their usefulness for theories of female representation, spectatorship and identity and for strategies for a feminist politics. **E. Ann Kaplan** in 'Feminism/Oedipus/postmodernism: the case of MTV', argues that Music Television is an appropriate case study, because its products are characteristic of what she describes as a postmodern television aesthetic. The question she poses is whether MTV's particular mix of 'modernist/avant-garde and popular aesthetic modes' transcend the binary oppositions of gender and offer relatively heterogeneous spectator positions. She sounds a note of warning against being seduced by the 'utopian' possibilities of the postmodern. She calls for feminist work to proceed strategically across a number of concerns within the production and analysis of culture.

A significant, if controversial, icon of female postmodernity is Madonna, who has attracted attention from feminist writers (Scwichtenberg, 1993). These writings are informed by poststructuralist theories of subjectivity, identity, power and the body. They tend to celebrate Madonna's transgressive and subversive potential as she apparently refuses one identity, but enters the playground of multiple identities. **Susan Bordo** in ' "Material Girl": the effacements of postmodern culture' argues that Madonna's different identities are embedded within a culture in which the female body is sexualised and objectified, thus their transgressive potential is contained. Bordo is sceptical of theories of the body and subjectivity which do not take account of their historical location. She insists that the body must be seen as a 'battleground whose self determination has to be fought for'. This is poignantly the case in relation to black identities in the face of the dominant white culture where celebrations of 'difference' are the result of a political struggle.

References and further reading

ANG, I. and HERMES, J. 1991: Gender and/in media consumption. In Curran, J. and Gurevitch, M. (eds.), *Mass media and society*. London: Edward Arnold.

BAEHR, H. 1981: The impact of feminism on Media Studies – Just another commercial break? In Spender, D. (ed.), *Men's studies modified*. London: Pergamon.

BUSBY, L. 1975: Sex role research in the media. *Journal of Communication* 25 (4).

CREEDON, P. 1993: *Women in mass communication*. London: Sage.

FRIEDAN, B. 1963: *The feminine mystique*. London: Penguin.

GALLAGHER, M. 1992: Women and men in the media. *Communication Research Trends* 12 (1). (Available from: The Centre for the Study of Communication & Culture (CSCC), 321 N. Spring, PO Box 56907, St Louis, MO, 63156–0907, USA.)

GITLIN, T. 1978: Media sociology: the dominant paradigm. *Theory and Society* 6. 205–53.

GREER, G. 1971: *The female eunuch*. London: Paladin.

HALL, S. 1977: Culture, the media and the 'ideological effect'. In Curran, J., Gurevitch, M. and Woollacott, J. (eds.), *Mass communication and society*. London: Edward Arnold.

MATTELART, M. 1981: *Women, media and crisis: femininity and disorder*. London: Comedia.

McQUAIL, D. 1987: *Introduction to mass communication theory*. London: Sage.

RAKOW, L. 1986: Rethinking gender research in communication. *Journal of Communication* 36, 11–26.

SCWICHTENBERG, C. (ed.) 1993: *The Madonna connection: representational politics, subcultural identities and cultural theory*. Boulder/San Francisco/Oxford: Westview Press.

STEEVES, H. 1987: Feminist theories and media studies. *Critical Studies in Mass Communication* 4, 95–135.

VAN ZOONEN, L. 1994: *Feminist media studies*. London: Sage.

1

Research on sex roles in the mass media: toward a critical approach

Noreene Z. Janus

From *The Insurgent Sociologist* 7, 19–32 (1977)

There is a growing concern within the U.S. feminist movement over the sexist content of our mass media. The purpose of this paper is twofold. First, the paper examines the theoretical framework of the research on women and the mass media in terms of a) the posing of the problem, b) the methodology used, c) the research questions asked, and d) the conclusions drawn. I will show that in each of these areas the research suffers from what might be called a 'liberal feminist' bias, and that this bias limits the usefulness of the analysis especially when studying the *changing* images of women. Liberal feminists, coming out of a tradition of bourgeois thought, have tended to attribute the recent changes in mass media portrayal of women to consciousness-raising and protest within the liberal democratic framework. This paper, however, demonstrates the need for a redefinition of the problem of sexism in the media from a more critical perspective. [...]

For the purposes of this analysis it is necessary to examine the term 'feminist movement' more closely. The feminist movement actually includes many different subgroupings with many different theoretical positions and policy approaches. It is possible, however, in spite of the variations, to distill a set of underlying assumptions which unite in a basic way most of the strands of the feminist movement today. These assumptions support what I shall call 'liberal feminism' [...]

Liberal feminists pose the problem as one of males against females within a system which oppresses and exploits women on the basis of their sex. They assume that this is a human universal and therefore tend not to question the origins and historical specificity of male–female roles in other societies. In light of this universal oppression of women, men, who own and operate the mass media in our society, are seen as perpetuating their own domination over women by transmitting sexist content. Women appear as housewives and sex objects in the mass media because the men who make the films, the ads, or TV like to see them in those roles.

The inadequacy of this approach is its limited and fragmentary understanding of the structures of our social life. Studying sexism apart from its social context, including mode of production and structures of political organization, leads to superficial hypotheses and misdirected research strategies.

The studies of women and the mass media have relied almost exclusively on the method of content analysis. For our purposes certain limiting characteristics of the method must be noted. First, content analysis is designed to measure certain aspects of a given unit of communication; the results of that measurement will, however, depend entirely on the objectives of the researcher, the way in which the research is set up, and the specific questions that are asked about the content. This implies that, contrary to the idea that a given method or technique of analysis will produce unbiased descriptions of the world, content analysis is constructed from the biases or ideological position of the researcher.

Further, the description is often a static one in which the image is described at only one point in time. When the method is used to describe content at more than one point in time, it may serve to detect a change in content but it cannot furnish an explanation for that change.

But, for our purposes, several of the most important characteristics of content analysis are summarized by Burgelin (1968). He lists the limitations of the method as, first, the fact that mere quantification of measurable symbols or units or communication provides no information as to how those isolated parts fit into the total structure of the larger communication picture, such as the page, the paragraph, the program or the film. 'Above all, there is no reason to assume that the item which recurs most frequently is the most important or the most significant, for a text is, clearly, a *structured* whole and the place occupied by the different elements is more important than the number of times they recur.' (Burgelin, 1972: pp. 313–28).

Secondly, he notes that traditional content analysis does not differentiate well between form and content and does not integrate the two levels of meaning into a common framework. For example, an automobile may be advertised with either a woman in a swimming suit or a well-dressed saleswoman. The form changes but the content remains basically the same and traditional content analysis typically registers the change in form as if it were a change in content.

The third limitation of traditional content analysis, and one which is of special interest to the study of women and the mass media, is that the method focuses only on the manifest content and ignores latent or ideological meanings of that manifest content. A woman appearing in an advertisement for example, may symbolize sexuality, stability, material well-being, or many other qualities, but in traditional content analysis only the woman's *visible* characteristics will be enumerated while the underlying meaning of her use as a symbol is ignored. Research tools for the analysis of signs and symbols at the ideological level are at an early stage of development and do not yield the type of hard quantitative results that content analysis does. However, by limiting the analysis to those aspects that *can* be reliably quantified with well-developed tools, one often ignores important larger theoretical issues.

The point is not, however, to completely reject content analysis as a method. It can be a useful tool when used with a critical understanding of its merits and its limits. Marxists recognize that content analysis yields a quantitative description of manifest content, studied as atomized and isolated elements at a given point in time, and must be interpreted as such; bourgeois social scientists generally do not.

The results of a content analysis depend entirely on the kinds of research questions asked, which in turn depend on the theoretical perspective one takes. The studies of women and the mass media ask questions that reflect a liberal feminist theoretical perspective since they set up male vs. female categories. All males are counted together as a general category and contrasted with an all-female category, with no reference made to the class, race or cultural divisions *within* each of these categories. Instead, the subjects are distinguished on the basis of visible personal traits (marital status, age, physical appearance and so forth). Consequently the questions are ahistorical, apolitical, and in no way indicate how the images of women or men are related to the fundamental structures of society.

A list of the major research questions and some of the representative results follows:

1. How frequently do female characters appear in the content as compared with male characters?
   Males were found to greatly outnumber females in prime-time television (Gerbner, 1972), in children's television (Long and Simon, 1974; and Sternglanz and Serbin, 1974), and newspaper photographs (Miller, 1975). Female characters were shown about as often as male characters in television soap operas (Downing, 1974; and Katzman, 1972).
2. What types of behavior patterns do female characters exhibit as compared with those of males?
   In television advertisements women clean, launder and cook while men give orders and advice and eat the meals (Cantor, 1974). In television soap operas males were more likely to discuss professional matters and deviant behavior while women were more likely to discuss romantic relationships, health and domestic matters (Katzman, 1972) and were more likely to take a negative tone in their discussions (Katzman, 1972).
3. What personality characteristics do females express as compared with males?
   In children's television males are significantly more aggressive, constructive, succorant (Sternglanz and Serbin, 1974), ambitious, bossy, unaffectionate, competitive, adventuresome, knowledgeable, active, independent, brave, strong, dominant, logical, impatient (Busby, 1974a) and competent (Women on Words and Images, 1975). Females are more often deferent (Sternglanz and Serbin, 1974), silly, weak, over-emotional and dependent on males (Busby, 1974b, Long and Simon, 1974), affectionate, romantic, passive (Busby, 1974). [...]
4. What types of commercial products do women represent as compared with those with men representatives?
   Females in both television and magazine advertisements were most often shown representing cleaning products, food products, cosmetics, clothing and home appliances. Males were most often shown representing cars, travel, banks, industrial products, entertainment media (and

alcohol and cigarettes in magazines) (Courtney and Lockeretz, 1971; Dominick and Rauch, 1972; Cantor, 1974; Toronto Women's Media Committee, 1973).

These research questions imply that media content might be less sexist if:

(a) women characters were shown to have the same occupational distribution as male characters;
(b) women were shown advertising the same types of products as men;
(c) the marital and parental status of women were shown to the same degree as for men;
(d) women's voices were used for the voiceovers in advertisements to the same extent as men's.

These studies, then, are consistent with the liberal feminist objective of integrating women into the present system on an equal basis with men. The characteristics associated with 'maleness' in media images are those which have been defined implicitly as the goal for women in media images. This interpretation of the problem of sexism in the media carries through to the conclusions that are drawn from the studies listed above.

Liberal feminist research has in fact conclusively demonstrated that men and women of mass media content are not equal. However, the form and content of that demonstration (the posing of the problem, the methodology, the questions asked, and the conclusions drawn), being generated by the liberal feminist framework, lend themselves to a reaffirmation of the very framework which produced them. Their research emerges from and supports their same theoretical perspective. For example, even while they often recognize that the objectification of women's sexuality has been economically profitable to industries and advertisers (Friedan, 1963; Komisar, 1971; Ventura, 1974), they nevertheless hold that its major purpose is to uphold the most fundamental division in society – that based on sex. [...]

A liberal feminist, believing that the most important social division is between men and women, may set up research measuring the men against women and then conclude that the research proves that the sexual division is the most fundamental. [...]

The problem of sexism in the media must not be seen in terms of males oppressing females without at the same time demonstrating the historical development of sexism and its present relationship to capitalist relations of production. Male chauvinism must be seen as a very powerful mechanism for enforcing and perpetuating the class system and, hence, we must study the role of the media in the relationship between women and capitalism, rather than its role in the relationship between women and men.

The methodology employed must emerge from and reflect the manner in which the problem of sexism in the media is posed. It must go beyond the mere description of manifest content by studying the media as industries subject to the laws of capitalism and as transmitters of ideology which reproduce that system. When media content is studied, the individual units of analysis must be seen in relation to the whole message. Furthermore, those individual symbols must be studied not only in terms of their manifest content, but also for their latent ideological meanings. Then the entire message, analyzed from this holistic approach, must be placed within the context of the structures of capitalism. We might combine some of the techniques of content analysis with other techniques of analysis of content such as semiology, the study of signs and symbols. And content analysis would profit greatly by being carried out together with other forms of social analysis. For example, the changing images of women might be studied and correlated with a study of female participation in the labor force. [...]

A critical perspective will demonstrate not only that the women in the media are inferior to men, but also the limited and demeaning image of women are structurally related to the functioning of capitalism. The liberal feminist explanation of the *changing* images of women will be shown to be inadequate in that it deals with only the *passive* responses of the media to one limited level of the contradiction posed by women in society. Moreover, the liberal feminist strategy to change the media images of women, being based on an inadequate theoretical framework, have only encouraged media creators to make mere marginal or cosmetic changes – changes that are, in any case, consistent with and limited by ruling class hegemony.

References

BURGELIN, Oliver 1972: Structural analysis and mass communication. In McQuail, Denis (ed.), *Sociology of mass communications.* Middlesex, England: Penguin.

BUSBY, Linda J. 1974a: Mass media research needs: a media target for feminists. *The University of Michigan Papers in Women's Studies 1.*

— 1974b: *Sex roles as presented in commercial network television programs directed toward children: rationale and analysis.* PhD dissertation, University of Michigan.

— 1975: Sex-role research on the mass media. *Journal of Communication* 25 (4).

CANTOR, Muriel 1974: Comparison of tasks and roles of males and females in commercials aired by WRC-TV during composite week. In National Organization for Women, National Capitol Area Chapter, *Women in the wasteland fight back: a report on the image of women portrayed in TV programming.*

COURTNEY, A.E. and LOCKERETZ, S.W. 1971: Woman's place: an analysis of the roles portrayed by women in magazine advertisements. *Journal of Marketing Research* 8, February.

DOMINICK, Joseph R. and RAUCH, Gail E. 1972: The image of women in network TV commercials. *Journal of Broadcasting* 16 (3).

DOWNING, Mildred 1974: Heroine of the daytime serial. *Journal of Communication* 24 (2).

FRIEDAN, Betty 1963: *The feminine mystique.* New York: Dell.

GERBNER, George 1972: Violence in television drama: trends and symbolic functions. In *Television and social behavior.* Washington DC: U.S. Government Printing Office.

KATZMAN, Natan 1972: Television soap operas: what's been going on anyway? *Public Opinion Quarterly* 36 (2).

KOMISAR, Lucy 1971: The image of women in advertising. In Gornick, V. and Moran, B. (eds.), *Woman in sexist society.* New York: Basic Books.

LONG, Michael L. and SIMON, Rita J. 1974: The roles and statuses of women on children and family TV programs. *Journalism Quarterly* 51 (1).

MILLER, Susan H. 1975: The content of news photos: women's and men's roles. *Journalism Quarterly* 52 (1).

STERNGLANZ, S.H. and SERBIN, L. 1974: An analysis of the sex roles presented on children's television programs. *Developmental Psychology* 10 (5).

TORONTO WOMEN'S MEDIA COMMITTEE 1973: Images of women in Toronto Area television commercials. Unpublished.

VENTURA, Charlene 1974: The impact of the women's liberation movement on advertising trends. Xerox.

WOMEN ON WORDS AND IMAGES 1975: *Channeling children*. P.O. Box 2163, Princeton, New Jersey 08540.

2

Women's depiction by the mass media

Gaye Tuchman

From *Signs: Journal of Women in Culture and Society* 3, 528–42 (1979)

[...] An issue tackled by the nascent women's movement was the relation-ship between images of women in the mass media and social roles. Betty Friedan based *The Feminine Mystique* in part on a content analysis of women's magazines.[1] As early as 1967 some consciousness-raising groups sought to excise media stereotypes from their collective understanding of gender roles and stratification. During this same period other women, seek-ing concrete feminist projects and influenced by concern for children's development, examined materials aimed at youngsters.

Needless to say, all these activities assumed that images of women in the mass media have some sort of detrimental impact upon both individual consciousness and collective social life. That tenet permeates feminist actions, such as the challenge to WRC-TV's license mounted by the National Organization for Women, journalistic commentaries, and academic research.[2] [...]

Practical, like the field from which it derives, recent work on the media has tried to locate facts with which to flesh out a quasi-political attack on sexism in the media, its origins and impact. The argument ordering those facts explicitly concerns 'who,' 'what,' and 'with what effect' and is also implicit in Friedan's book, the NOW challenge to WRC-TV, journalistic work, and reviews of the existing literature by Busby, Janus, the U.S. Com-mission on Civil Rights, and myself.[3] It assumes a direct correspondence among media organizations, their content, and the everyday world. It states:

1. Few women hold positions of power in media organizations, and so:
2. The content of the media distorts women's status in the social world. The media do not present women who are viable role models, and therefore:
3. The media's deleterious role models, when internalized, prevent and impede female accomplishments. They also encourage both women and men to define women in terms of men (as sex objects) or in the context of the family (as wives and mothers).

   Although politically useful, this argument is mired in a naive literalness and propounds a theory of a vulgar and odd mimesis, that is, reality really will mirror the media. Consider the core of the argument: The media distort women's status in the social world and do not present viable role models.

[...] To be sure, there appear to be some differences between yesterday's and today's media, particularly with regard to minorities. However, minority women, about 2.9 percent of the people on television, are concentrated in family-centered situation comedies. But at least they now appear on television; in the early 1960s, the regular presence of a black woman on a prime-time show contributed to its cancellation. However, mere presence does not suffice. Lemon points out that on some shows men dominated women so much that the regular appearance of a female co-star seemed to increase the male dominance.[4] Presence also enables the reiteration of stereotypes: Dominance patterns in interactions on prime-time television contrast the 'black matriarch' with the less forceful position of the white woman within her family. And, the mass media so assume male superiority that men even give more advice about personal entanglements on the soap operas than women do. This finding seems particularly significant, because the soap operas[5] come closer to presenting a pseudoegalitarian world than other television programs and most other media.

Too frequently, the term used to characterize these findings is 'distortion.' Both political and pejorative, the term itself seems to transmute the literary theory of realism. However, the idea that a literature reflects its society is transformed into the statement that the media should reflect society and the charge that contemporary media do not properly reflect the position of women. Citing demography and data on the labor force and on family structure, and contrasting the presentation of men with that of women, studies imply there should be a direct, discernible correspondence between the depiction of women in the media and contemporary life. By political references to our culture's normative expectations that news should transcend distortion, the dominant models of women's presentation in the media suggest that entertainment *should* also be a veridical reproduction of social life, an accurate representation [...].

However, the very underrepresentation of women, including their stereotypic portrayal, may symbolically capture the position of women in American society – their real lack of power. It bespeaks their 'symbolic annihilation' by the media. For, according to Gerbner, just as representation in the media signifies social existence, so too underrepresentation and (by extension) trivialization and condemnation indicate symbolic annihilation.[6]

Gerbner's concept is more politically sensitive than the cry of distortion. Interacting with their environment, social movements seek fresh tactics to gain new or modified goals, and their environment, including the media, may seek to repel, consolidate, or coopt those efforts. Gerbner sees the gross statistical similarities between today's and yesterday's media as indicators of the media's espousal of the politics of cultural resistance.[7] Rather than keeping pace with, say, the increased participation of women in the labor force, the media discredit, isolate, and undercut: They discuss 'women's libbers,' present issues of liberation on shows distasteful to a general audience, and muddy the distinction between women's liberation and sexual liberation. Ever alert and energetic, they transform and absorb dissent.

Yet, although the idea of symbolic annihilation seems to be a theoretical advance, it too has been used to advocate a naively literal notion of mimesis.

There are two dominant explanations of the media's sexism, women's position in media organizations, and the socioeconomic organization of the media. The first both cites the wrong evidence and ignores pertinent existing evidence.[8] The second assumes that the media will change essentially as the status of women improves.[9]

Some researchers have announced or implied that the media offer a deleterious portrait of women because few women hold positions of responsibility within the media. Most of the data thought to support this explanation concern television stations and the networks. Following a spurt of hiring women around 1970, the increase in women holding administrative positions at television stations has fallen off. Although it is difficult to determine, because the forms designed by the Federal Communications Commission permit a minority woman to be counted twice, women and minorities seem to have similar patterns of authority: Both tend to be in such dead-end jobs as affirmative action officer, to be marginal to the organizational chart, and to be primarily supervising other women and minorities. Evidence of discrimination in hiring and promotion was strong enough for women employees to have won lawsuits or achieved substantial out-of-court settlements from each of the three television networks.

None of this evidence indicates that discrimination in employment leads to the symbolic annihilation of women. As Cantor points out, these data mostly pertain to television stations, but decisions about programming are dominated by the networks, and the programs themselves are made by production companies which are technically independent of the networks.[10] Furthermore, sensitivity to affirmative action and a concern with how women are presented do not necessarily indicate that a corporation is free of sexism. The Public Broadcasting Corporation charged Isber and Cantor to prepare a report on its personnel and programs, which revealed an insistent definition of women as a special interest group and a consistent display of sex stereotypes.[11] Yet the corporation did not significantly change its policies. Equally important, the content and staffing characteristic of other media indicate that women frequently create 'sexist' content.

Consider journalists. Using survey data, Phillips finds that women's judgments about general news resemble those of men.[12] Merritt and Gross affirm that female editors of women's pages have virtually the same priorities and preferences as their male counterparts.[13] According to Orwant and Cantor's study of journalism students, women seem to have the same stereotypes of women as men do. Although these women students are interested in politics, not the traditional content of the women's pages, they believe that they are unusual and that other women are interested in the traditional fare.[14] In part the maintenance of stereotypes derives from the culture (an unfortunately diffuse explanation), in part from professionalism. Even when women do see a topic differently from men, professionalism limits the possible presentations and defuses radical critiques.[15] More generally, it is difficult for women employees to resist ideas and attitudes associated with success in their profession, even if those ideas disparage women, for sexism, like racism, is best understood as an institutional, not a personal, phenomenon.

The second explanation for media sexism, the socioeconomic organization of the media, appears to be more sensitive to institutional issues. For instance, it records that professionalism serves organizational interests in both journalism and entertainment. One observational study finds that both male and female members of a talk show may elicit sexist comments from celebrities in the preinterview preparatory to the network show; both may seek to defuse expressions of feminism in order to appease stations airing their program, much as they also seek to blunt other radical critiques.[16] For television writers, professionalism includes not offending the networks. And, the development of professionalism in the media is associated with the growth of the media as complex and capitalist bureaucracies. [...]

Notes

1. Betty Friedan, *The Feminine Mystique* (New York: Dell Books, 1963).
2. National Organization for Women (National Capitol Area Chapter), *Women in the Wasteland Fight Back* (Washington, D.C.: NOW, 1972).
3. Linda Busby, 'Sex-Role Research on the Mass Media,' *Journal of Communication* 25, no. 4 (1975): 107–31; Noreene Janus, 'Research on Sex Roles in the Mass Media,' *Insurgent Sociologist* 7 (Summer 1977): 19–31; U.S. Commission on Civil Rights, *Window Dressing on the Set* (Washington, D.C.: Government Printing Office, 1977); and Gaye Tuchman, 'Introduction: The Symbolic Annihilation of Women by the Mass Media,' in *Hearth and Home: Images of Women in the Mass Media*, ed. Gay Tuchman, Arlene Kaplan Daniels, and James Benét (New York: Oxford University Press, 1978). Useful references may also be found in Maurine Beasley and Sheila Silver, *Women in Media: A Documentary Source Book* (Washington, D.C.: Women's Institute for Freedom of the Press, 1977); Marion Marzolf, *Up from the Footnote: A History of Women Journalists* (New York: Hastings House, 1977); and Matilda Butler and William Paisley, *Women and the Mass Media: A Sourcebook* (New York: Human Sciences Press, 1979).
4. Judith Lemon, 'Dominant or Dominated? Women on Prime-Time Television,' in Tuchman *et al.*, pp. 51–68.
5. Joseph Turow, 'Advising and Ordering: Daytime, Primetime,' *Journal of Communication* 24, no. 2 (1974): 138–41.
6. George Gerbner, 'Violence in Television Drama: Trends and Symbolic Functions,' in *Media Content and Control: Television and Social Behavior* ed. George C. Comstock and Eli A. Rubinstein (Washington, D.C.: Government Printing Office, 1972), 28–187. The extension is developed in Tuchman, 'The Symbolic Annihilation of Women.'
7. George Gerbner, 'The Dynamics of Cultural Resistance,' in Tuchman *et al.*
8. This material is reviewed by Muriel Cantor, 'Will More Women Make a Difference? A Sociological Perspective on Employment and Portrayal in Television,' prepared for Telecommunications Policy Research Conference (Arlie, Virginia, May 11, 1978).
9. This criticism is raised by Janus of the 'reflection hypothesis' developed in Tuchman, 'Symbolic Annihilation of Women.'

10. See n. 8.
11. See Isber and Cantor; and Muriel Cantor, 'Where Are the Women in Public Broadcasting?' in Tuchman *et al.*
12. E. Barbara Phillips, 'The Artists of Everyday Life: Journalists, Their Craft and Their Consciousness' (Ph.D. diss., Syracuse University, 1975).
13. Sharyne Merritt and Harriet Gross, 'Women's Page/Life Style Editors: Does Sex Make a Difference?' *Journalism Quarterly,* vol. 55 (August 1978).
14. Jack E. Orwant and Muriel Cantor, 'How Sex Stereotyping Affects Perceptions of News Preferences,' *Journalism Quarterly* 54 (Spring 1977): 99–108, 139.
15. Gaye Tuchman, 'The Topic of the Women's Movement,' in *Making News: A Study in the Construction of Knowledge* (New York: Free Press, 1978).
16. Gaye Tuchman, 'Assembling a Television Talk Show,' in *The TV Establishment: Programming for Power and Profit*, ed. Gaye Tuchman (Englewood Cliffs, N.J.: Prentice-Hall Spectrum, 1974).

3

What do people do all day? Class and gender in images of women

Jo Spence

From *Screen Education* 29, 29–45 (1978–79)

This article follows on from the ideas about 'Ideology, Photography and Education' outlined by Terry Dennett and myself in *Screen Education* 21. Those were worked through as part of the collective work of Photography Workshop, a group of photographers developing radical photographic theory and practice. One of the group's current projects is to analyse representations of different types of labour, both historical and contemporary. [...] What this makes clear is the necessity of extending the ways in which representations of women are studied.

Much of the work in this area has been based on two concepts:

1. that woman is signified in relation to the male: there is a binary opposition within systems of signification in which what is present is definable only in relation to what is absent;[1] and
3. that we decode images by looking at what is present in the image itself, trying to locate its various 'signs and meanings'.

Such approaches have sometimes undervalued the ways that the meaning of an image is determined by the historical and institutional context of its production and reception.[2] In looking at images of women, they may also concentrate solely on the binary opposition male/female at the expense of other possible oppositions, notably that of labour/capital. Usually the woman's symbolic lack (of the phallus) and her exclusion from the patriarchal order have been stressed: but can the concept of woman as sign also illuminate her place in the 'symbolic order' of capitalism? In other words, I want to broaden the question of decoding images of women to take into account not just the symbolic sexual lack, but also the exploitation of women's labour power under capitalism.

[...] This is important in trying to understand the connection between changes in the ways that women's labour power is exploited in the labour process, and changes in visual representations of women.

Some light can be shed on this relationship by looking at the special case of how women were pictured in World War II, especially as these images are so often trotted out as evidence as some sort of past achievement for women. This 'case study' comes out of some more general research which has included looking at the illustrated news magazine *Picture Post* from its inception in October 1938 through to 1947. It is possible to see some clear shifts in the ways that women were represented there during that time.

One effect of the war was to make the National Government intervene far more directly in the social division of labour than it had done before – specifically, it had to mobilise large numbers of women into the workforce. By 1941, as women were increasingly exhorted to 'go to work in the factories', it is not surprising to find many more representations (like Fig. 3.1) in which the primary signification of *women as labour* is clearly indicated both in image and text. These appeared in *Picture Post*'s news and feature stories. The old ideas about women did not disappear, though. The need for 'beauty' had been a running thread in early *Picture Post* editorials. In February 1941, a Woman's Editor was appointed to provide articles of 'interest to women', dealing with 'fashion, beauty, decoration, sewing and knitting, cooking, gardening, ideas for comfort...stressing the words beauty and comfort'. So the idea of woman as domestic and narcissistic was only displaced in the separate features on women in industry and in the armed forces. (Women's 'sexuality' also seemed to be hived off, in this case into articles about women in show business. These continued to use the traditional types of display.)

What about the advertisements in *Picture Post*? They often used news-type photographs or realist line drawings and it didn't take long for specific class stereotypes to emerge – the industrial worker (like the woman at her lathe in Fig. 3.2), the land girl, the bus conductress. The advertisers took up the theme of women at war with great gusto. Advertisements showed woman doing two jobs and filled out the 'human detail' that news

Fig. 3.1 *Picture Post* 5.7.41

Picture Post, February 21, 1942

THE MEN CALL HER "MUSCLE"!
Mother of three saws two-ton gun barrels—then does the washing

MRS. ELSIE RAMSCAR is known as "Muscle" in the North-Western war factory where she does a man's job sawing gun barrels weighing 2 tons apiece.

"Hard work keeps you young, I reckon," she says. She wants to keep young for the sake of a very nice husband in the Forces!

Mrs. Ramscar lives near the factory, so goes home to get dinner for her three children—all school age. The washing she fits in according to her "shifts."

She does it the Rinso no-boil way—lets the clothes soak for 12 minutes in Rinso and hot water from the tap. Even her dirty overalls come clean without boiling if she smooths a little dry Rinso on the worst places. "This method saves me an hour and a half's hard work," says Mrs. Ramscar.

Hitler can't win so long as women like Elsie Ramscar keep a happy home around them while they make the weapons to defend it!

R. S. Hudson Limited

Fig. 3.2   *Picture Post* 21.2.42

and feature stories couldn't handle. They offered products which would enable her to function better as a 'working mother', keep her health, safety and strength up, to do the washing and cooking more quickly. Although the research from which these examples are drawn is still incomplete, it is possible to show at this stage that there were clear differences between representations of the same stereotype. I would relate these to the distinction between the point of production (the *labour* represented in the news) and the point of consumption represented in the advertisements. To do that, it is necessary to examine the ideological shifts involved.

Particularly valuable in this research has been Stuart Hall's article on *Picture Post*, in which he comments on the limitations of the news photograph.

> 'Its (*Picture Post*'s) "social eye" was a clear lens. But its "political" eye was far less decisive. It pinpointed exploitation, misery and social abuse, but always in a language which defined these as "problems" to be tackled with energy and goodwill. It never found a way ... of relating the *surface images* of these problems to their structural foundation.'[3]

Looking at the illustration from *Picture Post* in the light of this concept of 'limitation', we can get some idea of how some advertisements have been *doubly* stripped of their potential 'meanings'. News photographs like Fig. 3.1 cannot reveal that while women were being conscripted and coerced in the name of patriotism to enter the labour force, their average pay packet was just half that of men. It cannot show that it was illegal to strike, or that (as an article in May 1944 reported) nearly 24,000 workers were prosecuted for industrial offences not punishable before the war, and 1,807 actually sent to jail.

A typical advertisement (like Fig. 3.2) *shows* a woman at work, contributing to the war effort. But, bearing its 'limitations' in mind again, it is possible to read it differently. Not only is the woman producing surplus value for someone else and being encouraged to 'buy back' the commodities produced by workers like herself: as a 'mother of three' she is assumed to perform unpaid domestic labour and reproduce the future workforce needed for capitalist production. Such images do suggest quite clearly that industrial needs for changes in the social division of labour had some effect on the types of images of women that were produced during the war. This also seems to be borne out by what happened after it finished. Just as the 'new' images emerged when women were needed in the labour force, so the idea of 'two jobs' soon collapsed back into 'one job' when women were encouraged to re-enter the domestic sphere during the massive task of re-employing demobbed labour. (See Fig. 3.3.)

Of course the war *was* a special case – the historical socio-economic determinants of particular stereotypes are seldom so blatant. But it does underline the potential usefulness of the binary opposition labour/capital as well as that of male/female. At this stage, it is difficult to be precise about signification of class in these examples. For a start we are dealing with women from *many* social backgrounds, some of whom had previously been confined to the domestic sphere. (We can be sure, though, that working class women actually got working class jobs.) Then, as now, women inhabited different social and economic spheres – the world of home (reproduction) and the world of work (production) – and the ways in which 'class' was signalled were very different in each of them. With the onset of war the depictions of extremes in social classes became less pronounced, and there

Fig. 3.3 *Picture Post* 16.2.46

were regularly features showing women at work. Nonetheless, the repertoire of signs connoting class (or class power) is far more limited than those
connoting gender. Class relations are *structural* and, therefore, in visual
terms, 'absent': they were, in Hall's terms, beyond the scope of *Picture Post*'s
'political' eye. A class *identity*, though, is – like sexuality – constructed
through a system of representation. [...]

Notes

1. I am using the term 'sign' in its semiotic sense. The sign consists of two inter-
   locking elements: the *signifier* (the visual 'thing' itself) and the *signified* (the
   'meaning(s)' which can be read off). For a stringent analysis of 'the sign' see J.
   Williamson, *Decoding Advertisements* (Boyars, 1978); on its relation to women in
   particular, see E. Cowie, 'Woman as Sign' in *m/f* 1 1978.
2. On such determinants of production see J. Tagg, 'The Currency of the Photograph' in *Screen Education* 28 Autumn 1978; on those of reception, see S. Hall,
   'Encoding and Decoding in the TV Discourse' (Birmingham CCCS Stencilled
   Paper 7).
3. S. Hall, 'The Social Eye of *Picture Post*', in *Working Papers in Cultural Studies* 2 (my
   emphasis).

4

Rethinking stereotypes

T.E. Perkins

From M. Barrett, P. Corrigan, A. Kuhn and J. Wolff (eds.), *Ideology and cultural production* (Croom Helm 1979)

[...] The work situation of the housewife is such that she develops the capacity to cope with several things at once and learns not to concentrate on one thing so hard that she is not aware of what else is going on and cannot switch skills instantaneously. It will not encourage the capacity for analytical (critical) thought but will call considerably on the emotional side of her personality and for quick emotional responses. Her organisational skills may be highly developed in a limited area. Similarly, the work situation of a manual worker will encourage a decline in his/her capacity for creative or critical thought, while that of a junior executive will exercise his/her decision making capacity and necessarily develop 'human-relation' skills related to his/her position of authority (that is, leadership skills).

These are gross oversimplifications no doubt, but illustrative of the sort of determining influences material conditions have on consciousness. In each situation there are factors which counteract these tendencies, but they are weaker and tend either to be non-typical features of the work situation, or to be typical but subject to social sanctions thereby weakening their potential influence. These three examples illustrate one of the ways in which stereotypes are structurally reinforced. Part of the stereotype of women concerns their inability to concentrate on one issue at a time, their mental flightiness, scattiness and so on. In the middle of a conversation about one issue they skip to something completely different. This is all part of the 'irrational, illogical, inconsistent' (female logic) stereotype. Now what this seems to me to relate to is a mode of thinking which is essential to the housewife's job. Most other jobs demand concentration on a single issue and the application of one skill at a time; the capacity to keep shifting attention back and forth, and changing skills, is characteristic of a housewife's job. What the stereotype does is to identify this feature of the woman's job situation, place a negative evaluation on it, and then establish it as an innate female characteristic, thus inverting its status so that it becomes a cause rather than an effect. It is these features of stereotypes which explain why stereotypes appear to be false – indeed, *are* false. The point at the moment is to identify their validity, because the strength of stereotypes lies in this combination of validity and distortion.

Whether or not I am correct in identifying this capacity as one which is produced by the housewife's situation is something only research could tell us. Undoubtedly it is a difference which cartoonists recognise, as shown by all those cartoons of father sitting at the breakfast table immersed in the newspaper while all hell lets loose around him. This characterisation of women as incapable of sticking to a single topic is a good example of flexibility – gross exaggerations occur in comedy and cartoons – but a more realistic version is used in everyday life.

[...] Stereotypes short-circuit critical thinking; their effectiveness depends in part on our willingness to short-circuit. Our willingness derives from two things: firstly, it may simply make life easier, more convenient; the other is that information may be limited and our critical faculties may be underdeveloped, and effectively we may often have no other choice but to short-circuit. This is true of all of us sometimes. But the more limited our knowledge and training then the greater the area will be where short-circuiting is the only solution. This characteristic of stereotypes appears to locate them firmly in the area of 'common sense', one of whose distinguishing features, according to Gramsci, is its unworked-out character. However, though this may be their main arena, we cannot limit our analysis of stereotypes to this level. Common sense also contains 'scientific ideas' and 'philosophical currents'. So too do stereotypes and our understanding of their location in systematic worked out ideology, in legislation and so on, is essential to an understanding of how they function ideologically.

[...] I have said that stereotypes are often 'valid'; that they are often effective in so far as people define themselves in terms of the stereotypes about them; that they are structurally reinforced; that they refer to role performances, and so on. However, having said all this there are important senses in which stereotypes are inaccurate or false. [...] Stereotypes are similar to ideology in that they are both (apparently) true and (really) false at the same time. [...] Two main points about their falsity are to be made: Firstly, stereotypes present interpretations of groups which conceal the 'real' cause of the group's attributes and confirm the legitimacy of the group's oppressed position. Secondly, stereotypes are selective descriptions of particularly significant or problematic areas and to that extent they are exaggerations.

[...] Stereotypes are selective descriptions – they select those features which have particular ideological significance. Hence, remarkably few stereotypes refer to such qualities as kindness, compassion, integrity – or even honesty (nor their opposites). Personality traits can be subdivided into: mental, sexual and personal. However it is the mental attributes which are definitive and which seem to 'dictate' the rest of the content. Other attributes become linked to mental characteristics in a non-reciprocal way. Dumb does not imply dirty; 'dirty' as a social description does imply 'stupidity'. The reason mental characteristics are dominant is that they are ideologically the most significant (and therefore convincing). Briefly, economic differentiation is the most important differentiation. The ideological criterion for economic differentiation in our capitalist society is primarily intelligence; and only secondly 'contribution' to the society and possession of skills which are necessary but 'supposedly' scarce (for example, decision-making, responsibility, leadership qualities). The most important and the *common* feature of the stereotypes of the major structural groups relates to their mental abilities. In each case the oppressed group is characterised as innately less intelligent. It is particularly important for our ideology that attributes should be conceived of as being innate characteristics either of human nature in general (competitiveness) or of women/men/blacks in particular, since this supports the belief that they are not the effect of the socioeconomic system (and the order of things appears to be inevitable – the survival of the fittest and may the best man win). The fact that stereotypes do so often present attributes as if they were 'natural' is not a feature of stereotyping *per se*, so much as an indication that they are ideological concepts. [...]

5

Woman is an island: femininity and colonisation

Judith Williamson

From Tania Modleski (ed.), *Studies in entertainment* (Indiana University Press 1986)

[...] Living in liberal democracies, we are accustomed to 'difference' appearing as a form of validation – whether in the form of 'balance' as we are shown opposing points of view in controversial TV programs, or in the form of 'choice,' as we are able to choose between different brands of corn-flakes when shopping. The whole drive of our society is toward displaying as much difference as possible within it while eliminating where at all possible what is different from it: the supreme trick of bourgeois ideology is to be able to produce its opposite out of its own hat. And those differences represented within, which our culture so liberally offers, are to a great extent reconstructions of captured external differences. Our culture, deeply rooted in imperialism, needs to destroy genuine difference, to capture what is beyond its reach; at the same time, it needs *constructs* of difference in order to signify itself at all. What I intend to focus on is not just the representation of difference and otherness within mass culture, but on the main *vehicle* for this representation: 'Woman.' (Fig. 5.1)

[...] In our society women stand for the side of life that seems to be outside history – for personal relationships, love and sex – so that these aspects of life actually seem to become 'women's areas.' But they are also, broadly speaking, the arena of 'mass culture.' Much of mass culture takes place, or is consumed, in the 'feminine' spheres of leisure, family or personal life, and the home; and it also focuses on these as the subject matter of its representations. The ideological point about these areas, the domain of both 'the feminine' and 'mass culture,' is that they function across class divisions. If ideology is to represent differences while drawing attention away from social inequality and class struggle, what better than to emphasize differences which cut across class – the 'eternal' sexual differences – or those which are bigger than class, like nationality? The most likely Other for a white working-class man, is either a woman [...] or a foreigner – in particular somebody black. It is *not* likely to be someone from the class which controls his livelihood.

So one of the most important aspects of 'femininity' in mass culture is not what they reveal, but what they conceal. If 'woman' means home, love, and sex, what 'woman' *doesn't* mean, in general currency, is work, class, and

Fig. 5.1 The fashion for tans shows most clearly of all the necessity of difference in producing meaning, and also reveals how the relation of ideological phenomena to production is frequently central to their meaning (despite the supposed outdating of this concept within contemporary Marxism). When the nature of most people's productive work, outdoors, made a suntan the norm for working people, a pale skin was much prized, a mark of luxury: not just a symbol but an indexical sign of leisure time, a measure of distance from the masses' way of life. Now, however, a deep suntan stands for exactly the same things – leisure, wealth, and distance – for it must involve not being at work for the majority of people, and therefore suggests having the wealth for both leisure and travel.

In fact, this ad for Ambre Solaire offers you self-tanning lotion which doesn't require hours in the sun; however, the fake tan it produces only has a meaning because it does suggest time in the sun, leisure, etc. It is typical within ideology that the method of the product, the self-tanning, actually denies what it means, which is 'real suntan' – making the inaccessible accessible, while simultaneously boasting that it is uniquely hard to obtain. In theory, anyone and everyone could buy fake-tan lotion and get a tan, yet the tan still represents difference, as the caption shows.

There is another kind of difference which this provocative caption completely ignores. 'Isn't it nice to be brown when everyone else is white?' Yes, but only if you were white to start with. The racism of a white colonial society isn't very nice.

politics. This is not to suggest that domestic, personal or sexual dimensions of life are not political: far from it. It is just that questions of class power frequently hide behind the omnipresent and indisputable gender difference, the individual fascination of which overrides political and social divisions we might prefer to forget. [...] In mass culture this phenomenon appeared in, for example, the Valentine's Day headline of the *Daily Mirror* – 'Mr

Britain, This is Your Wife' – with a series of mother and child photos that were successfully non-specific in terms of class, standing for a universal/national wife and motherhood. In academic circles the same syndrome is often equally apparent in the stress on sexual (rather than class) interpellation, in the concern with the construction of the (raceless, classless) gendered subject, and above all, in the current preoccupation with 'desire.' Obviously these areas are important, yet the focus on them seems to have gone hand in hand with neglect of other issues. For example, speech and writing have as much to do with class as with 'desire.' But sexuality and 'desire' are special to us *all*. [...]

As soon as one stops talking about 'masculinity' and 'femininity' as timeless psychoanalytic universals and looks at the particular historical structures which have led up to our present culture, the idea of a sort of 'pure'

Fig. 5.2 These two posters provide a perfect example of the division between male-work-social and female-leisure-natural. The ad for beer shows a man in a hard hat, obviously thirsty from work, consuming a pint of Harp lager. He is presented as culturally specific: it would be possible to guess his job within perhaps half a dozen guesses — construction worker, engineer, builder, oil worker: someone who works outdoors in a blue denim shirt. Firmly located in time and place, his clothes show that he could only be in the present; and he is fair-skinned, blond, obviously a white American or European.

The advertisement for Colman's mustard on the left is the flip-side of the lager ad. Despite the fact that the woman in it appears to be eating a piece of Kentucky Fried Chicken, she herself is the feast that is offered. Her pose places her not as consumer, but as up for consumption: though her remark is addressed to the product, her body is addressed to the passing viewer. Sprawled on a tiger skin in front of an ornate but historically unplaceable fireplace, she is, like it, waiting to be lit, and a leopard is bringing her the mustard from back right of frame.

We are back to jungle imagery, the tiger and leopard suggesting a wildness and sexuality that are quite outside culture (even though they are awaiting a cultural product, the Colman's mustard, to burst into flame). The woman is fairly dark and not easy to place ☞

signification of difference evaporates, and we can see *what* differences are expressed by the m/f divide.[1] We live today to a great extent in carefully divided spheres: work/leisure, public/private, political/domestic, economic life/emotional life, and so on. (Fig. 5.2.) The political value of these divisions is manifest. If there is a strike (the sphere of work/politics), then 'ordinary people,' 'housewives,' 'consumers' (those in the domestic/individual sphere) suffer. The fact that the same people literally straddle both spheres becomes forgotten. [...] But it is difference that makes meaning possible, and though in reality these spheres are *not* separate, it is their separation into sort of ideological pairs that gives them meaning. What 'home' means to a working man is something opposite to work, though for a woman whose work-place it is, it may *not* have the same meaning of 'leisure.' One of the reasons mass culture is so little concerned with work

either historically or geographically: she has a slightly Eastern appearance, but is impossible to locate in time. Although she is surrounded by cultural accoutrements, they are ones which signify wildness and exoticism, making them appear natural and connecting her sexuality and availability with the natural instincts of the beasts. Sexual difference is suggested in that her surroundings are far from 'feminine': it is unlikely that she killed the tiger whose skin she is lying on, and whoever did is presumably the masculine presence (or absence) which is required to light her fire. Femininity needs the 'other' in order to function, even as it provides 'otherness.'

A fire to be lit, and a fire to be put out: he needs the product with a drive that comes from his own masculinity, his activity at work; while she needs the product to bring alive her universal femininity, which is represented as passive and completely separate from the social world. He is a particular man: she is Woman, femininity, all women. But her placement with the wild beasts, *outside* culture, conversely places her culture, the culture of the Colman's mustard, *within nature*. The social construct of female 'sexuality' does not appear as class-specific; it offers each and every one of us a hot line back to the wild, an escape from the mundane problems of the present.

or political movements is that most people turn on the TV to forget about these things. This obvious but important point is frequently overlooked by those of us whose work it is to observe and write about mass culture, as the function of these artifacts in daily life tends to be overshadowed by the process of detailed textual analysis. This rigid separation of work and leisure *feels* necessary because, since most of working life is so exploitative and much of social and political life so oppressive, people want to 'get away from it all.'

Not only are activities divided: the drive to escape into personal life arises from the way that values are divided too in equally schizophrenic fashion, so that all the things society claims to value in private and family life (caring, sharing, freedom, choice, personal development) – the kind of values that every tabloid runs its human warmth or heartbreak stories on – are regarded as entirely inappropriate in the sphere of political, social and economic life. Their lack there can be covered up, however, by locating these qualities in women and in the family, as cornerstones of our culture. Women, the guardians of 'personal life,' become a kind of dumping ground for all the values society wants off its back but must be perceived to cherish: a function rather like a zoo, or nature reserve, whereby a culture can proudly proclaim its inclusion of precisely what it has *ex*cluded. It is as if Western capitalism can hold up an image of freedom and fulfillment and say, 'look, our system offers this!' while in fact the reason these values are squeezed into personal life (and a tight squeeze it is, too) is that they are exactly what the economic system fundamentally negates, based as it is on the values of competition and profit, producing lack of control, lack of choice and alienation. In this sea of exploitation it does indeed appear that *Woman Is an Island*. (Fig. 5.3.)

Thus, while we seem to have little choice over, for example, nuclear weapons, we tend to think of ourselves as having freedom or happiness inasmuch as these qualities are manifested in our personal lives, the part of life represented by femininity. And the sphere which is supposedly most different from the capitalist system is crucial to it, both economically and in producing its meanings. The family provides the most lucrative market for modern consumer economies; in Britain 80% of all shopping is done by women. The 'natural' phenomena of the family and sexuality throw back an image of a 'natural' economy, while the economy penetrates and indeed constructs these 'natural' and 'personal' areas through a mass of products – liberally offering us our own bodies as sites of difference [. . .].

It is in consuming that we appear to have choice, and in personal relations that we appear to have freedom. As long as women are carrying those values individually, *for* society, they do not have to be put into operation socially. Women who protest 'as women' against the bomb are either engaging in a very effective use of society's own values against itself or accepting society's ideologial definition of themselves as inherently more caring. Whatever their uses, the values of interpersonal relations, feeling, and caring are loaded onto women in direct proportion to their off-loading from the realities of social and economic activity.

This can be seen in everyday terms, as the 'personal life' that is set up in opposition to work becomes the justification for work: men (as if only men

Fig. 5.3 Woman and colony become completely confused here: Fiji is an island but has been appropriated as nothing but a perfume; while the wearer of perfume, Woman, has been turned into an island, generalized, non-specific, but reeking of exoticism. The feminine and the exotic are perfectly merged, as both are colonized by The French Quarter, which wraps its red, white and blue flag round the lot. (The picture is bordered in red, white and blue, the same colors as on the tie of the 'Q' around the bottom left caption.) Woman is an island because she is mysterious, distant, a place to take a holiday; but she is also an island within ideology – surrounded and isolated, as the colony is by the colonizer, held intact as the 'Other' within a sea of sameness. If Fidji can be wrapped up in the chic French scarf of femininity, femininity is equally enclosed, gift-wrapped within culture, not as one of its own products but as a package tour of the natural.

go out to work) are exhorted to work harder, so as to earn more, so as to insure their home and family, invest for their children, enhance their leisure time, buy more exciting holidays, etc. The daily grind appears meaningful only because of the life outside it. The social structure is justified not in social but in personal and individual terms. This shows how separation and difference, the opposition between terms, produce meaning not just in theory but in day-to-day life. Similarly, the idea of 'woman' and the 'personal' as a repository for the values society wants to be rid of can be seen literally in current social policies in Britain – policies which have deliberately replaced social services for the handicapped and elderly with the explicit assumption that women will perform these services individually, unpaid, in the home. The government then seems to be the champion of the individual, the home, and family – which is exactly where it is dumping its unwanted burden! This illustrates in practice the separation of sign and referent: the 'return to the family' *stands* for something quite different from the hardship, disguised as responsibility, which is in fact being 'returned' to real families.

If this kind of 'concrete semiotics' seems a little far-fetched, one might ask what other kind of semiotics could possibly be of any use politically? I see a Marxist semiotics as an enterprise that tries to understand both a structure and its content – concerned with a system of meaning, but one whose meanings function within actual historical systems. The need of our society both to engulf Others and to exploit 'otherness' is not only a structural and ideological phenomenon; it has been at the root of the very development of capitalism, founded as it is on the imperialist relations [. . .] If woman is the great Other in the psychology of patriarchal capitalist culture, the Other on which that culture has depended for its very existence is the colony which [. . .] it needed simultaneously to exploit and to destroy. Capitalism is not a system which can function alone in equilibrium. It always needs some imbalance, something other than itself: riddled with contradictions, it is not internally sufficient. Our current standard of living derives in part from the incredibly cheap labor exploited by multinational companies in 'developing countries,' which produce many of our consumer goods on wages that would be unacceptable to us, and from the control of markets internationally. Western banks make enormous loans, at enormous interest, to impoverished [. . .] countries. Economically, we need the Other, even as politically we seek to eliminate it.

So, with colonial economies as with the family, capitalism feeds on different value systems and takes control of them, while nourishing their symbolic differences from itself. The 'natural' and 'exotic', the mystery of foreign places and people, appear both as separate from our own culture and as its most exciting product [. . .]. Travel and holiday advertising offers us the rest of the world in commodity form, always represented as completely different from the fast pace of Western 'culture,' yet apparently easily packaged by it nonetheless. Rather as, in individual psychology, the repressed, instead of disappearing, is represented or replaced by a symptom or dream image, so in global terms different systems of production (colonial, feudal) which are *sup*pressed by capitalism are then incorporated into its imagery and ideological values: as 'otherness,' old-fashioned, charming, exotic, natural, primitive, universal. (Fig. 5.4.)

What is taken away in reality, then, is re-presented in image and ideology so that *it stands for itself* after it has actually ceased to exist. The travel images of 'colorful customs,' of exotic cultures, of people apparently more 'natural' than ourselves but at the same time expressing our own 'naturalness' for us – all these images of 'otherness' have as their referent an actual Otherness which was and is still being systematically destroyed, first by European then by American capital. Yet it is the *idea* of 'natural' and 'basic' cultures which seems to guarantee the permanence (and, ironically, the uni-

Fig. 5.4 This woman-in-sea-with-garland image is the typical representation of the exotic; conversely, femininity is represented by the 'woman of the islands': half-naked, dark-haired, tanned. Yet her features make her equally likely to be a white American or European woman who has *acquired* the 'natural tan of the islands.' It is striking that the deep-tan advertising genre, and the exotic 'southern' images, never use either African-looking models or politically contentious places: in this ad 'the islands' are obviously Hawaii, but in general there are many imaginary 'islands' in make-up, suntan, and perfume ads which serve to represent an 'other' place and culture without actually having to recognize any real other country and its culture. The 'desert island' is the ideal location for the 'other'; it is more easily colonized than an entire continent (the early capitalist pioneer Robinson Crusoe did well in this respect) and picturing the colony as female makes it so much more conquerable and receptive.

Of course, when the caption offers its product 'to all skin types for a safe, dark, natural tan' it doesn't really mean a 'natural tan.' If one were naturally dark, of course, one would be black — a contingency not anticipated by the ad, which clearly does *not* address 'all skin types' but, like almost all public imagery, assumes its audience to be white.

versality) of capitalist culture. It is the value system of our own society that we 'read off' other societies; we seek to naturalize our own power structures in the mirror of 'natural' life as pictured outside capitalism. Other societies can be used in the same way that the family is used to show work without revealing class; little wonder that, for example, car advertising selects so many images of women and peasants, since their labor can be presented as 'natural' and autonomous.[2] But just as the commodity which expresses another's value loses its own identity in the process, so those 'primitives' – women and foreigners – who are so valuable in reflecting capitalism's view of itself are robbed of their own meanings and speech, indeed are reduced to the function of commodities. We are the culture that knows no 'other,' and yet can offer myriad others, all of which seem to reflect, as if they were merely surfaces, our own supposed natural and universal qualities. To have something 'different' captive in our midst reassures us of the liberality of our own system and provides a way of re-presenting real difference in tamed form. [...] We do not like real Others but need to construct safe ones out of the relics of the Others we have destroyed – like the Stepford Wives, the perfect, robotically feminine wives manufactured by the men of Stepford from selected components of their original, human wives. The real women are killed in the process. [...]

Notes

In reprinting these extracts from Judith Williamson's article, the editors have changed the order in which some of the illustrations appear and have done so by permission of the author.

1. In her article, 'Woman as Sign,' in *m/f* no. 1 (1978), Elizabeth Cowie explores the place of women as bearers of meaning in societies from both a psychoanalytic and an anthropological point of view. However, in locating 'woman' as a sign produced entirely through exchange, her argument becomes tautological, as women come to signify nothing but difference, and difference is signified simply through the fact that women are exchanged while men are not. 'Woman is produced as a sign within exchange systems in as much as she is the signifier of a difference in relation to men, i.e., women are exchanged rather than men.... The position of women as sign in exchange therefore has no relation to *why* women are exchanged, in other words, it has no relation to the "idea" of women in society' (p. 56). This particular analysis, which is important in that it was one of the first to examine women not as signified but as sign, stops short at the formal production of the sign and never looks at what that sign means, the content of the signifying system. What woman the sign means, according to this account, is the concept 'woman,' which in itself means simply exchangeability.
2. I have gone into this argument in more detail in 'The History of Photographs Mislaid', *Photography/Politics: One* (London: Photography Workshop, 1979).

6

Feminism/Oedipus/postmodernism: the case of MTV

E. Ann Kaplan

From her (ed.) *Postmodernism and its discontents* (Verso 1988)

[...] I want to explore the implications of postmodernism as a putative new cultural moment, as a theoretical and critical concept, and as a variously valued (anti-)aesthetic for feminist theories of narrative as sketched briefly above, particularly in the light of Craig Owens's observation that discussions of sexual difference have been signally absent from writings about postmodernism.[1] How does postmodernism as a theory and as deployed in popular culture affect feminist theory and aesthetic practice?[2] Does postmodernism change female representation, female spectatorship? Does it hinder or advance feminist cultural aims? I will consider these questions through the optic of Music Television as a postmodern cultural institution: specific rock videos exhibited on the channel will help to clarify theoretical points.

[...] Music Television [...] is a commercial station, produced and exhibited within a profit-making institution. Its postmodern (anti-)aesthetic strategies need to be considered within that larger context rather than in and for themselves. If some of the devices approximate those used in the 'utopian' postmodern texts, we must nevertheless ask if such a text can be produced within the commercial framework.

Several critics who include popular texts in their discussion of the 'utopian' postmodern appear to accept that possibility. Some apply to the latter area theories not originally developed with popular culture in mind; or they use a theorist like Bakhtin, who wrote about a very different kind of popular culture preceding mechanization. Indeed, many such scholars look to Bakhtin as the one thinker who can provide a theoretical opening to a utopian text or to cultural alternatives.[3] Bakhtin's concept of dialogism, as rewritten by Kristeva, has seemed particularly useful in avoiding the traps and dead-ends of binarism. As is well known, the early Kristeva searches for a text where sex and other differences are transcended, where the metaphysical category of difference no longer exists: we see this in her concept of the 'semiotic' and in her reworking of Bakhtin's notion of the carnivalesque, 'where discourse attains its "potential infinity" ... where prohibitions (representation, "monologism") and their transgression (dream, body, "dialogism") coexist'.[4] It is what she finds in Sollers's *H* which is 'music that is inscribed in language, becoming the object of its own reasoning, ceaselessly, and until saturated, overflowing, and dazzling sense has been exhausted ... It whisks you from your comfortable position; it breaches a gust of dizziness into you, but lucidity returns at once, along with music [...]'. (p. 7).

Similarly, the following theorists seem to be agreed in imagining a kind of art that does not take its shape from running counter to the dominant system, but is anti-essentialist, plural, where discourses are not hierarchically ordered, where sex and other differences are transcended, where the metaphysical category of difference no longer exists. This is what White and Stallybrass demand when they note the need for a concept of carnival to be linked to notions of transgression and symbolic inversion if it is to designate 'not just an infraction of binary structures, but movement into an absolutely negative space beyond the structure of significance itself'.[5]

This is what Lyotard is reaching for in his rejection of the master narratives of the past, and in his nostalgic attempt to return to something preceding modernism but nevertheless beyond it;[6] Robert Stam similarly envisions 'a fundamentally non-unitary, constantly shifting cultural field in which the most varied discourses exist in shifting multi-valenced oppositional relationships'.[7] And it seems to be what Fred Pfeil has in mind in his discussion of possibilities within what he calls 'the culture of the PMC' (i.e. the Professional-Managerial Class), when he hopes that 'much of what we now call postmodernism might be turned and engaged in more progressive political directions [...]'. Pfeil is fully aware that the figurations he has in mind 'are at present no more than trace elements of a dream whose concrete realization would require on all sides enormous amounts of hard work and painful struggle'.[8]

Recently certain feminist film and literary theorists have begun to consider this same option. Teresa de Lauretis, for example, speaks about the need for texts that construct a new aesthetic in a specific female and heterogeneous address – an address which insists on a series of different spectator positions through which one becomes involved in a process toward subjectivity, rather than being fixed.[9] And Alice Jardine has raised the possibilities for new ways of thinking woman in her exploration of 'gynesis' as this has been recently deployed in texts by French male theorists.[10]

This sort of utopian postmodernism builds on, and carries to its own subversive ends, certain strands of high modernism. Not all modernism was co-opted into mainstream culture: resistant trends (Eisenstein, Buñuel, Brecht – what Paul Willemen calls the 'true' avant-garde because it subverted art's autonomy in favor of a reintegration of art and life)[11] may be seen as precursors of the utopian postmodern briefly outlined above.

Let me now return to the question of whether this sort of art can ever be produced within dominant *commercial* culture: if not, how does the commercial institutional context constrain meanings and influence reception? The question is complicated because what is new about much recent popular culture – especially MTV – and what marks it as different from high modernism is the very intermingling of modernist/avant-garde and popular aesthetic modes that may also be characteristic of the 'utopian' postmodern. Some theorists (e.g. Stam and Pfeil) obviously believe that commercial culture provides at least limited space for a subversive post-modern, although they are scarcely clear about precisely what aesthetic terrain they have in mind when they speak about the utopian possibilites. We can imagine texts which transcend binary categories within an avant-garde context of production and exhibition (largely the terrain on which people like Kristeva, Cixous, de Lauretis think); but I am wary of such claims being made for the sphere of popular culture as it exists at present. Or at least, we need to address the contradictions and constraints of any 'spaces' we may find in mass texts. Do mixings of the popular and the avant-garde transcend binary oppositions or decenter the subject in a way that leads to something new? Or are they rather an example of Baudrillard's implosion or collapsing of meanings into something undesirable?

The answer to this question is intricately tied to one's theory about the TV apparatus. This phrase refers to the complex of elements including the machine itself and its various sites of reception from the living-room to the bathroom; its technological features (the way it produces and presents images); its mixture of texts, inclusion of ads, commentaries, displays; the central relationship of programming to the sponsors, whose own texts, the ads, are arguably the *real* TV texts;[12] the unbounded nature of the texts and reception; the range of potentialities one can produce through operating the machine.

Baudrillard's image is compelling: 'With the television image – television being the ultimate and perfect object for this era – our own body and the whole surrounding universe become a control screen.'[13] Situated in the illusory position of mastery and control, the spectator can play with various possibilities, none of which, however, makes the slightest difference to anything. Have we (as Baudrillard would argue) replaced Marx's 'drama of alienation' with the 'ecstasy of communication', and Freud's old 'hot sexual obscenity' with 'the contactual and motivational obscenity of today'?[14] Is TV, as Kroker and Cook argue, 'the real world of postmodern culture which has *entertainment* as its ideology, the *spectacle* as the emblematic sign of the commodity form, *lifestyle advertising* as its popular psychology, pure, empty *seriality* as the bond which unites the simulacrum of the audience, *electronic images* as its most dynamic, and only form of social cohesion ... the diffusion of a *network of relational power* as its real product'?[15]

I am persuaded by much of Baudrillard's and Kroker's and Cook's scenario for where high culture is headed, and the role the TV and the computer screens play in it. The somewhat complicit vision in texts like *Blade Runner, Videodrome* and *Max Headroom* on the one hand, or the more subversive one in those like *The Man Who Fell to Earth* or *Brazil*, no longer seem impossible. I agree with Kroker that the enemy is partly liberal humanist philosophy with its easy compromises and denials; but I have trouble with Baudrillard's notion that the resistance of the object (i.e. 'infantilism, hyper-conformism, total dependence, passivity, idiocy') is the proper response to the dangerous 'hegemony of meaning'.[16] In either case, however, once the signifiers have been freed from their signifieds, once the fixed frameworks and constraints of traditional gender-based genres have been relinquished, we have no way of controlling what comes into the space Both positive and negative things may happen, particularly for women.

MTV is a useful area within which to debate competing claims about postmodernism, and by which to distinguish the postmodern from the transgressive text. It also provides an occasion to ask how we can create a popular culture that will move beyond dominant binary oppositions (and the classical realism within which such binarisms are encased), without the collapse of oppositions being recuperated through their reduction to empty surfaces.

Many rock videos have been seen as postmodern insofar as they abandon the usual binary oppositions on which dominant culture depends.[17] That is, videos are said to forsake the usual oppositions between high and low culture; between masculine and feminine; between established literary and filmic genres; between past, present and future; between the private and the public sphere; between verbal and visual hierarchies; between realism and anti-realism, etc. This has important implications for the question of narrative as feminists have been theorizing it, in that these strategies violate the paradigm pitting a classical narrative against an avant-garde anti-narrative, the one supposedly embodying complicit, the other subversive, ideologies. The rock video reveals the error in trying to align an aesthetic strategy with any particular ideology, since all kinds of positions emerge from an astounding mixture of narrative/anti-narrative/non-narrative devices. The five video types I have outlined elsewhere in an effort to organize the multitude of rock videos on the channel are only broad categories that by no means cover all the various possible combinations of narrational strategies.[18]

Narrative/non-narrative is no longer a useful category within which to discuss videos. What is important is, first, whether or not any position manifests itself across the hectic, often incoherent flow of signifiers which are not necessarily organized into a chain that produces a signified, and, second, what are the implications of the twenty-four-hour flow of short (four-minute or less) texts that all more or less function as ads.

In line with Baudrillard's theory, MTV partly exploits the imaginary desires allowed free play through the various sixties liberation movements, divesting them, for commercial reasons, of their originally revolutionary implications.[19] The apparatus itself, in its construction of a decentered, fragmented spectator through the rapid flow of short segments, easily reduces politics to the 'radical chic' (USA For Africa) or the pornographic (Rolling Stones' 'She Was Hot').

Yet, paradoxically, MTV's chosen format of short texts enables exhibition of thematic and aesthetic positions that criticize the status quo. That is, MTV's twenty-four-hour rapid flow of short segments on the one hand renders all of its texts 'postmodern' because of the manner of their exhibition (i.e. a stream of jumbled, hectic signifiers for which no signified was intended or has time to be communicated; the reduction of all to surfaces/textures/sounds/the visceral and kinaesthetic; the hypnotizing of the spectator into an exitless, schizophrenic stance by the unceasing image series); yet, on the other hand, if we rather artificially 'stop the flow', we can find individual texts that in their four-minute airplay do offer subversive subject positions.

Since the subject positions the channel offers are important for the female spectator, let me 'stop the flow' for the purposes of analysis, fully aware that what one finds in this process differs from what one experiences as a 'normal' spectator. The existence of alternative subject positions is theoretically important, even if such positions are normally swept up in the plethora of more oppressive ones. Hence, I will look briefly at strategies in a typical 'postmodern' video having negative results for women, and then at videos leaning in the avant-garde, transgressive direction descending from high modernism and opening up useful space for the female spectator.

Take for instance Tom Petty and the Heartbreakers' 'Don't Come Around Here No More'. This video, like many others, stands in a strange intertextual relationship to a well-known original – here Lewis Carroll's *Alice In Wonderland*. The text cannot be labelled 'parody' in the modernist sense that Jameson has outlined: and yet it is clearly playing off the original. It thus falls between parody and actually moving beyond the binarisms of conventional narrative. The issue of the gaze becomes confused: we have a sense of the text playing with oedipal positionings in the apparent sadism enacted on Alice's body, in the monstrous father torturing the child; but it deflects this reading by the semi-comic, self-conscious stance it takes toward what it is doing, and by the brilliance of its visual strategies. One becomes entranced by the visual and aural dimensions, which overwhelm all others. One holds in abeyance the reaching for a signified and is absorbed in the surfaces/textures/shapes/sounds which dominate reception channels.

The pastiche mode makes it difficult to say that the text is taking a sado-masochistic pleasure in violence against women, so that while the imagery offends the female spectator she fears she is being trapped into taking it too seriously. The video just might be intending reference to the sadism in the original *Alice*; it might even be 'exposing' male abuse of the female body through the grotesque image of Alice's body being eaten as cake. But one cannot be sure. The spectator is made to doubt through this sort of play, which characterizes the co-opted postmodern.

Madonna's successful 'Material Girl' positions the spectator equally uncomfortably, while not addressing or moving beyond established polarities in the manner of the utopian text. 'Material Girl' stands in a strange intertextual relationship to Howard Hawks's film, *Gentlemen Prefer Blondes*. It offers a pastiche of Monroe's 'Diamonds Are a Girl's Best Friend' number, while declining any critical comment upon that text. In this video, Madonna may be said to represent a postmodern feminist stance by combining seductiveness with a gutsy kind of independence. She incorporates the qualities of both Jane Russell and Monroe in Hawks's film, creating a self-confident, unabashedly sexual image that is far more aggressive than those of the Hollywood stars.

It is perhaps Madonna's success in articulating and parading a desire to be desired – the opposite of the self-abnegating urge to lose oneself in the male evident in many classical Hollywood films – that attracts the hordes of twelve-year-old fans to her performances and videos. A cross between a bag-lady and a bordello queen, Madonna's image is a far cry from the 'patriarchal feminine' of women's magazines; yet it remains within those constraints in still focusing on the 'look' as crucial to identity. Madonna's narcissism and self-indulgences co-opt her texts back into a consumerist postmodernism, as do also the seductive participatory rhythms of this and other pop rock melodies. Such melodies bind the female spectator to the images so that the repressive aspects slip by unnoticed because of the comforting, appealing beat.

Some videos on the channel do use the new form in ways reminiscent of a transgressive/modernist mode. They use narrative in differing degrees and in various ways, much as did the great modernists, and they employ realist or non-realist strategies as befits a particular moment in a text. There is no set form for videos offering a critique of dominant female representations or of woman's position in male culture as signs for something in the male unconscious. The videos range from the black-comedy parody in Julie Brown's 'The Home Coming Queen's Got A Gun', to a sophisticated feminist critique of female representations and of woman's construction as passive sexual object in Annie Lennox's and Aretha Franklin's 'Sisters Are Doin' It for Themselves' and Tina Turner's 'Private Dancer'; to Laurie Anderson's anti-narrative, deconstructive video 'Language is a Virus', which attacks dominant bourgeois culture generally and commercial TV in particular.

We can thus see how difficult it is to make a case for MTV as progressive or retrogressive in its narrative modes. In a sense, those categories do not apply. MTV is something else – or it is elsewhere. It defies our usual critical categories while not setting up something we can recognize as liberating in new ways such as those Derrida and Kristeva search for.

Let me conclude by summarizing the contradictory aspects of postmodernism for feminist cultural concerns. Contemporary feminism, as a political and cultural discourse, has assumed a set of strategic subjectivities in order to attack the old patriarchal theorists. Feminists have both made use of and criticized the powerful, often subversive discourses of both Marx and Freud in creating the feminist stance against dominant gender constructs. If those discourses are seen as no longer relevant, on what ground can any strategic feminism stand? We might hope that we no longer needed such feminism, that we could work toward transcending 'death-dealing binary oppositions of masculinity and femininity', but events like the recent 'Baby M' case show how distant is American culture from any such stage. Does postmodernism make feminism archaic as a theory, while refusing to address the remaining oppressive discourses that perpetuate woman's subordination? For Kroker and Cook, technology is the only remaining ideology: feminists, however, can see in the Baby M case how various gender ideologies interact with new technologies in a complex, often contradictory manner.

The postmodernism that is produced by the collapse of the enlightenment project and of the belief in the transcendental (male) subject benefits women when it leads to the utopian postmodernism text discussed earlier. And even in the commercial postmodernism exemplified in MTV, we saw that there are benefits for the female spectator: the breaking up of traditional realist forms sometimes entails a deconstruction of conventional sex-role representations that opens up new possibilities for female imagining. The four-minute span does not permit regression to the oedipal conflicts of the classical Hollywood film that oppresses women. Meanwhile, the fragmentation of the viewing subject perhaps deconstructs woman's conventional other-centered reception functions – woman positioned as nurturer, caregiver – releasing new ways for the female spectator to relate to texts. Postmodernism offers the female spectator pleasure in sensations – color, sound, visual patterns – and in energy, body movement. Madonna represents new possibilities for female desire and for the empowered woman, even if we would want these forms of desire and empowerment to be only a transitional phase.

On the other hand, we could argue that commercial postmodern culture builds on and satisfies already dominant masculine qualities such as violence, destruction, consumption, phallic sexuality, and appropriation of the female in the non-male image. In much postmodernism, the domestic and the familial – modes that in the past offered some satisfaction to women – no longer function. It is possible that the new 'universe of communication' is attractive to some male theorists seeking relief from Baudrillard's old 'Faustian, Promethean (perhaps Oedipal) period of production and consumption', just because women have begun, through feminist discourse, to make and win demands within that system and to challenge male dominance there.

But the postmodern discourse theorized by Kroker and Cook is not anti-feminist; rather, it envisions a world beyond feminism as we have known it in the past twenty-five years. In the postmodern world, both men and women are victims; all bodies are 'invaded' and exploited because they are no longer adequate to the advanced technologies. Marilouise and Arthur Kroker are concerned about the (ab)use of women's bodies in fashion and about the reduction of woman to a baby-making 'machine' through new reproductive technologies. These devices alienate woman from her body and disconnect her from the baby she produces. But the Krokers also point out the new 'fallen' image of the penis in the age of AIDS and other sexual viruses, and many other ways in which humans, as we have conceived of them for centuries, are being drastically altered by electronic implants and additions.

Indeed, a movie like *Videodrome* is surprising more for its representation of the male than of the female body. Female figures in the film interestingly fall back into traditional stereotypes (the masculinized 'bitch' woman, the oversexed, masochistic woman), but we see the male body invaded and made monstrous in the hero's machine-produced hallucinations. It is true that the horrific deformation of the body involves its turning into a kind of vagina-like, bloody opening,[20] but this is a reference to the horror of technology that deforms all bodies and blurs their gender distinction. There are as many images of castration (the deformed arm, the powerless gun) as of female orifices. The point is that the hero's body turns into a playback machine: the body is controlled by electronic frequencies that prevent the owner from controlling himself. We have entered a Baudrillardean world (Brian Oblivion being a thinly disguised Baudrillard) in which there is no 'reality' other than video; the human body is reduced to the video machine – it and the TV set are one and the same.

As feminists we need to listen to the discourse for what it can tell us about the possible future: as an ethics of description, the postmodern discourse of this kind may warn against the devastating results of the abuse of science and technology by capital. Popular culture theory needs to attend to the Baudrillard/Kroker accounts, while avoiding their more seductive but improbable extremism. In what is hopefully only a transitional phase, we need more than ever to construct critical analyses of the new cultural scene, and the shift in consciousness wrought by science and technology; we need to engage in work that will redress dangerous directions, or prevent what is envisaged from coming to be. As humans implicated against our wills in the effects of new technologies, we also still exist as historical subjects in specific political contexts; we must continue feminist struggles wherever we live and work, at the same time being aware of the larger cultural constructions that implicate us and for which feminist ideologies may no longer be adequate.

In terms of cultural studies, the first two of my trilogy of male theorists (i.e. Barthes and Bakhtin) are useful particularly as they have been theorized by French feminists (Kristeva, Cixous, Montrelay); Lacan, Althusser and Foucault are equally important, again in connection with French feminists (Cixous, Irigaray). Let me conclude by listing the different kinds of cultural work that feminists need to be doing: I will discuss this work in terms of the three main categories discussed above, namely: a) the modernist/transgressive text; b) the 'utopian' postmodern text; and c) the 'popular/commercial' postmodern text.

First, feminists must continue to make use of transgressive strategies, as some feminist film-makers have been doing (e.g. Mulvey and Wollen's *Riddles of the Sphinx*, Sally Potter's *Thriller* or her *Gold-diggers*, Sigmund Freud's *'Dora'*; Trinh T. Minh-ha's *Naked Spaces – Living Is Round*, among others). In this way, feminists can continue to question and undo the patriarchal construction of femininity, to pose the problem of representation, to demonstrate the social constructions of gender. Unlike the high modernists (most of whom were male, many misogynist), such feminists have the benefit of recent work on deconstruction, and can employ sophisticated theories of representation and gender that have also recently been developed through semiotics and psychoanalysis. Inevitably, such texts will be produced and exhibited mainly in alternate spaces, given the demands they make on the viewer through their counter-text strategies. However, we should not underestimate the impact of such texts, now that they are making their way into the academy.

Such texts vary in their strategies, particularly in relation to the use or non-use of narrative. Some feminists, like Teresa de Lauretis, keenly aware that narrative movement is that of masculine desire, 'the movement of a passage, an actively experienced transformation of the human being into... man', nevertheless are wary of the automatic adoption of anti-narrative devices. De Lauretis argues that we must create a new kind of narrative, based not on male desire but rather on a different kind of desiring. Other feminists believe that all narrative involves essentializing (i.e., positing some 'female' desire in place of the prior 'male' desire) and that, therefore, we can offer a truly transgressive position only through anti-narrative techniques.

This work needs to be differentiated from a second feminist concern, which we could position within the 'utopian' postmodernism discussed above.   Here, feminists theorize and try to construct texts that radically decenter, disrupt and refuse all categories hitherto central in Western thought, much in the manner of Derrida. The efforts in the transgressive sort of text should provide the groundwork for the utopian postmodernist text in leading us through the problems and tangles of binary oppositions toward a glimpse of how the beyond might appear.

An important third area of work needs to address the possibilities within what I have called the dominant 'co-opted' postmodernism of our time. Here it seems to me that we can bring to bear tools developed just prior to the postmodern moment in analyzing women in popular culture (the classical Hollywood melodrama), 1950s television, the soaps). An important issue here is the degree to which the new co-opted postmodernism is an aggressive attempt to recover popular culture, traditionally linked to a scorned 'feminine', for males. We can begin to analyze the implications of the changes in films and in television shows that earlier addressed a specifically female audience – and that therefore spoke to women's special needs, fantasies and desires within partriarchy. If postmodernism takes away such gaps, perhaps it offers other possibilities. We need to explore fully the contradictions involved in 'co-opted' postmodernism, for once the fixed frameworks and traditional gender-oriented genres are relinquished, once signifiers are freed from the constraints such frameworks and genres impose, then both negative and positive outcomes for women may occur. Since co-opted postmodernism addresses a mass female audience, it is perhaps the most important terrain for feminist cultural studies. We need actively to resist and challenge the male qualities of violence, aggression and misogyny that mark much co-opted postmodernism and toward which women are being drawn in the mistaken belief, perhaps, that this offers liberation from earlier 'feminine' constraints. We also need to recognize the genuine places where new possibilities are offered to the female spectator by virtue of prior genre constraints being lifted.

We cannot expect a commercial medium like MTV to resist the pressures of what may indeed be a deep cultural change. And we need to see postmodernism of both kinds in the context of the great modernist movement, of the search for an alternative consciousness, cultural practice and representation to the dominant. Unfortunately, we cannot actually produce the positive or utopian postmodernism until we have managed to challenge the symbolic order sufficiently to permit its articulation. That is, we have to work through the binary oppositions by constantly challenging them before we can be beyond them. Much utopian postmodernism does just that: it stands on the shoulders of modernism and the great modernist thinkers, while struggling to move beyond their critical categories and aesthetic strategies. It moves through them by meditating upon the possibility of transcending them.

But much of what people celebrate as liberating in what I call 'co-opted' postmodernism is an avoidance of the struggle, an attempt to sidestep the task of working through the constraining binary oppositions, including sexual difference. The liberating elements in some popular culture like rock videos are important, but often superficial. Women are invested in culture's move beyond dysfunctional gender polarities, but a superficial collapsing of previously distinct female representations, for instance, gets us nowhere. This sort of strategy, as many others evident in rock videos, is preferable to the old 'realist-talking-heads', essentializing and monolithic (male) discourse of the past. But we must still be wary of making too extreme claims for what is going on. We must also be wary of assuming the acceptance by historical female subjects of the co-opted postmodernist world. Work needs to be done on the various kinds of resistances these subjects devise in the face of the commercial and technological onslaughts.

As cultural workers, we do not want to return to the error of insisting upon fixed points of enunciation, labelled 'truth'; rather, as Tony Bennett and Ernesto Laclau have both pointed out,[21] we must continue to articulate oppositional discourses – recognizing them as discourses rather than an ontological truth that theory has cast doubt on – if we are to construct new subjects capable of working toward the utopian postmodernism we all hope will be possible. This means not validating or celebrating the erosion of all categories and differences and boundaries – as Baudrillard and his followers sometimes appear to do. Feminists in particular need to continue to construct strategic subjectivities, and to use the category 'woman' as a tool to prevent the too easy and too early collapsing of a difference that continues to organize culture. As long as that difference operates, we need to counter it with the only tools we have, while simultaneously working toward a much more difficult transcendence – or, in Craig Owens's words,[22] toward a concept of difference without opposition.

Notes

1. See Craig Owens, 'The Discourse of Others: Feminists and Postmodernism', in Hal Foster, ed. *The Anti-Aesthetic: Essays on Postmodern Culture* (Port Townsend, WA: The Bay Press, 1983), p. 61.
2. Given the focus of this article, it will not be possible to deal with how postmodernism affects all the different kinds of feminisms; hence, I shall beg the reader's indulgence for an analysis positing a generalized 'feminism' that necessarily embodies my own biases.
3. The reasons for this are fascinating, and perhaps have to do with Bakhtin's links to both Freud and semiotics, while not adhering to either theory fully. See Robert Stam's essay in this volume.
4. See Julia Kristeva, 'Word, Dialogue, and Novel', in *Desire in Language: A Semiotic Approach to Literature and Art*, ed. Leon S. Roudiez; trans. Thomas Gora, Alice Jardine and Leon S. Roudiez (New York: Columbia University Press, 1980), p. 79. Subsequent page references appear parenthetically.
5. See Allon White and Peter Stallybrass, *The Politics and Poetics of Transgression* (London: Methuen, Inc., 1986), p. 18.
6. Jean-François Lyotard, *The Postmodern Condition: A Report on Knowledge*, trans. Geoff Bennington and Brian Massumi (Minneapolis: University of Minnesota Press, 1984).
7. Robert Stam, 'Mikhail Bakhtin and Left Cultural Critique', in this volume.
8. Fred Pfeil, 'Makin' Flippy-Floppy: Postmodernism and the Baby-Boom PMC', in *The Year Left: An American Socialist Yearbook*, I, ed. Mike Davis, Fred Pfeil and Michael Sprinker (London: Verso, 1985), pp. 272, 292.
9. See Teresa de Lauretis, 'Aesthetic and Feminist Theory: Rethinking Women's

Cinema', *New German Critique* 34 (winter 1985), pp. 154–75.

10. Alice A. Jardine, *Gynesis: Configurations of Woman and Modernity* (Ithaca and London: Cornell University Press, 1985).

11. See Paul Willemen, 'An Avant Garde for the Eighties', *Framework* 24 (spring 1984), pp. 53–73. One of the issues complicating the debates about postmodernism has of course been the different theories of modernism from which critics start. Willemen's article is a useful clarification of some of the confusions around modernism.

12. See Sandy Flitterman, 'The *Real* Soap Operas: TV Commercials', in E. Ann Kaplan, ed., *Regarding Television: Critical Approaches – An Anthology* (Los Angeles: The American Film Institute, 1983), pp. 84–97.

13. Jean Baudrillard, 'The Ecstasy of Communication', in Hal Foster, ed., p. 127.

14. Ibid., pp. 130–31.

15. Arthur Kroker and David Cook, *the Postmodern Scene: Excremental Culture and Hyper-Aesthetics* (New York: St Martin's Press, 1986), p. 279.

16. Jean Baudrillard, 'The Implosion of Meaning in the Media and the Implosion of the Social in the Masses', in K. Woodward, ed., *The Myths of Information: Technology and Postindustrial Culture* (Madison: Coda Press, 1980), pp. 138–48.

17. For example, see the issue of the *Journal of Communication Inquiry* 10, 1 (winter 1986), devoted to Music Television.

18. See my *Rocking Around the Clock: Music Television, Postmodernism and Consumer Culture* (London and New York: Methuen, Inc., 1987). Chapter 3.

19. Let me note here to avoid confusion that in the following comments I am talking about the 'model' spectator the apparatus constructs, rather than about the possible modes of specific reception – including resistance – individual historical spectators may engage in. In interviews with teenagers, it became clear that historical subjects are not necessarily *tabulae rasae*, soaking up spectator positions, but employ a number of strategies to subvert or alter what they are given. Some teenagers turn off the sound and put on their own, preferred music to accompany images; others talk and comment about the images, ridiculing and spoofing the stars. Female spectators apparently manifest less of this behaviour, but a complexly organized reception study would be necessary to establish the validity of generalization.

20. See Tania Modleski, 'The Terror of Pleasure: The Contemporary Horror Film and Postmodern Theory', in Tania Modleski, ed., *Studies in Mass Entertainment: Critical Approaches to Mass Culture* (Madison, WI: University of Wisconsin Press, 1986), p. 163.

21. See Tony Bennett, 'Texts in History: The Determinations of Readings and Their Texts', in D. Attridge, G. Bennington and R. Young, eds. *Post-Structuralism and the Question of History* (Cambridge: Cambridge University Press, 1987); and Ernesto Laclau, 'Populist Rupture and Discourse', *Screen Education*, 34 (spring 1980).

22. See Craig Owens, 'The Discourse of Others: Feminists and Postmodernism', in Hal Foster, ed., *The Anti-Aesthetic*, pp. 57–82.

7

'Material Girl': the effacements of postmodern culture

Susan Bordo

From her *Unbearable weight: feminism, western culture, and the body* (University of California Press 1993)

[...] Academics do not usually like to think of themselves as embodying the values and preoccupations of popular culture on the plane of high theory or intellectual discourse. We prefer to see ourselves as the demystifyers of popular discourse, bringers-to-consciousness-and-clarity rather than unconscious reproducers of culture. Despite what we would *like* to believe of ourselves, however, we are always within the society that we criticize, and never so strikingly as at the present postmodern moment. All the elements of what I have here called postmodern conversation – intoxication with individual choice and creative *jouissance*, delight with the piquancy of particularity and mistrust of pattern and seeming coherence, celebration of 'difference' along with an absence of critical perspective differentiating and weighing 'differences,' suspicion of the totalitarian nature of generalization along with a rush to protect difference from its homogenizing abuses – have become recognizable and familiar in much of contemporary intellectual discourse. Within this theoretically self-conscious universe, moreover, these elements are not merely embodied [...] but explicitly thematized and *celebrated*, as inaugurating new constructions of the self, no longer caught in the mythology of the unified subject, embracing of multiplicity, challenging the dreary and moralizing generalizations about gender, race, and so forth that have so preoccupied liberal and left humanism.

For this celebratory, academic postmodernism, it has become highly unfashionable – and 'totalizing' – to talk about the grip of culture on the body. Such a perspective, it is argued, casts active and creative subjects as passive dupes of ideology; it gives too much to dominant ideology, imagining it as seamless and univocal, overlooking both the gaps which are continually allowing for the eruption of 'difference' and the polysemous, unstable, open nature of all cultural texts. To talk about the grip of culture on the body (as, for example, in 'old' feminist discourse about the objectification and sexualization of the female body) is to fail to acknowledge, as one theorist put it, 'the cultural work by which nomadic, fragmented, active subjects confound dominant discourse.'[1]

So, for example, contemporary culture critic John Fiske is harshly critical of what he describes as the view of television as a 'dominating monster' with 'homogenizing power' over the perceptions of viewers. Such a view, he argues, imagines the audience as 'powerless and undiscriminating' and overlooks the fact that:

> Pleasure results from a particular relationship between meanings and power ... There is no pleasure in being a 'cultural dope.' ... Pleasure results from the production of meanings of the world and of self that are felt to serve the interests of the reader rather than those of the dominant. The subordinate may be disempowered, but they are not powerless. There is a power in resisting power, there is a power in maintaining one's social identity in opposition to that proposed by the dominant ideology, there is a power in asserting one's own subcultural values against the dominant ones. There is, in short, a power in being different.[2]

Fiske then goes on to produce numerous examples of how *Dallas, Hart to Hart*, and so forth have been read (or so he argues) by various subcultures to make their own 'socially pertinent' and empowering meanings out of 'the semiotic resources provided by television.'

Note, in Fiske's insistent, repetitive invocation of the category of power, a characteristically postmodern flattening of the terrain of power relations, a lack of differentiation between, for example, the power involved in creative *reading* in the isolation of one's own home and the power held by those who control the material production of television shows, or the power involved in public protest and action against the conditions of that production and the power of the dominant meanings – for instance, racist and sexist images and messages – therein produced. For Fiske, of course, there *are* no such dominant meanings, that is, no element whose ability to grip the imagination of the viewer is greater than the viewer's ability to 'just say no' through resistant reading of the text. That ethnic and subcultural meaning *may* be wrested from *Dallas* and *Hart to Hart* becomes for Fiske proof that dominating images and messages are only in the minds of those totalitarian critics who would condescendingly 'rescue' the disempowered from those forces that are in fact the very medium of their creative freedom and resistance ('the semiotic resources of television').

Fiske's conception of power – a terrain without hills and valleys, where all forces have become 'resources' – reflects a very common postmodern misappropriation of Foucault. Fiske conceives of power as in the *possession* of individuals or groups, something they 'have' – a conception Foucault takes great pains to criticize – rather than (as in Foucault's reconstruction) a dynamic of noncentralized forces, its dominant historical forms attaining their hegemony, not from magisterial design or decree, but through multiple 'processes, of different origin and scattered location,' regulating and normalizing the most intimate and minute elements of the construction of time, space, desire, embodiment.[3] This conception of power does *not* entail that there are no dominant positions, social structures, or ideologies emerging from the play of forces; the fact that power is not held by any *one* does not mean that it is equally held by *all*. It is in fact not 'held' at all; rather, people and groups are positioned differentially within it. This model is particularly useful for the analysis of male dominance and female subordination, so much of which is reproduced 'voluntarily,' through our self-normalization to everyday habits of masculinity and femininity. Within such a model, one can acknowledge that women may indeed contribute to the perpetuation of female subordination (for example, by embracing, taking pleasure in, and even feeling empowered by the cultural objectification and sexualization of the female body) without this entailing that they have power in the production and reproduction of sexist culture.

Foucault does insist on the *instability* of modern power relations – that is, he emphasizes that resistance is perpetual and unpredictable, and hegemony precarious. This notion is transformed by Fiske (perhaps under the influence of a more deconstructionist brand of postmodernism) into a notion of resistance as *jouissance*, a creative and pleasurable eruption of cultural 'difference' through the 'seams' of the text. What this celebration of creative reading as resistance effaces is the arduous and frequently frustrated historical struggle that is required for the subordinated to articulate and assert the value of their 'difference' in the face of dominant meanings – meanings which often offer a pedagogy directed at the reinforcement of feelings of inferiority, marginality, ugliness. During the early fifties, when *Brown v. the Board of Education* was wending its way through the courts, as a demonstration of the destructive psychological effects of segregation black children were asked to look at two baby dolls, identical in all respects except color. The children were asked a series of questions: which is the nice doll? which is the bad doll? which doll would you like to play with? The majority of black children, Kenneth Clark reports, attributed the positive characteristics to the white doll, the negative characteristics to the black. When Clark asked one final question, 'Which doll is like you?' they looked at him, he says, 'as though he were the devil himself' for putting them in that predicament, for forcing them to face the inexorable and hideous logical implications of their situation. Northern children often ran out of the room; southern children tended to answer the question in shamed embarrassment. Clark recalls one little boy who laughed, 'Who am I like? That doll! It's a nigger and I'm a nigger!'[4]

Failing to acknowledge the psychological and cultural potency of normalizing imagery can be just as effective in effacing people's experiences of racial oppression as lack of attentiveness to cultural and ethnic differences – a fact postmodern critics sometimes seem to forget. This is not to deny what Fiske calls 'the power of being different'; it is, rather, to insist that it is won through ongoing political *struggle* rather than through an act of creative interpretation. Here, once again, although many postmodern academics may claim Foucault as their guiding light, they differ from him in significant and revealing ways. For Foucault, the metaphorical terrain of resistance is explicitly that of the 'battle'; the 'points of confrontation' may be 'innumerable' and 'instable,' but they involve a serious, often deadly struggle of embodied (that is, historically situated and shaped) forces.[5] Barbara Kruger exemplifies this conception of resistance in a poster that represents the contemporary contest over reproductive control through the metaphor of the body as battleground (Fig. 7.1). Some progressive developers of children's toys have self-consciously entered into struggle with racial and other forms of normalization. The Kenya Doll (Fig. 7.2) comes in three different skin tones ('so your girl is bound to feel pretty and proud') and attempts to create a future in which hair-straightening *will* be merely

Fig. 7.1

one decorative option among others. Such products, to my mind, are potentially effective 'sites of resistance' precisely because they recognize that the body is a battleground whose self-determination has to be fought for.

The metaphor of the body as battleground, rather than postmodern playground, captures, as well, the *practical* difficulties involved in the political struggle to empower 'difference.' *Essence* magazine has consciously and strenuously tried to promote diverse images of black strength, beauty, and self-acceptance. Beauty features celebrate the glory of black skin and lush lips; other departments feature interviews with accomplished black women writers, activists, teachers, many of whom display styles of body and dress that challenge the hegemony of white Anglo-Saxon standards. The magazine's advertisers, however, continually play upon and perpetuate consumers' feelings of inadequacy and insecurity over the racial characteristics of their bodies. They insist that, in order to be beautiful, hair must be straightened and eyes lightened; they almost always employ models with fair skin, Anglo-Saxon features, and 'hair that moves,' insuring association of their products with fantasies of becoming what the white culture most prizes and rewards.

This ongoing battle over the black woman's body and the power of its 'differences' ('differences' which actual black women embody to widely

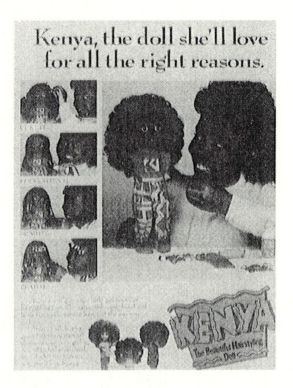

Kenya, the doll she'll love for all the right reasons.

Fig. 7.2

varying degrees, of course) is made manifest in the twentieth-anniversary issue, where a feature celebrating 'The Beauty of Black' faced an advertisement visually legislating virtually the opposite (and offering, significantly, 'escape') (Figs 7.3 and 7.4). This invitation to cognitive dissonance reveals what *Essence* must grapple with, in every issue, as it tries to keep its message of African American self-acceptance clear and dominant, while submitting to economic necessities on which its survival depends. Let me make it clear here that such self-acceptance, not the reverse tyranny that constructs light-skinned and Anglo-featured African Americans as 'not black enough,' is the message *Essence* is trying to convey, against a culture that *denies* 'the Beauty of Black' at every turn. This terrain, clearly, is not a playground but a minefield that constantly threatens to deconstruct 'difference' *literally* and not merely literarily.

'Material Girl': Madonna as postmodern heroine

John Fiske's conception of 'difference,' in the section quoted above, at least imagines resistance as challenging specifiable historical forms of dominance. Women, he argues, connect with subversive 'feminine' values leaking through the patriarchal plot of soap operas; blacks laugh to themselves

Fig. 7.3

at the glossy, materialist cowboy culture of *Dallas*. Such examples suggest a resistance directed against *particular* historical forms of power and subjectivity. For some postmodern theorists, however, resistance imagined as the refusal to embody *any* positioned subjectivity at all; what is celebrated is continual creative escape from location, containment, and definition. So, as Susan Rubin Suleiman advises, we must move beyond the valorization of historically suppressed values (for example, those values that have been

Fig. 7.4

culturally constructed as belonging to an inferior, female domain and generally expunged from Western science, philosophy, and religion) and toward 'endless complication' and a 'dizzying accumulation of narratives.'[6] She appreciatively (and perhaps misleadingly) invokes Derrida's metaphor of 'incalculable choreographies'[7] to capture the dancing, elusive, continually changing subjectivity that she envisions, a subjectivity without gender, without history, without location. From this perspective, the truly resistant female body is, not the body that wages war on feminine sexualization and objectification, but the body that, as Cathy Schwichtenberg has put it, 'uses simulation strategically in ways that challenge the stable notion of gender as the edifice of sexual difference ... [in] an erotic politics in which the female body can be refashioned in the flux of identities that speak in plural styles.'[8] For this erotic politics, the new postmodern heroine is Madonna.

This celebration of Madonna as postmodern heroine does not mark the first time Madonna has been portrayed as a subversive culture-figure. Until the early 1990s, however, Madonna's resistance has been interpreted along 'body as battleground' lines, as deriving from her refual to allow herself to be constructed as a passive object of patriarchal desire. John Fiske, for example, argues that this was a large part of Madonna's original appeal to her 'wanna-bes' – those hordes of middle-class pre-teeners who mimicked

Madonna's moves and costumes. For the 'wanna-bes,' Madonna demonstrated the possibility of a female heterosexuality that was independent of patriarchal control, a sexuality that defied rather than rejected the male gaze, teasing it with her own gaze, deliberately trashy and vulgar, challenging anyone to call her a whore, and ultimately not giving a damn how she might be judged. Madonna's rebellious sexuality, in this reading, offered itself, not as coming into being through the look of the 'other,' but as self-defining and in love with, happy with itself – an attitude that is rather difficult for women to achieve in this culture and that helps to explain, as Fiske argues, her enormous appeal for pre-teen girls.[9] 'I like the way she handles herself, sort of take it or leave it; she's sexy but she doesn't need men ... she's kind of there all by herself,' says one. 'She gives us ideas. It's really women's lib, not being afraid of what guys think,' says another.[10]

Madonna herself, significantly and unlike most sex symbols, has never advertised herself as disdainful of feminism or constructed feminists as man-haters. Rather, in a 1985 *Time* interview, she suggests that her lack of inhibition in 'being herself' and her 'luxuriant' expression of 'strong' sexuality constitute her brand of feminist celebration.[11] Some feminist theorists would agree. Molly Hite, for example, argues that 'asserting female desire in a culture in which female sexuality is viewed as so inextricably conjoined with passivity' is 'transgressive':

> Implied in this strategy is the old paradox of the speaking statue, the created thing that magically begins to create, for when a woman writes – self-consciously from her muted position as a woman and not as an honorary man – about female desire, female sexuality, female sensuous experience generally, her performance has the effect of giving voice to pure corporeality, of turning a product of the dominant meaning-system into a producer of meanings. A woman, conventionally identified with her body, writes about that identification, and as a consequence, femininity – silent and inert by definition – erupts into patriarchy as an impossible discourse.[12]

Not all feminists would agree with this, of course. For the sake of the contrast I want to draw here, however, let us grant it, and note, as well, that an argument similar to Fiske's can be made concerning Madonna's refusal to be obedient to dominant and normalizing standards of female *beauty*. I am now talking, of course, about Madonna in her more fleshy days. In those days, Madonna saw herself as willfully out of step with the times. 'Back in the fifties,' she says in the *Time* interview, 'women weren't ashamed of their bodies.' (The fact that she is dead wrong is not relevant here.) Identifying herself with her construction of that time and what she calls its lack of 'suppression' of femininity, she looks down her nose at the 'androgynous' clothes of our own time and speaks warmly of her own stomach, 'not really flat' but 'round and the skin is smooth and I like it.' Contrasting herself to anorectics, whom she sees as self-denying and self-hating, completely in the thrall of externally imposed standards of worthiness, Madonna (as she saw herself) stood for self-definition through the assertion of her own (traditionally 'female' and now anachronistic) body-type (Fig. 7.5).

Of course, this is no longer Madonna's body type. Shortly after her 1987 marriage to Sean Penn she began a strenuous reducing and exercise pro-

Fig. 7.5

gram, now runs several miles a day, lifts weights, and has developed, in obedience to dominant contemporary norms, a tight, slender, muscular body (Fig. 7.6). Why did she decide to shape up? 'I didn't have a flat stomach anymore,' she has said. 'I had become well-rounded.' Please note the sharp about-face here, from pride to embarrassment. My goal here, however, is not to suggest that Madonna's formerly voluptuous body was a non-alienated, freely expressive body, a 'natural' body. While the slender body is the current cultural ideal, the voluptuous female body is a cultural form, too (as are all bodies), and was a coercive ideal in the fifties. My point is that in terms of Madonna's own former lexicon of meanings – in which feminine voluptuousness and the choice to be round in a culture of the lean were clearly connected to spontaneity, self-definition, and defiance of the cultural gaze – the terms set by that gaze have now triumphed. Madonna has been normalized; more precisely, she has self-normalized. Her 'wanna-bes' are following suit. Studies suggest that as many as 80 percent of nine-year-old suburban girls (the majority of whom are far from overweight) are making rigorous dieting and exercise the organizing discipline of their lives.[13] They do not require Madonna's example, of course, to believe that they must be thin to be acceptable. But Madonna clearly no longer provides a model of resistance or 'difference' for them.

Fig. 7.6

None of this 'materiality' – that is, the obsessive body-praxis that regulates and disciplines Madonna's life and the lives of the young (and not so young) women who emulate her – makes its way into the representation of Madonna as postmodern heroine. In the terms of this representation (in both its popular and scholarly instantiations) Madonna is 'in control of her image, not trapped by it'; the proof lies in her ironic and chameleon-like approach to the construction of her identity, her ability to 'slip in and out of character at will,' to defy definition, to keep them guessing.[14] In this coding of things, as in the fantasies of the polysurgical addict [. . .], *control* and *power*, words that are invoked over and over in discussions of Madonna,

have become equivalent to *self-creating*. Madonna's new body has no material history; it conceals its continual struggle to maintain itself, it does not
reveal its pain. (Significantly, Madonna's 'self-exposé', the documentary
Truth or Dare, does not include any scenes of Madonna's daily workouts.)
It is merely another creative transformation of an ever-elusive subjectivity.
'More Dazzling and Determined Not to Stop Changing,' as *Cosmopolitan*
describes Madonna: '. . . whether in looks or career, this multitalented daz-
zler will never be trapped in *any* mould!'[15] The plasticity of Madonna's subjectivity is emphasized again and again, in the popular press, particularly
by Madonna herself. It is how she tells the story of her 'power' in the industry: 'In pop music, generally, people have one image. You get pigeonholed.
I'm lucky enough to be able to change and still be accepted . . . play a part,
change characters, looks, attitudes.'[16]

Madonna claims that her creative work, too, is meant to escape definition. 'Everything I do is meant to have several meanings, to be ambiguous,'
she says. She resists, however (in true postmodern fashion), the attribution
of serious artistic intent; rather (as she told *Cosmo*), she favors irony and
ambiguity, 'to entertain myself' and (as she told *Vanity Fair*) out of 'rebel-
liousness and a desire to fuck with people.'[17] It is the postmodern nature of
her music and videos that has most entranced academic critics, whose acco-
lades reproduce in highly theoretical language the notions emphasized in
the popular press. Susan McClary writes:

> Madonna's art itself repeatedly deconstructs the traditional notion of the uni-
> fied subject with finite ego boundaries. Her pieces explore . . . various ways
> of constituting identities that refuse stability, that remain fluid, that resist def-
> inition. This tendency in her work has become increasingly pronounced; for
> instance, in her recent controversial video 'Express Yourself' . . . she slips in
> and out of every subject position offered within the video's narrative context
> . . . refusing more than ever to deliver the security of a clear, unambiguous
> message or an 'authentic' self.[18]

Later in the same piece, McClary describes 'Open Your Heart to Me,'
which features Madonna as a porn star in a peep show, as creating 'an
image of open-ended *jouissance* – an erotic energy that continually escapes
containment.'[19] Now, many feminist viewers may find this particular video
quite disturbing, for a number of reasons. First, unlike many of Madonna's
older videos, 'Open Your Heart to Me' does not visually emphasize
Madonna's subjectivity or desire – as 'Lucky Star,' for example, did through
frequent shots of Madonna's face and eyes, flirting with and controlling the
reactions of the viewer. Rather, 'Open Your Heart to Me' places the viewer
in the position of the voyeur by presenting Madonna's body as object, now
perfectly taut and tightly managed for display. To be sure, we do not identify with the slimy men, drooling over Madonna's performance, who are
depicted in the video; but, as E. Ann Kaplan has pointed out, the way men
view women *in* the filmic world is only one species of objectifying gaze.
There is also the viewer's gaze, which may be encouraged by the director
to be either more or less objectifying.[20] In 'Open Your Heart to Me,' as in
virtually all rock videos, the female body is offered to the viewer purely as
a spectacle, an object of sight, a visual commodity to be consumed.
Madonna's weight loss and dazzling shaping-up job make the spectacle of

her body all the more compelling; we are riveted to her body, fascinated by it. Many men and women may experience the primary reality of the video as the elicitation of desire *for* that perfect body; women, however, may also be gripped by the desire (very likely impossible to achieve) to *become* that perfect body.

These elements can be effaced, of course, by a deliberate abstraction of the video from the cultural context in which it is historically embedded – the continuing containment, sexualization, and objectification of the female body – and in which the viewer is implicated as well and instead treating the video as a purely formal text. Taken as such, 'Open Your Heart to Me' presents itself as what E. Ann Kaplan calls a 'postmodern video': it refuses to 'take a clear position vis-à-vis its images' and similarly refuses a 'clear position for the spectator within the filmic world . . . leaving him/her decentered, confused.'[21] McClary's reading of 'Open Your Heart to Me' emphasizes precisely these postmodern elements, insisting on the ambiguous and unstable nature of the relationship depicted in the narrative of the video, and the frequent elements of parody and play. 'The usual power relationship between the voyeuristic male gaze and object' is 'destabilized,' she claims, by the portrayal of the male patrons of the porno house as leering and pathetic. At the same time, the portrayal of Madonna as porno queen–object is deconstructed, McClary argues, by the end of the video, which has Madonna changing her clothes to those of a little boy and tripping off playfully, leaving the manager of the house sputtering behind her. McClary reads this as 'escape to androgyny,' which 'refuses essentialist gender categories and turns sexual identity into a kind of play.' As for the gaze of the viewer, she admits that it is 'risky' 'to invoke the image of porn queen in order to perform its deconstruction,' but concludes that the deconstruction is successful: 'In this video, Madonna confronts the most pernicious of her stereotypes and attempts to channel it into a very different realm: a realm where the feminine object need not be the object of the patriarchal gaze, where its energy can motivate play and nonsexual pleasure.'[22]

I would argue, however, that despite the video's evasions of clear or fixed meaning there *is* a dominant position in this video: it is that of the objectifying gaze. One is not *really* decentered and confused by this video, despite the 'ambiguities' it formally contains. Indeed, the video's postmodern conceits, I would suggest, facilitate rather than deconstruct the presentation of Madonna's body as an object on display. For in the absence of a coherent critical position telling us how to read the images, the individual images themselves become preeminent, hypnotic, fixating. Indeed, I would say that ultimately this video is entirely about Madonna's body, the narrative context virtually irrelevant, an excuse to showcase the physical achievements of the star, a video centerfold. On this level, any parodic or destabilizing element appears as cynically, mechanically tacked on, in bad faith, a way of claiming trendy status for what is really just cheesecake – or, perhaps, soft-core pornography.

Indeed, it may be worse than that. If the playful 'tag' ending of 'Open Your Heart to Me' is successful in deconstructing the notion that the objectification, the sexualization of women's bodies is a serious business, then

Madonna's *jouissance* may be 'fucking with' her youthful viewer's perceptions in a dangerous way. Judging from the proliferation of rock and rap lyrics celebrating the rape, abuse, and humiliation of women, the message – not Madonna's responsibility alone, of course, but hers among others, surely – is getting through. The artists who perform these misogynist songs also claim to be speaking playfully, tongue-in-cheek, and to be daring and resistant transgressors of cultural structures that contain and define. Ice T, whose rap lyrics gleefully describe the gang rape of a woman – with a flashlight, to 'make her tits light up' – claims that he is only 'telling it like it is' among black street youth (he compares himself to Richard Wright), and he scoffs at feminist humorlessness, implying, as well, that it is racist and repressive for white feminists to try to deny him his indigenous 'style.' The fact that Richard Wright embedded his depiction of Bigger Thomas within a critique of the racist culture that shaped him, and that *Native Son* is meant to be a *tragedy*, was not, apparently, noticed in Ice T's postmodern reading of the book, whose critical point of view he utterly ignores. Nor does he seem concerned about what appears to be a growing fad – not only among street gangs, but in fraternity houses as well – for gang rape, often with an unconscious woman, and surrounded by male spectators. (Some of the terms popularly used to describe these rapes include 'beaching' – the woman being likened to a 'beached whale' – and 'spectoring,' to emphasize how integral a role the onlookers play.)

My argument here is a plea, not for censorship, but for recognition of the social contexts and consequences of images from popular culture, consequences that are frequently effaced in postmodern and other celebrations of 'resistant' elements in these images. To turn back to Madonna and the liberating postmodern subjectivity that McClary and others claim she is offering: the notion that one can play a porno house by night and regain one's androgynous innocence by day does not seem to me to be a refusal of essentialist categories about gender, but rather a new inscription of mind/body dualism. What the body does is immaterial, so long as the imagination is free. This abstract, unsituated, disembodied freedom, I have argued in this essay, glorifies itself only through the effacement of the material praxis of people's lives, the normalizing power of cultural images, and the continuing social realities of dominance and subordination.

Notes

1. This was said by Janice Radway in an oral presentation of her work, Duke University, Spring, 1989.
2. John Fiske, *Television Culture* (New York: Methuen, 1987), p. 19.
3. Michael Foucault, *Discipline and Punish* (New York: Vintage, 1979), p. 138.
4. Related in Bill Moyers, 'A Walk Through the Twentieth Century: The Second American Revolution,' PBS Boston.
5. Foucault, *Discipline and Punish*, pp. 26–27.
6. Susan Rubin Suleiman, '(Re)Writing the Body: The Politics and Poetics of Female Eroticism,' in Susan Rubin Suleiman, ed., *The Female Body in Western Culture* (Cambridge: Harvard University Press, 1986), p. 24.
7. Jacques Derrida and Christie V. McDonald, 'Choreographies,' *Diacritics* 12, no.

2 (1982): 76.

8. Cathy Schwichtenberg, 'Postmodern Feminism and Madonna: Toward an Erotic Politics of the Female Body,' paper presented at the University of Utah Humanities Center, National Conference on Rewriting the (Post)Modern: (Post)Colonialism/Feminism/Late Capitalism, March 30–31, 1990.

9. John Fiske, 'British Cultural Studies and Television,' in Robert C. Allen, ed., *Channels of Discourse* (Chapel Hill: University of North Carolina Press, 1987), pp. 254–90.

10. Quoted in John Skow, 'Madonna Rocks the Land,' *Time* (May 27, 1985): 77.

11. Skow, 'Madonna Rocks the Land,' p. 81.

12. Molly Hite, 'Writing – and Reading – the Body: Female Sexuality and Recent Feminist Fiction,' in *Feminist Studies* 14, no. 1 (Spring 1988): 121–22.

13. 'Fat or Not, 4th Grade Girls Diet Lest They Be Teased or Unloved,' *Wall Street Journal*, Feb. 11, 1986.

14. Catherine Texier, 'Have Women Surrendered in MTV's Battle of the Sexes?' *New York Times*, April 22, 1990, p. 31.

15. *Cosmopolitan* (July 1987): cover.

16. David Ansen, 'Magnificent Maverick,' *Cosmopolitan* (May 1990): 311.

17. Ansen, 'Magnificent Maverick,' p. 311; Kevin Sessums, 'White Heat,' *Vanity Fair* (April 1990): 208.

18. Susan McClary, 'Living to Tell: Madonna's Resurrection of the Fleshy,' *Genders*, no. 7 (Spring 1990): 2.

19. McClary, 'Living to Tell,' p. 12.

20. E. Ann Kaplan, 'Is the Gaze Male,' in Ann Snitow, Christine Stansell, and Sharon Thompson, eds., *Powers of Desire: The Politics of Sexuality* (New York: Monthly Review Press, 1983), pp. 309–27.

21. E. Ann Kaplan, *Rocking Around the Clock: Music Television, Postmodernism and Consumer Culture* (New York: Methuen, 1987), p. 63.

22. McClary, 'Living to Tell,' p. 13.

Section II

Genre: textuality, femininity, feminism

Much of the early feminist research within media studies, as reflected in the previous section, concentrated on investigating representations of women in and through different media forms. The late 1970s saw a significant development when feminist scholars turned their attention to those aspects of media which were specifically addressed to, and furthermore had tremendous appeal for, women. This shift can be understood as part of the growing theoretical work on understanding femininity, female identity and the politics of culture. It can be argued that work emerging from the feminist insistence on examining specific, and especially *popular* generic characteristics and the pleasures they offered to women, initiated a much broader attention to popular pleasures and related questions of identity (Dyer *et al.*, 1981; Brunsdon, 1981; Hobson, 1982; Modleski, 1982; Ang, 1985; Brown, 1990).

This section begins with **Annette Kuhn**'s 'Women's genres', published in 1984, which explores the critical issues involved in such a topic. The question she posits is a deceptively simple one: 'what does "aimed at a female audience" mean?' She tackles this with reference to soap opera and film melodrama. By looking at the different ways in which feminist film studies and media studies have responded to this problematic, she draws attention to the distinctive theoretical development of both and the consequences for the conceptualisation of 'audience' in recognising 'women's genres'. This article serves to contextualise much feminist work on genre and insists that we pay attention to the audience in our understanding of the resilience of such popular female genres.

Soap opera can serve as the prime example of a popular television narrative form aimed at a female audience and has therefore been the focus of much attention from media and cultural studies (Brunsdon, 1981; Hobson, 1982; Cantor and Pingree, 1983; Allen, 1985; Ang, 1985). **Christine Geraghty**'s work on the generic characteristics of soap opera – narrative mode, central female characters, mass appeal to women – is represented in her piece 'A woman's space' in which she explores the ways in which soap opera offers particular pleasures for women, specifically by comparing the genre to other forms of television. She does this in the recognition that prime time soaps have employed strategies to attract a less specifically female audience. This raises pertinent questions in relation to viewing and female identity, and what it is to 'read as a woman'.

Along with Geraghty, a number of feminists have acknowledged the potential of popular genres with mass appeal to women. They are seen to offer a celebration of female culture and validation of 'competencies' attributed to women and more recently for subversion of dominant modes of 'femininity'. **Kathleen Rowe**'s study of 'Roseanne: unruly woman as domestic goddess' examines what is arguably one of the most conservative forms of popular television, the situation comedy (Neale and Krutnik, 1990). She sees *Roseanne* in terms of its subversive possibilities, invoking an historical understanding of the figure of the 'female transgressor' and her disruptive effect. However, Rowe argues that Roseanne Barr was able, through the eventual success of the programme, to take control over aspects of production, particularly in relation to the development of her character, and describes this as 'an unruly act *par excellence*'.

If the 'soap opera' can be described as the quintessential women's TV genre, then the equivalent within print media is the 'woman's magazine'. This is not to say that men neither watch nor read these products, but to acknowledge that both are concerned with female subjectivity, offering particular feminine identities to their viewers and readers. The ways in which, historically, different types of women's magazines construct particular versions of femininity has been of great interest to feminists (White, 1970; Ferguson, 1983) and especially in relation to their role in constructing and reconstructing women as consumers (Winship, 1987). In their 'A critical analysis of women's magazines', **Ros Ballaster, Margaret Beetham, Elizabeth Frazer** and **Sandra Hebron** introduce some of the key characteristics of women's magazines, identified through different critical approaches, in particular with regard to their construction of gender relations and the fragmentary and multiple nature of 'femininity' which they invite their readers to inhabit. Central to this process is consumption, both in terms of the economic organisation and textuality of the magazines and the range of identities and 'life styles' offered to the female reader.

Ellen McCracken's 'The cover: window to the future self' argues that the covers of women's magazines are particularly condensed forms of communication, vying for our attention on the news-stands, and as such are the most important advertisement in the magazine. The covers therefore offer idealized mirror images and an invitation into the particular world of the magazine constructed around a notion of feminine identity. Her analysis seeks to understand how these images work, particularly in establishing different genres of women's magazine.

References and further reading

ALLEN, R. 1985: *Speaking of soap operas*. Chapel Hill: University of North Carolina Press.
ANG, I. 1985: *Watching Dallas: soap opera and the melodramatic imagination*. London:

Methuen.

BROWN, M. E. 1990: *Television and women's culture: the politics of the popular.* London/Newbury Park/New Delhi: Sage.

BRUNSDON, C. 1981: 'Crossroads' – notes on soap opera. *Screen* 22, 32–37.

CANTOR, M. G. and PINGREE S. 1983: *The soap opera.* Beverley Hills/London/New Delhi: Sage.

DYER, R., GERAGHTY, C., LOVELL, T., JORDAN, M., PATERSON, R. and STEWART, J. 1981: *Coronation Street.* London: British Film Institute.

FERGUSON, M. 1983: *Forever feminine: women's magazines and the cult of femininity.* London: Heinemann.

HOBSON, D. 1982: *Crossroads: the drama of a soap opera.* London: Methuen.

MODLESKI, T. 1982: *Loving with a vengeance.* Hamden, Conn: Archon.

NEALE, S. and KRUTNIK, F. 1990: *Popular film and television comedy.* London/New York: Routledge.

WHITE, C. L. 1970: *Women's magazines 1693–1968.* London: Michael Joseph.

WINSHIP, J. 1987: *Inside women's magazines.* London/New York: Pandora Press.

8

Women's genres

Annette Kuhn

From *Screen* 25, 18–28 (1984)

Television soap opera and film melodrama, popular narrative forms aimed at female audiences, are currently attracting a good deal of critical and theoretical attention. Not surprisingly, most of the work on these 'gyno-centric' genres is informed by various strands of feminist thought on visual representation. Less obviously, perhaps, such work has also prompted a series of questions which relate to representation and cultural production in a more wide-ranging and thoroughgoing manner than a specifically feminist interest might suggest. Not only are film melodrama (and more particularly its subtype the 'woman's picture') and soap opera directed at female audiences, they are also actually enjoyed by millions of women. What is it that sets these genres apart from representations which possess a less gender-specific mass appeal?

One of the defining generic features of the woman's picture as a textual system is its construction of narratives motivated by female desire and processes of spectator identification governed by female point-of-view. Soap opera constructs woman-centred narratives and identifications, too, but it differs textually from its cinematic counterpart in certain other respects: not only do soaps never end, but their beginnings are soon lost sight of. And whereas in the woman's picture the narrative process is characteristically governed by the enigma-retardation-resolution structure which marks the classic narrative, soap opera narratives propose

> competing and intertwining plot lines introduced as the serial progresses. Each plot ... develops at a different pace, thus preventing any clear resolution of conflict. The completion of one story generally leads into others and ongoing plots often incorporate parts of semi-resolved conflicts.[1]

Recent work on soap opera and melodrama has drawn on existing theories, methods and perspectives in the study of film and television, including the structural analysis of narratives, textual semiotics and psychoanalysis, audience research, and the political economy of cultural institutions. At the same time, though, some of this work has exposed the limitations of existing approaches, and in consequence been forced if not actually to abandon them, at least to challenge their characteristic problematics. Indeed, it may be contended that the most significant developments in film and TV theory in general are currently taking place precisely within such areas of feminist concern as critical work on soap opera and melodrama.

In examining some of this work, I shall begin by looking at three areas in which particularly pertinent questions are being directed at theories of representation and cultural production. These are, firstly, the problem of gendered spectatorship; secondly, questions concerning the universalism as against the historical specificity of conceptualisations of gendered spectatorship; and thirdly, the relationship between film and television texts and their social, historical and institutional contexts. Each of these concerns articulates in particular ways with what seems to me the central issue here – the question of the audience, or audiences, for certain types of cinematic and televisual representation.

Film theory's appropriation to its own project of Freudian and post-Freudian psychoanalysis places the question of the relationship between text and spectator firmly on the agenda. Given the preoccupation of psychoanalysis with sexuality and gender, a move from conceptualising the spectator as a homogeneous and androgynous effect of textual operations[2] to regarding her or him as a gendered subject constituted in representation seems in retrospect inevitable. At the same time, the interests of feminist film theory and film theory in general converge at this point in a shared concern with sexual difference. Psychoanalytic accounts of the formation of gendered subjectivity raise the question, if only indirectly, of representation and feminine subjectivity. This in turn permits the spectator to be considered as a gendered subject position, masculine or feminine: and theoretical work on soap opera and the woman's picture may take this as a starting point for its inquiry into spectator-text relations. Do these 'gynocentric' forms address, or construct, a female or a feminine spectator? If so, how?

On the question of film melodrama, Laura Mulvey, commenting on King Vidor's *Duel in the Sun*,[3] argues that when, as in this film, a woman is at the centre of the narrative, the question of female desire structures the hermeneutic: 'What does *she* want?' This, says Mulvey, does not guarantee the constitution of the spectator as feminine so much as it implies a contradictory, and in the final instance impossible, 'phantasy of masculinisation' for the female spectator. This is in line with the author's earlier suggestion that cinema spectatorship involves masculine identification for spectators of either gender.[4] If cinema does thus construct a masculine subject, there can be no unproblematic feminine subject position for any spectator. [...]

Writers on TV soap opera tend to take views on gender and spectatorship rather different from those advanced by film theorists. Tania Modleski, for example, argues with regard to soaps that their characteristic narrative patterns, their foregrounding of 'female' skills in dealing with personal and domestic crises, and the capacity of their programme formats and scheduling to key into the rhythms of women's work in the home, all address a female spectator. Furthermore, she goes as far as to argue that the textual processes of soaps are in some respects similar to those of certain 'feminine' texts which speak to a decentred subject, and so are 'not altogether at odds with ... feminist aesthetics'.[5] Modleski's view is that soaps not only address female spectators, but in so doing construct feminine subject positions which transcend patriarchal modes of subjectivity.

Different though their respective approaches and conclusions might be, however, Mulvey, Cook and Modleski are all interested in the problem of gendered spectatorship. The fact, too, that this common concern is informed by a shared interest in assessing the progressive or transformative potential of soaps and melodramas is significant in light of the broad appeal of both genres to the mass audiences of women at which they are aimed.

But what precisely does it mean to say that certain representations are aimed at a female audience? However well theorised they may be, existing conceptualisations of gendered spectatorship are unable to deal with this question. This is because spectator and audience are distinct concepts which cannot – as they frequently are – be reduced to one another. [...] [I]t is important to note a further problem for film and television theory, posed in this case by the distinction between spectator and audience. Critical work on the woman's picture and on soap opera has necessarily, and most productively, emphasised the question of gendered spectatorship. In doing this, film theory in particular has taken on board a conceptualisation of the spectator derived from psychoanalytic accounts of the formation of human subjectivity.

Such accounts, however, have been widely criticised for their universalism. Beyond, perhaps, associating certain variants of the Oedipus complex with family forms characteristic of a patriarchal society and offering a theory of the construction of gender, psychoanalysis seems to offer little scope for theorising subjectivity in its cultural or historical specificity. Although in relation to the specific issues of spectatorship and representation there may, as I shall argue, be a way around this apparent impasse, virtually all film and TV theory – its feminist variants included – is marked by the dualism of universalism and specificity.

Nowhere is this more evident than in the gulf between textual analysis and contextual inquiry. Each is done according to different rules and procedures, distinct methods of investigation and theoretical perspectives. In bringing to the fore the question of spectator-text relations, theories deriving from psychoanalysis may claim – to the extent that the spectatorial apparatus is held to be coterminous with the cinematic or televisual institution – to address the relationship between text and context. But as soon as any attempt is made to combine textual analysis with analysis of the concrete social, historical and institutional conditions of production and reception of texts, it becomes clear that the context of the spectator/ subject of psychoanalytic theory is rather different from the context of production and reception constructed by conjunctural analyses of cultural institutions.

[...] In work on television soap opera as opposed to film melodrama, the dualism of text and context manifests itself rather differently, if only because – unlike film theory – theoretical work on television has tended to emphasise the determining character of the contextual level, particularly the structure and organisation of television institutions. Since this has often been at the expense of attention to the operation of TV texts, television theory may perhaps be regarded as innovative in the extent to which it attempts to deal specifically with texts as well as contexts. Some feminist critical work has in fact already begun to address the question of TV as text, though always with characteristic emphasis on the issue of gendered spectatorship. This emphasis constitutes a common concern of work on both TV soaps and the woman's picture, but a point of contact between text and context in either medium emerges only when the concept of social audience is considered in distinction from that of spectator.

Each term – spectator and social audience – presupposes a different set of relations to representations and to the contexts in which they are received. Looking at spectators and at audiences demands different methodologies and theoretical frameworks, distinct discourses which construct distinct subjectivities and social relations. The *spectator*, for example, is a subject constituted in signification, interpellated by the film or TV text. This does not necessarily mean that the spectator is merely an effect of the text, however, because modes of subjectivity which also operate outside spectator-text relations in film or TV are activated in the relationship between spectators and texts.

This model of the spectator/subject is useful in correcting more deterministic communication models which might, say, pose the spectator not as actively constructing meaning but simply as a receiver and decoder of preconstituted 'messages'. In emphasising spectatorship as a set of psychic relations and focusing on the relationship between spectator and text, however, such a model does disregard the broader social implications of filmgoing or televiewing. It is the social act of going to the cinema, for instance, that makes the individual cinemagoer part of an audience. Viewing television may involve social relations rather different from filmgoing, but in its own ways TV does depend on individual viewers being part of an audience, even if its members are never in one place at the same time. A group of people seated in a single auditorium looking at a film, or scattered across thousands of homes watching the same television programme, is a *social audience*. The concept of social audience, as against that of spectator, emphasises the status of cinema and television as social and economic institutions.

Constructed by discursive practices both of cinema and TV and of social science, the social audience is a group of people who buy tickets at the box office, or who switch on their TV sets; people who can be surveyed, counted and categorised according to age, sex and socio-economic status.[6] The cost of a cinema ticket or TV licence fee, or a readiness to tolerate commercial breaks, earns audiences the right to look at films and TV programmes, and so to be spectators. Social audiences become spectators in the moment they engage in the processes and pleasures of meaning-making attendant on watching a film or TV programme. The anticipated pleasure of spectatorship is perhaps a necessary condition of existence of audiences. In taking part in the social act of consuming representations, a group of spectators becomes a social audience.

The consumer of representations as audience member and spectator is involved in a particular kind of psychic and social relationship: at this point, a conceptualisation of the cinematic or televisual apparatus as a regime of pleasure intersects with sociological and economic understandings of film and TV as institutions. Because each term describes a distinct set of relationships, though, it is important not to conflate social audience with spectators. At the same time, since each is necessary to the other, it is equally important to remain aware of the points of continuity between the two sets of relations.

These conceptualisations of spectator and social audience have particular implications when it comes to a consideration of popular 'gynocentric' forms such as soap opera and melodrama. Most obviously, perhaps, these centre on the issue of gender, which prompts again the question: what does 'aimed at a female audience' mean? What exactly is being signalled in this reference to a gendered audience? Are women to be understood as a subgroup of the social audience, distinguishable through discourses which construct *a priori* gender categories? Or does the reference to a female audience allude rather to gendered spectatorship, to sexual difference constructed in relations between spectators and texts? Most likely, it condenses the two meanings; but an examination of the distinction between them may nevertheless be illuminating in relation to the broader theoretical issues of texts, contexts, social audiences and spectators.

The notion of a female social audience, certainly as it is constructed in the discursive practices through which it is investigated, presupposes a group of individuals already formed as female. For the sociologist interested in such matters as gender and lifestyles, certain people bring a pre-existent femaleness to their viewing or film and TV. For the business executive interested in selling commodities, TV programmes and films are marketed to individuals already constructed as female. Both, however, are interested in the same kind of woman. On one level, then, soap operas and women's melodramas address themselves to a social audience of women. But they may at the same time be regarded as speaking to a female, or a feminine, spectator. If soaps and melodramas inscribe femininity in their address, women – as well as being already formed *for* such representations – are in a sense also formed *by* them.

In making this point, however, I intend no reduction of femaleness to femininity: on the contrary, I would hold to a distinction between femaleness as social gender and femininity as subject position. For example, it is possible for a female spectator to be addressed, as it were, 'in the masculine', and the converse is presumably also true. Nevertheless, in a culturally pervasive operation of ideology, femininity is routinely identified with femaleness and masculinity with maleness. Thus, for example, an address 'in the feminine' may be regarded in ideological terms as privileging, if not necessitating, a socially constructed female gender identity.

The constitutive character of both the woman's picture and the soap opera has in fact been noted by a number of feminist commentators. Tania Modleski, for instance, suggests that the characteristic narrative structures and textual operations of soap operas both address the viewer as an 'ideal mother' – ever-understanding, ever-tolerant of the weaknesses and foibles of others – and also posit states of expectation and passivity as pleasurable:

the narrative, by placing ever more complex obstacles between desire and ful-filment, makes anticipation of an end an end in itself.[7]

In our culture, tolerance and passivity are regarded as feminine attributes, and consequently as qualities proper in women but not in men.

Charlotte Brunsdon extends Modleski's line of argument to the extra-tex-tual level: in constructing its viewers as competent within the ideological and moral frameworks of marriage and family life, soap opera, she implies, addresses both a feminine spectator and female audience.[8] Pointing to the centrality of intuition and emotion in the construction of the woman's point-of-view, Pam Cook regards the construction of a feminine spectator as a highly problematic and contradictory process: so that in the film melo-drama's construction of female point-of-view, the validity of femininity as a subject position is necessarily laid open to question.[9]

This divergence on the question of gendered spectatorship within femi-nist theory is significant. Does it perhaps indicate fundamental differences between film and television in the spectator-text relations privileged by each? Do soaps and melodramas really construct different relations of gen-dered spectatorship, with melodrama constructing contradictory identifica-tions in ways that soap opera does not? Or do these different positions on spectatorship rather signal an unevenness of theoretical development – or, to put it less teleologically, reflect the different intellectual histories and epistemological groundings of film theory and television theory?

Any differences in the spectator-text relations proposed respectively by soap opera and by film melodrama must be contingent to some extent on more general disparities in address between television and cinema. Thus film spectatorship, it may be argued, involves the pleasures evoked by look-ing in a more pristine way than watching television. Whereas in classic cin-ema the concentration and involvement proposed by structures of the look, identification and point-of-view tend to be paramount, television specta-torship is more likely to be characterised by distraction and diversion.[10] This would suggest that each medium constructs sexual difference through spec-tatorship in rather different ways: cinema through the look and spectacle, and television – perhaps less evidently – through a capacity to insert its flow, its characteristic modes of address, and the textual operations of dif-ferent kinds of programmes into the rhythms and routines of domestic activities and sexual divisions of labour in the household at various times of day.

It would be a mistake, however, simply to equate current thinking on spectator-text relations in each medium. This is not only because theoreti-cal work on spectatorship as it is defined here is newer and perhaps not so developed for television as it has been for cinema, but also because con-ceptualisations of spectatorship in film theory and TV theory emerge from quite distinct perspectives. When feminist writers on soap opera and on film melodrama discuss spectatorship, therefore, they are usually talking about different things. This has partly to do with the different intellectual histories and methodological groundings of theoretical work on film and on television. Whereas most TV theory has until fairly recently existed under the sociological rubric of media studies, film theory has on the whole been based in the criticism-oriented tradition of literary studies. In consequence, while the one tends to privilege contexts over texts, the other usually privileges texts over contexts.

However, some recent critical work on soap opera, notably work produced within a cultural studies context, does attempt a *rapprochement* of text and context. Charlotte Brunsdon, writing about the British soap opera *Crossroads*, draws a distinction between subject positions proposed by texts and a 'social subject' who may or may not take up these positions.[11] In considering the interplay of 'social reader and social text', Brunsdon attempts to come to terms with problems posed by the universalism of the psychoanalytic model of the spectator/subject as against the descriptiveness and limited analytical scope of studies of specific instances and conjunctures. In taking up the instance of soap opera, then, one of Brunsdon's broader objectives is to resolve the dualism of text and context.

'Successful' spectatorship of a soap like *Crossroads*, it is argued, demands a certain cultural capital: familiarity with the plots and characters of a particular serial as well as with soap opera as a genre. It also demands wider cultural competence, especially in the codes of conduct of personal and family life. For Brunsdon, then, the spectator addressed by soap opera is constructed within culture rather than by representation. This, however, would indicate that such a spectator, a 'social subject', might – rather than being a subject in process of gender positioning – belong after all to a social audience already divided by gender.

The 'social subject' of this cultural model produces meaning by decoding messages or communications, an activity which is always socially situated.[12] Thus although such a model may move some way towards reconciling text and context, the balance of Brunsdon's argument remains weighted in favour of context: spectator-text relations are apparently regarded virtually as an effect of socio-cultural contexts. Is there a way in which spectator/subjects of film and television texts can be thought in a historically specific manner, or indeed a way for the social audience to be rescued from social/historical determinism?

Although none of the feminist criticism of soap opera and melodrama reviewed here has come up with any solution to these problems, it all attempts, in some degree and with greater or lesser success, to engage with them. Brunsdon's essay possibly comes closest to an answer, paradoxically because its very failure to resolve the dualism which ordains that spectators are constructed by texts while audiences have their place in contexts begins to hint at a way around the problem. Although the hybrid 'social subject' may turn out to be more a social audience member than a spectator, this concept does suggest that a move into theories of discourse could prove to be productive.

Both spectators and social audience may accordingly be regarded as discursive constructs. Representations, contexts, audiences and spectators would then be seen as a series of interconnected social discourses, certain discourses possessing greater constitutive authority at specific moments than others. Such a model permits relative autonomy for the operations of texts, readings and contexts, and also allows for contradictions, oppositional readings and varying degrees of discursive authority. Since the state of a discursive formation is not constant, it can be apprehended only by means of inquiry into specific instances or conjunctures. In attempting to deal with the text-context split and to address the relationship between spectators and social audiences, therefore, theories of representation may have to come to terms with discursive formations of the social, cultural and textual.

[...] The popularity of television soap opera and film melodrama with women raises the question of how it is that sizeable audiences of women relate to these representations and the institutional practices of which they form part. It provokes, too, a consideration of the continuity between women's interpellation as spectators and their status as a social audience. In turn, the distinction between social audience and spectator/subject, and attempts to explore the relationship between the two, are part of a broader theoretical endeavour: to deal in tandem with texts and contexts. The distinction between social audience and spectator must also inform debates and practices around cultural production, in which questions of context and reception are always paramount. For anyone interested in feminist cultural politics, such considerations will necessarily inform any assessment of the place and the political usefulness of popular genres aimed at, and consumed by, mass audiences of women.

Notes

1. Muriel G. Cantor and Suzanne Pingree, *The Soap Opera* (Beverley Hills, Sage Publications, 1983), p. 22. Here 'soap opera' refers to daytime (US) or early evening (UK) serials ... not prime-time serials like *Dallas* and *Dynasty*.
2. See Jean-Louis Baudry, 'Ideological Effects of the Basic Cinematographic Apparatus', *Film Quarterly* vol. 28 no. 2 (1974–5), pp. 39–47; Christian Metz, 'The Imaginary Signifier', *Screen* Summer 1975, vol. 16 no. 2, pp. 14–76.
3. Laura Mulvey, 'Afterthoughts on "Visual Pleasure and Narrative Cinema"', *Framework* nos. 15/16/17 (1981), pp. 12–15.
4. Laura Mulvey, 'Visual Pleasure and Narrative Cinema', *Screen* Autumn 1975, vol. 16 no. 3, pp. 6–18.
5. Tania Modleski, *Loving With a Vengeance: Mass Produced Fantasies for Women* (Hamden Connecticut, The Shoe String Press, 1982), p. 105. See also Tania Modleski, 'The Search for Tomorrow in Today's Soap Operas', *Film Quarterly* vol. 33 no. 1 (1979), pp. 12–21.
6. Methods and findings of social science research on the social audience for American daytime soap operas are discussed in Cantor and Pingree, op. cit., Chapter 7.
7. Modleski, *Loving With a Vengeance*, op. cit., p. 88.
8. Charlotte Brunsdon, 'Crossroads: Notes on Soap Opera', *Screen*, vol. 22 no. 4 (1981), pp. 32–37.
9. Pam Cook, 'Melodrama and the Women's Picture', in Sue Aspinall and Robert Murphy (eds.), *Gainsborough Melodrama* (London, BFI, 1983), p. 10.
10. John Ellis, *Visible Fictions* (London, Routledge and Kegan Paul, 1982).
11. Brunsdon, op. cit., p. 32.
12. A similar model is also adopted by Dorothy Hobson in *Crossroads: the Drama of a Soap Opera* (London, Methuen, 1982).

9

A woman's space

Christine Geraghty

From *Women and soap opera: a study of prime time soaps* (Polity 1991)

[...] The assumption that soaps are for women is widely held and the interest shown in soaps by both feminist critics and the more traditional
women's magazines stems from this appeal to a predominantly female
audience.[1] This chapter attempts to explore the way in which the programmes offer particular enjoyment to female viewers and to point to the
ways in which they differ in this respect from other TV programmes. One
of [my] central arguments is that the prime time soaps I am examining
have changed in their attempts to attract a less specifically female-domi-
nated audience. Nevertheless, it is still possible to map out the traditional
framework which had been established by programmes like *Coronation
Street* and *Crossroads* over many years and to examine the nature of the
appeal of more recent soaps like *Dallas* and *Dynasty* to women. This is a
complex area in which we need to distinguish between the position offered
to the woman viewer by the programmes; the social subject positioned
through race, gender and class; and the responses of individual viewers.
As Charlotte Brunsdon has argued, a distinction needs to be made 'between
the subject positions that a text constructs, and the social subject who may
or may not take these positions up'.[2] A particular view on abortion, for
instance, may be proposed by a soap but it may not be adopted by women
in the audience. The individual woman viewer may reject the positions and
pleasures offered by soaps, as David Morley found in interviewing women
in South London who saw themselves as different from other women
because they did not like or watch soaps.[3] Even those who accept the invitation may do so for different reasons than those implied by the programmes, taking pleasure in the spectacle of *Dallas* for instance but refusing
its emotional demands. Enjoyment will be affected by the way in which
the woman viewer is herself positioned within the home as
mother/wife/daughter, for instance, and her activities outside it. The
teenage girl watching *Dallas* may enjoy different things from her mother.
So in assuming an audience in which women predominate neither pro-
gramme-maker nor critic can assume that women are a consistent or
unchanging category. Nevertheless, the importance of soaps in Western culture as one of the litmus tests of the 'feminine' still needs to be considered.

What is it about soaps that makes a male viewer assert, 'it's not manly to talk about soaps'?[4]

The concerns of soaps have traditionally been based on the commonly perceived split between the public and the personal, between work and leisure, reason and emotion, action and contemplation. This tradition not only offers a set of oppositions but consistently values what are seen to be the more active modes – those of the public sphere – over those whose terrain is the personal and hence deemed to be less effective and more passive. The use of such distinctions are endemic in our culture and are as common for instance among left-wing trade unionists as among right-wing businessmen, both emphasising work as primary, action as necessary and cooperation between people (race and gender immaterial) as being essential for progress and change. This is not to say that both groups operate in the same way, let alone have the same aims, but that the vocabulary of the public world springs to their lips because their aims, however different, are to affect what they perceive as the public arena. The ultimate pair of oppositions, on which such differences rest, is masculine and feminine and it is feminists who in different ways have been questioning the naturalness of such dichotomies. In some cases, the task has been to bring the personal into the public sphere and thus to repair the split (the introduction of child care and sexuality issues into trade union activity, for example); in others, it has been to celebrate the specificity of women's pleasures and to re-evaluate them against the grain of male denigration.

In this context, it becomes possible to see why soaps are not merely seen as silly but positively irritating and even unmanly. Soaps overturn the deeply entrenched value structure which is based on the traditional oppositions of masculinity and femininity. Compared with other TV programmes, such as police series or the news, the actions in soaps, while heavily marked, lack physical weight. Bobby's periodic punch-ups with JR hardly compare with the regular confrontations even in *Hill Street Blues* let alone *Miami Vice*. Instead, the essence of soaps is the reflection on personal problems and the emphasis is on talk not on action, on slow development rather than the immediate response, on delayed retribution rather than instant effect. All television relies on the repetition of familiar characters and stories but soaps more than other genres offer a particular type of repetition in which certain emotional situations are tested out through variations in age, character, social milieu and class. Personal relationships are the backbone of soaps. They provide the dramatic moments – marriage, birth, divorce, death – and the more day-to-day exchanges of quarrels, alliances and dilemmas which make up the fabric of the narrative. The very repetition of soap opera plots allows them to offer a paradigm of emotional relationships in which only one element needs to be changed for the effect to be different. Soaps offer a continually shifting kaleidoscope of emotional relationships which allow the audience to test out how particular emotional variations can or should be handled.

On a broad level, soap stories may seem to be repetitive and over familiar. One set of stories, for example, deals with the relationships between men and women, offering a recognisable scenario of courtship, marriage and separation through quarrels, divorce or death. At the micro level, however, the differences become crucial since the testing-out process depends on the repetition of a number of elements but with one significantly changed. The audience is engaged by the question 'What would happen if ...?' and given the opportunity to try out a set of variants. *Coronation Street* offers a good example of this process in its handling of the courtship-marriage scenario. It invites the audience to consider a number of pairings as if to test out which is the most satisfying and durable. What happens to a marriage, it asks, if the husband is the local liberal conscience of the community and the wife lively, sociable and previously married to a ne'er-do-well [...], if a stolid middle-aged grocer marries a flighty blonde with a dubious past [...]; if 'one of the lads' marries a woman who is more mature and sensible than he is [...]; if 'one of the lads' marries an irresponsible but determined young girl with a mind of her own [...].[5] The same stories yield a rich vein of plots in which the differences in age, character and status are minutely explored. The same variety can be seen in other general plots – those concerned with parent–child relationships for example or with the parameters of community and friendship. This testing-out process is, of course, carried out within the serial by the commentary of the characters, some of whom achieve an almost chorus-like function, underlining the nuances of the changing situation. [...] Viewing soaps with friends or family is often accompanied by a commentary of informed advice to the characters – 'she shouldn't trust him', 'if he hadn't said that, it would have been alright', 'how could she forget?' When the popular press asked their agony aunts whether Deirdre Barlow in *Coronation Street* should remain with her husband or leave him for her lover, they were making concrete (and using one of the sources chosen for support by women themselves) the conversations which were taking place in homes and workplaces all over the country.[6] The weighing up of the qualities of the two men against Deirdre's own character, the financial situation, the needs of the child involved – all these factors had to be taken into account and the pleasure for the female viewer in rehearsing the decision-making process without the responsibility for its consequences should not be underestimated.

For it is still women who are deemed to carry the responsibility for emotional relationships in our society – who keep the home, look after the children, write the letters or make the phone calls to absent friends, seek advice on how to solve problems, consult magazines on how to respond 'better' to the demands made on them. It is this engagement with the personal which is central to women's involvement with soaps but it is important to be precise about how that involvement works. It is not just that soap operas have a domestic setting. Much of television takes place either in home settings or leisure venues. Nor is it that social problems are made personal or manageable in soaps. It could be argued that many different types of TV programmes, including police series and the news, use the same mode. Nor is it just the fact that soaps feature strong women in major roles though the pleasures of that are certainly substantial. It is the process which is important, the way in which soaps recognise and value the emotional work which women undertake in the personal sphere. Soaps rehearse to their female audience the process of handling personal relationships – the balancing of each individual's needs, the attention paid to every word and gesture so as to understand its emotional meaning, the recognition of competing demands for attention.

This engagement of the audience in a constant rehearsal of emotional dilemmas has been articulated in a number of ways. Two of the most important contributors to the debate, Tania Modleski and Charlotte Brunsdon, have specifically looked at the structures by which soap operas address their female audience in a way which chimes with the construction outside the programmes of women as the emotional centre of the home and family. Modleski, in her influential study of US daytime soaps, argues that 'the formal properties of daytime television ... accord closely with the rhythms of women's work in the home'.[7] She describes two different kinds of women's work, to be both 'moral and spiritual guides and household drudges'[8] and sees the daytime soaps as permitting and indeed supporting both roles. For the household drudge, the soap operas, with their slow pace, repetition, dislocated and overlapping story lines and their emphasis on the ordinary rather than the glamorous, provide a narrative which can be understood without the concentration required by prime time television. 'Unlike most workers in the labor force,' Modleski suggests, 'the housewife must beware of concentrating her energies too exclusively on any one task – otherwise, the dinner could burn or the baby could crack its skull'.[9] The soap opera form replicates this fragmented and distracted approach and makes it pleasurable. Modleski argues that the housewife's 'duties are split among a variety of domestic and familial tasks, and her television programs keep her from desiring a focused existence by involving her in the pleasures of a fragmented life'.[10] In doing so, the soap opera 'reflects and cultivates the "proper" psychological disposition of the woman in the home'.[11]

On the moral and emotional front, Modleski ascribes to soaps a similar function of reinforcing the work ascribed to women of nurturing relationships and holding the family together. Again, she adroitly links the formal properties of the genre with its subject matter and proposes that 'soap operas invest exquisite pleasure in the central condition of a woman's life; waiting – whether for her phone to ring, for the baby to take its nap, or for the family to be reunited after the day's final soap opera has left its family still struggling against dissolution'.[12] It is important to Modleski's argument that soaps do not, as they are sometimes accused, present ideal families able to achieve harmony and resolution. Instead, the literally endless tales with their variety of insoluble dilemmas offer reassurance that the woman viewer is not alone in her inability to reconcile and hold together the family unit. What is demanded by the soaps is the tolerance of the good mother who is able to see that there is no right answer and who is understanding and sympathetic to 'both the sinner and the victim'.[13] 'Soap operas convince women that their highest goal is to see their families united and happy, while consoling them for their inability to realise this ideal and bring about familial harmony'.[14] And indeed the goal is unrealisable in more ways than one since Modleski points out that the soap opera does not offer a mirror image of the viewer's own family but 'a kind of *extended* family, the direct opposite of her own isolated nuclear family'.[15] What the housewife experiences is an isolation rooted in her real experience for which soap operas offer a form of consolation.

Modleski does offer the housewife/viewer an outlet for the frustrations and contradictions implicit in her dual role. Here she cites the delight viewers take in despising the soap opera villainess who uses situations such as pregnancy and marriage, which frequently trap women in soaps, to her own selfish ends. The villainess's refusal to appreciate, let alone acquiesce in, the needs of others is in contrast to the passive role of the other characters (and indeed the viewer) and provides 'an outlet for feminine anger'.[16] But because the villainess is a bad figure, Modleski argues that women's frustration is directed 'against the one character who refuses to accept her own powerlessness, who is unashamedly self-seeking'.[17] Soap operas continually acknowledge the existence of women's contradictory impulses – the demise of one villainess leads to the creation of another – but they are, in Modleski's view, rendered harmless since 'woman's anger is directed at woman's anger, and an eternal cycle is created'.[18]

Loving with a Vengeance deals with US daytime soaps which in their scheduling and format are different from the soaps discussed in this book. Nevertheless, there is much here which rings true, particularly in Modleski's account of the way in which soaps encourage the viewer to take into account a number of viewpoints on the same story and provide, over a period of time, explanations (or perhaps excuses) for ill-advised or even wrong actions. It is sometime unclear, however, whether Modleski is analysing the position of the good mother which soaps encourage their viewers to adopt or is describing the housewife/viewer as a social subject, formed by her own social and economic circumstances. This is, as we have seen, a difficult distinction but in either case the female viewer seems curiously passive and isolated. Despite her argument that soap opera is in the vanguard of all popular narrative art and her appeal to feminists to build on rather than reject the fantasy of community offered by soaps Modleski's viewer comes close to the model offered by less sympathetic critics. She is distracted, lonely, unable to make judgements or to discriminate; her anger is internalised, directed at her own scarcely expressed desire for greater power. She waits for the nonexistent family to return so that she can perform her role as ideal mother but is denied even 'this extremely flattering illusion of her power'[19] by the genre's insistence on the insolubility of the problems it is the mother's task to solve. Almost despite herself, Modleski seems to share the doubts which feminists and others have expressed that soap operas, like other forms of women's fiction, serve only to keep women in their place. The depressing nature of this place seems to come about not merely because of the low economic status of 'the housewife' but also because her very pleasure in soap opera is based on a masochistic acknowledgement of her powerlessness and the uselessness of her own skills.

Other feminist critics have taken a more positive approach which, while not doubting the oppression imposed on women in and outside the home, has argued that it is important not to underrate women's role in the personal sphere. Charlotte Brunsdon, in her article on *Crossroads*, examines the notion of a gendered audience in an attempt to come to terms with the pleasures offered to the female viewer. Brunsdon argues that the scheduling of the programme in the late afternoon/early evening and the advertising and spin-offs surrounding it – interview material, cookbooks, knitting patterns – are addressed to the feminine consumer, the viewer who is constructed in her gender-based role of wife, mother, housewife, and that these extra-textual factors 'suggest that women are the target audience for *Crossroads*'.[20] Drawing attention to the distinction made between public and personal life, Brunsdon defines 'the ideological problematic of soap opera' as that of 'personal life in its everyday realisation through personal relationships' and argues that 'it is within this realm of the domestic, the personal, the private, that feminine competence is recognised'.[21] She acknowledges the incoherence of *Crossroads* in terms of its spatial and temporal organisation, its narrative interruptions and repetitions and its dramatic irresolution but argues that its coherence, for those (feminine) viewers who know how to read it, is articulated through the moral and ideological frameworks which the programme explores; '*Crossroads* is in the business not of creating narrative excitement, suspense, delay and resolution, but of constructing moral consensus about the conduct of personal life'.[22] The competent viewer needs to be skilled in three areas – that of generic knowledge (familiarity with soap opera as a genre), that of serial-specific knowledge (knowledge of narrative and character in *Crossroads*) and that of cultural knowledge of the way in which one's personal life is (or should be) conducted. It is this last competence to which Brunsdon draws particular attention for it is the basis of her argument that *Crossroads* as a text (rather than through its extratextual factors) implies a gendered audience; 'it is the culturally constructed skills of femininity – sensitivity, perception, intuition and the necessary privileging of the concerns of personal life – which are both called on and practised in the genre'.[23] *Crossroads* requires skilled readers to make it pleasurable and the competencies necessary for that process are the very ones which are valued in the soaps themselves.

The process of testing out emotional situations which I described earlier clearly owes much to Brunsdon's notion of competence in personal life. Brunsdon does not take up Modleski's suggestion of the viewer as the 'ideal mother' possessed of endless tolerance, although she agrees that *Crossroads*, like the US daytime soaps, offers a 'range of different opinions and understandings' and 'a consistent holding off of *denouement* and knowledge'.[24] Nevertheless, the article does imply that the viewer is called on to make judgements about characters even while recognising that events next week might change the basis of that judgement once more. Brunsdon emphasises the importance of stories which centre on lies and deceit when the audience knows more than the characters involved and 'can see clearly what and who is "right"'.[25] She adds that the question determining a soap opera narrative is not 'What will happen next?' but 'What kind of person is this?' – a question which both acknowledges the importance of the individual character and implies a moral/social judgement about that character. I emphasise this, perhaps against the grain of other parts of the article, because it seems to me that it is this acknowledgement of the capacity to judge which enables Brunsdon, unlike Modleski, to value the process she describes. The judgements may not be firm or final; certainly the moral framework is not fixed – two similar actions (the breaking off of an engagement, for example) may require different decisions and the viewer may indeed decide to postpone judgement until a more suitable time, in itself an active decision rather than a passive one. But until we replace the model of the tolerant viewer accepting everything with that of Brunsdon's competent viewer weighing the emotional dilemmas put before her, we are always going to underestimate the position offered to the female viewer of soap operas.

The question of judgement is the more important because it is tied in with one of the most consistent pleasures offered to women by soaps – that of being on our side. Again this is not just a question of a domestic setting or an emphasis on a particular type of story both of which could apply to situation comedies without the same kind of effect. It is more that soap operas, not always, not continuously, but at key points, offer an understanding from the woman's viewpoint that affects the judgements that the viewer is invited to make. This sense of being 'down among the women' is crucial to the pleasures of recognition which soaps offer women – a slightly secretive, sometimes unspoken understanding developed through the endless analysis of emotional dilemmas which Modleski and Brunsdon describe. This effect is achieved in a number of ways but essential to it is the soap's basic premise that women are understandable and rational, a premise that flies in the face of much TV drama.

Because soaps are rooted in the personal sphere, the actions of the women in them become explicable and often, though not always, correct. In itself this runs counter to much television drama in which women's association with the personal is deemed to be a disadvantage because it clouds their judgement. In soaps, competence in the personal sphere is valued and women are able to handle difficult decisions well because of it. One simple example of this occurred in *Crossroads* when, following the death of Diane, a long-standing and well-loved character, her friends Jill and Adam Chance (married but at the time separated) discuss funeral arrangements with the undertaker. Throughout the interview, Adam urges a commonsense view that Diane would not want too much money spent while Jill tries to insist that they have the best. This exchange would not be unusual in any other TV drama. What is striking, however, is that Jill is not exposed as hysterical or overemotional but as trying appropriately to recognise her own loss and Diane's worth; the viewer is invited to understand Jill's concern and her approach is presented as rational and appropriate.

Such small moments are common in soaps. On a larger scale, consistent recognition is given to the emotional situations which women are deemed to share. At its most obvious, this sense of a common feeling marks major events such as birth, marriage, the death of a child or the development of a romance. When such a moment occurs for a female character, the other women are seen to understand it even while they might not welcome it. Thus, Pam in *Dallas* was sympathetic to Miss Ellie's fears when the 'new' Jock Ewing appeared and encouraged her to talk about her sexual and emotional feelings. Sue Ellen, though very dubious about what would happen, accompanied and supported Pam in her search for Mark in Hong Kong. Similarly, Deirdre Barlow in *Coronation Street* supported her step-daughter's decision to have an abortion and argued with Mike Baldwin that he should be looking to his wife Susan's needs rather than his own desire to have a child. Even when the women are at odds with each other they share a common sense of what is at stake. When Nicola in *Crossroads* tried to explain to her long-lost daughter why she had given her away at birth, Tracy was angry and upset. But she and Nicola were able to conduct a dialogue from which the men were excluded either because of ignorance or from a desire to rush to hasty judgement. In *Dynasty*, Karen, Dana and Alexis had opposing and competing interests in Adam but shared common feelings around maternity when Karen bore Adam's child and Dana went so far as to risk Adam's loss of his son through expressing in court her own sympathy for Karen's right as the natural mother to keep the child.

This sense of common feeling is often more rueful than celebratory, rooted in a shared perception that men can never live up to the demands women make of them. Mavis and Rita, in *Coronation Street*'s corner shop, comment, the one wistfully, the other sardonically, on the behaviour of men while, on one memorable occasion, Sue Ellen, so often the butt of other women's sympathetic glances, commiserated with some satisfaction with Miss Ellie and Jenna on the absence of their men from that morning's breakfast table. (Bobby's night out was later explained of course by his death.) In both cases, the sense of a common situation is strong even when reactions to it differ. Traditionally, soaps value this sense of female solidarity and have worked on the assumption that women have common attitudes and problems, 'are sisters under the skin' as the respectable Annie Walker once acknowledged to the rather less respectable Elsie Tanner in *Coronation Street*. Women in soaps define themselves as different from men and pride themselves on the difference, a position which the programmes endorse. 'Despite everything,' says Angie in *EastEnders*, 'I'm still glad I'm not a man.' 'You've got to remember they're like children,' Lou Beale tells her granddaughter Michelle in the same programme, voicing another common feeling shared by women characters in soaps. In addition, the women frequently console each other at the end of a romance, as Bet Lynch did with Jenny in *Coronation Street*, with a variation on 'There's not one of them worth it.' This expression of an underlying solidarity based on a shared position persists even when the women appear to be on opposite sides. Pam Ewing helped Sue Ellen remove her child from Southfork, emphasising that she understood Sue Ellen's feeling in a way in which the men could not. In return, Sue Ellen commented 'I don't want us to lose our friendship ... we have to try hard not to get into their fights.' 'Take more than a couple of fellas to split us up,' Rita Fairclough tells Mavis in *Coronation Street* in a similarly explicit acknowledgement of the importance of female friendship.

A further factor in establishing a shared female viewpoint is indeed the range of emotional relationships in which the women characters are involved. It is too often assumed that soaps emphasise male–female relationships at the expense of others. In fact, because the central husband–wife relationship is such hard work for the women characters, they need to be supported by other friendships which are more reliably sustaining. The relationship between mother and daughter, for instance, is central to many soaps, providing an irresistible combination of female solidarity and family intimacy. [...] Equally important, perhaps, is the emphasis placed on female friendship and the time spent showing women talking together. [. . .] The programmes continually show women talking to each other, sometimes in moments of high drama, sometimes in a routine way as if it were an everyday occurrence that needed no emphasis. When *EastEnders* devoted a whole episode to Ethel and Dot, reminiscing, quarrelling, spilling secrets, making tea, it was unusual only in that it was drawing specific attention to the fact that female conversation is the backbone of the traditional soap.

The centrality of women in soaps has the effect of making them the norm by which the programmes are understood. They are not peripheral to the stories; they are not mysterious, enigmatic or threatening as they so often are in thrillers or crime stories. They handle the complex web of relationships which make up a soap opera with a care and intensity which makes the men seem clumsy and uncomprehending. Even when the women are wrong they are transparent and understandable, an unusual characteristic for women in a culture in which they are deemed most desirable when they are most opaque and enigmatic. This is not to say that soaps present women more realistically as feminists sometimes demand of representations of women. Neither Sue Ellen nor Angie Watts would be deemed particularly realistic representations and in some ways their characters are presented as particularly and conventionally feminine. Married to men who emotionally abuse them, apparently irrational and sometimes devious, volatile, brittle and soft-hearted, Angie and Sue Ellen, it could be argued, represent gender stereotyping of a high degree. Yet it is also important that the audience is not only consistently presented with information and comment on what these women do but is also continually implicated in their actions by being drawn into their logic. The baffled assertion of commonsense in the face of women's emotions still permeates much of TV fiction as it did mainstream film genres like film noir. In soaps, such a lack of understanding is impossible for the male as well as the female viewer because we have been led through every step of the woman character's way.

This shift is accompanied by a move away from the male figure as the agent of the action. TV fiction took over from mainstream film the narrative structure in which 'the man's role' is 'the active one of forwarding the story, making things happen'.[26] Even in *Hill Street Blues*, for example, the stories are initiated by men making things happen or by women having things happen to them. But in soap operas, not only do women take action but the audience is led through that process with them. In *EastEnders*, for instance, the traditional triangle of Den manoeuvering between his wife Angie and his mistress Jan might have given the impression that it was the man who was, if not in control of the situation, at least the active agent. Nothing could be further from the truth because the audience was aware not merely of Angie's plans to fight for her marriage through her lies about her illness, for instance, but also of Jan's determination to push for her own needs. Only the man remained baffled, frustrated and incoherent in the centre of an emotional maelstrom. What is important here is not so much the outcome of the action (Angie's stratagems failed in this instance) but the fact that the audience was prevented from sharing Den's bafflement. Whatever judgements are made about the women's behaviour, the reasons for their actions are laid out in detail to the audience and are meticulously worked over as the triangle of relationships shifts. In the same way, the saga of JR's dealings with Sue Ellen did not allow the audience to find her actions incomprehensible. Different viewers might have arguments about how far she could have avoided the saga of drink, injudicious affairs and madness, but the reasons for her behaviour, the desperate attempts to get JR's attention without losing control of her son, were always crystal clear.

It would be overstating the case to assert that, in prime time soaps, the position of men as narratively active, women as passive, is reversed. The action of male characters is crucial and often provokes, as in the examples above, the action taken by the women. Nevertheless, the position of engagement with the women characters which the audience is encouraged to adopt is based on the transparency of the women's behaviour; our understanding is invoked by the process of going through the narrative with them. Surprisingly often in soaps men are caught in a position of baffled impotence. 'Women', they say to each with resigned incomprehension 'who can understand them?' If this were said in a thriller or a police series, the male characters would be speaking from a position of superiority, asserting the irrationality of feminine behaviour. In soaps, such remarks are made from a position of ignorance, allowing the female viewer the satisfaction of knowing more and understanding more than these enraged and frustrated men. This is one of the central pleasures offered to women by soaps, a recognition based not so much on a realistic representation of women's everyday lives but on what it feels like to have so much invested in the personal sphere while men are unable to live up to or even be aware of its demands – Den and JR, the apparently powerful, caught in close-up at the end of the episode, floored once again by their inability to keep up with the women's ability to operate in the personal sphere.

Notes

1. Although soaps are still derided by TV critics and by many in the TV industry, the work of Brunsdon, Ang, Feuer and Modleski, among others, has, rather ironically, given soaps a higher status in the academic world of cultural studies and media theory.
2. Charlotte Brunsdon, ' "Crossroads" – Notes on Soap Opera', *Screen* vol. 22, no. 4, p. 32. For a more extensive discussion of work in this area, see Annette Kuhn, 'Women's genres', in Christine Gledhill (ed.), *Home is Where the Heart is* (British Film Institute, London, 1987).
3. David Morley, *Family Television: Cultural Power and Domestic Leisure* (Comedia, London, 1986), p. 164.
4. Male viewer in ITV's *Watching Us, Watching You*, 6 April 1987.
5. For a fuller discussion of the way narrative variants are organised in soaps, see Christine Geraghty, 'The Continuous Serial – a Definition', and Richard Paterson and John Stewart, 'Street Life', both in Richard Dyer (ed.), *Coronation Street* (British Film Institute, London, 1981).
6. *The Sun* (28 January 1983), for instance, ran contrasting articles on Deirdre's dilemma – 'Yes, why not have a fling?' by the Women's Editor, Wendy Henry, and 'No, don't fall for Mike's charms' by the Problems Columnist, Deirdre Sanders.
7. Tania Modleski, *Loving with a Vengeance* (Methuen, New York, 1982), p. 102.

8. ibid., p. 101.
9. ibid., p. 100.
10. ibid., p. 101.
11. ibid., p. 98.
12. ibid., p. 88.
13. ibid., p. 93.
14. ibid., p. 92.
15. ibid., p. 108.
16. ibid., p. 97.
17. ibid., p. 98.
18. ibid., p. 98.
19. ibid., p. 92.
20. Brunsdon, ' "Crossroads" – Notes on Soap Opera', p. 34.
21. ibid., p. 34.
22. ibid., p. 35.
23. ibid., p. 36.
24. ibid., p. 35.
25. ibid., pp. 35–6.
26. Laura Mulvey, 'Visual Pleasure in Narrative Cinema', in Philip Rosen (ed.), *Narrative, Apparatus, Ideology* (Columbia University Press, New York, 1986), p. 204.

10

Roseanne: unruly woman as domestic goddess

Kathleen K. Rowe

From *Screen* 31, 408–19 (1990)

[...] Questions about television celebrities often centre on a comparison with cinematic stars – on whether television turns celebrities into what various critics have called 'degenerate symbols' who are 'slouching toward stardom' and engaging in 'dialogues of the living dead'.[1] This article examines Roseanne Barr, a television celebrity who has not only slouched but whined, wisecracked, munched, mooned and sprawled her way to a curious and contradictory status in our culture explained only partially by the concept of stardom, either televisual or cinematic. Indeed, the metaphor of decay such critics invoke, while consistent with a strain of the grotesque associated with Barr, seems inappropriate to her equally compelling vitality and *jouissance*. In this paper, I shall be using the name 'Roseanne' to refer to Roseanne Barr-as-sign, a person we know only through her various roles and performances in the popular discourse. My use follows Barr's lead in effacing the lines among her roles: Her show, after all, bears her name and in interviews she describes her 'act' as 'who she is'.

Nearing the end of its second season, her sitcom securely replaced *The Cosby Show* at the top of the ratings. The readers of *People Weekly* identified her as their favorite female television star and she took similar prizes in the People's Choice award show this spring. Yet 'Roseanne', both person and show, has been snubbed by the Emmies, condescended to by media critics and trashed by the tabloids (never mind the establishment press). Consider *Esquire*'s solution of how to contain Roseanne. In an issue on its favorite (and least favorite) women, it ran two stories by two men, side by side – one called 'Roseanne – Yay', the other 'Roseanne – Nay'. And consider this from *Star*: 'Roseanne's shotgun "wedding from hell" – Dad refuses to give pregnant bride away –"Don't wed that druggie bum!" '; 'Maids of honor are lesbians – best man is groom's detox pal'; 'Ex-hubby makes last-ditch bid to block ceremony'; 'Rosie and Tom wolf two out of three tiers of wedding cake'. (6 Feb 1990) Granted that tabloids are *about* excess, there's often an edge of cruelty to that excess in Roseanne's case, and an effort to wrest her definition of herself from the comic to the melodramatic.

Such ambivalence is the product of several phenomena. Richard Dyer might explain it in terms of the ideological contradictions Roseanne plays upon – how, for example, the body of Roseanne-as-star magically reconciles the conflict women experience in a society that says 'consume' but look as if you don't. Janet Woollacott might discuss the clash of discourses inherent in situation comedy – how our pleasure in Roseanne's show arises not so much from narrative suspense about her actions as hero, nor from her one-liners, but from the economy or wit by which the show brings together two discourses on family life: one based on traditional liberalism and the other on feminism and social class. Patricia Mellencamp might apply Freud's analysis of wit to Roseanne as she did to Lucille Ball and Gracie Allen, suggesting that Roseanne ventures farther than her comic foremothers into the masculine terrain of the tendentious joke.[2]

All of these explanations would be apt, but none would fully explain the ambivalence surrounding Roseanne. Such an explanation demands a closer look at gender and at the historical representations of female figures similar to Roseanne. These figures, I believe, can be found in the tradition of the 'unruly woman', a *topos* of female outrageousness and transgression from literary and social history. Roseanne uses a 'semiotics of the unruly' to expose the gap she sees between the ideals of the New Left and the Women's Movement of the late 60s and early 70s on the one hand, and the realities of working class family life two decades later on the other.

Because female unruliness carries a strongly ambivalent charge, Roseanne's use of it both intensifies and undermines her popularity. Perhaps her greatest unruliness lies in the presentation of herself as *author* rather than actor and, indeed, as author of a self over which she claims control. Her insistence on her 'authority' to create and control the meaning of *Roseanne* is an unruly act *par excellence*, triggering derision or dismissal much like Jane Fonda's earlier attempts to 'write' her self (but in the genre of melodrama rather than comedy). I will explain this in three parts: the first takes a brief look at the tradition of the unruly woman; the second, at the unruly qualities of *excess* and *looseness* Roseanne embodies; and the third, at an episode of her sitcom which dramatizes the conflict between female unruliness and the ideology of 'true womanhood'.

The unruly woman is often associated with sexual inversion – 'the woman on top', according to social historian Natalie Zemon Davis, who fifteen years ago first identified her in her book *Society and Culture in Early Modern France*. The sexual inversion she represents, Davis writes, is less about gender confusion than about larger issues of social and political order that come into play when what belongs 'below' (either women themselves, or their images appropriated by men in drag) usurps the position of what belongs 'above'. This *topos* isn't limited to Early Modern Europe, but reverberates whenever women, especially women's bodies, are considered excessive – too fat, too mouthy, too old, too dirty, too pregnant, too sexual (or not sexual enough) for the norms of conventional gender representations. For women, excessive fatness carries associations with excessive wilfulness and excessive speech ('fat texts', as Patricia Parker explains in *Literary Fat Ladies*, a study of rhetoric, gender and property that traces literary examples of this connection from the Old Testament to the Twentieth Century).[3] Through body and speech, the unruly woman violates the unspoken feminine sanction against 'making a spectacle' of herself. I see the unruly woman as prototype of woman as subject – transgressive above all when she lays claim to her own desire.

The unruly woman is multivalent, her social power unclear. She has reinforced traditional structures, as Natalie Davis acknowledges.[4] But she has also helped sanction political disobedience for men and women alike by making such disobedience thinkable. She can signify the radical utopianism of undoing all hierarchy. She can also signify pollution (dirt or 'matter out of place', as Mary Douglas might explain). As such she becomes a source of danger for threatening the conceptual categories which organize our lives. For these reasons – for the power she derives from her liminality, her associations with boundaries and taboo – she evokes not only delight but disgust and fear. Her ambivalence, which is the source of her oppositional power, is usually contained within the licence accorded to the comic and the caranivalesque. But not always.

[...] The disruptive power of these women – carnivalesque and carnivalized – contains much potential for feminist appropriation. Such an appropriation could enable us to problematize two areas critical to feminist theories of spectatorship and the subject: the social and cultural norms of femininity, and our understanding of how we are constructed as gendered subjects in the language of spectacle and the visual. In her essay 'Female Grotesques', Mary Russo asks: 'In what sense can women really produce or make spectacles out of themselves? ... The figure of female transgressor as public spectacle is still powerfully resonant, and the possibilities of redeploying this representation as a demystifying or utopian model have not been exhausted'.[5] She suggests that the parodic excesses of the unruly woman and the comic conventions surrounding her provide a space to act out the dilemmas of femininity, to *make visible* and *laughable* what Mary Ann Doane describes as the 'tropes of femininity'.

Such a sense of spectacle differs from Laura Mulvey's. It accepts the relation between power and visual pleasure but argues for an understanding of that relation as more historically determined, its terms more mutable. More Foucaldian than Freudian, it suggests that visual power flows in multiple directions and that the position of spectacle isn't entirely one of weakness. Because public power is predicated largely on visibility, men have traditionally understood the need to secure their power not only by looking but by being seen – or rather, by fashioning, as author, a spectacle of themselves. Already bound in a web of visual power, women might begin to renegotiate its terms. Such a move would be similar to what Teresa de Lauretis advocates when she calls for the strategic use of narrative to 'construct other forms of coherence, to shift the terms of representation, to produce the conditions of representability of another – and gendered – social subject'.[6] By returning the male gaze, we might expose (make a spectacle of) the gazer. And by utilizing the power already invested in us as image, we might begin to negate our own 'invisibility' in the public sphere.

The spectacle Roseanne creates is *for* herself, produced *by* herself from a consciously developed perspective on ethnicity, gender and social class. This spectacle derives much of its power from her construction of it as her 'self' – an entity which, in turn, she has knowingly fashioned through interviews, public performances and perhaps most unambiguously her autobiography. This book, by its very existence, enhances the potency of Roseanne-as-sign because it grants a historicity to her 'self' and a materiality to her claims for authorship. The autobiography describes key moments in the development of 'Roseanne' – how she learned about female strength when for the first time in her life she saw a woman (her grandmother) stand up to a man, her father; how she learned about marginality and fear from her childhood as a Jew in Utah under the shadow of the Holocaust, and from her own experience of madness and institutionalization. Madness is a leitmotif both in her autobiography and in the tabloid talk about her.[7] Roseanne's eventual discovery of feminism and counter-culture politics led to disillusionment when the women's movement was taken over by women unlike her, 'handpicked', she writes, to be acceptable to the establishment.

Co-existing with the pain of her childhood and early adulthood was a love of laughter, the bizarre, a good joke. She always wanted to be a writer, not an actor. Performance, however, was the only 'place' where she felt safe. And because, since her childhood, she could always say what she wanted to as long as it was funny, *comic* performance allowed her to be a writer, to 'write' herself. While her decision to be a comedian was hampered by a difficulty in finding a female tradition in which to locate her own voice, she discovered her stance (or 'attitude') when she realized that she could take up the issue of female oppression by adopting its language. Helen Andelin's *Fascinating Womanhood* (1974) was one of the most popular manuals of femininity for the women of her mother's generation. It taught women to manipulate men by becoming 'domestic goddesses'. Yet, Roseanne discovered, such terms might also be used for 'self-definition, rebellion, truth-telling', for telling a truth that in her case is both ironic and affirmative. And so she built her act and her success on an exposure of the 'tropes of femininity' (the ideology of 'true womanhood', the perfect wife and mother) by cultivating the opposite (an image of the unruly woman).

Roseanne's disruptiveness is more clearly paradigmatic than syntagmatic, less visible in the stories her series dramatizes than in the image cultivated around her body: Roseanne-the-person who tattooed her buttocks and mooned her fans, Roseanne-the-character for whom farting and nose-picking are as much a reality as dirty dishes and obnoxious boy bosses. Both in body and speech, Roseanne is defined by *excess* and by *looseness* – qualities that mark her in opposition to bourgeois and feminine standards of decorum.

Of all of Roseanne's excesses, none seems more potent than her weight. Indeed, the very appearance of a 200-plus-pound woman in a weekly prime-time sitcom is significant in itself. Her body epitomizes the grotesque body of Bakhtin, the body which exaggerates its processes, its bulges and orifices, rather than concealing them as the monumental, static 'classical' or 'bourgeois' body does. Implicit in Bakhtin's analysis is the privileging of the female body – above all the *maternal* body which, through pregnancy and childbirth, participates uniquely in the carnivalesque drama of inside-out and outside-in, death-in-life and life-in death. Roseanne's affinity with the grotesque body is evident in the first paragraph of *Roseanne: My Life as a Woman*, where her description of her 'gargantuan appetites' even as a newborn brings to mind Bakhtin's study of Rabelais.[8] Roseanne compounds her fatness with a 'looseness' of body language and speech – she sprawls, slouches, flops on furniture. Her speech – even apart from its content – is loose (in its 'sloppy' enunciation and grammar) and excessive (in tone and volume). She laughs loudly, screams shrilly and speaks in a nasal whine.

In our culture, both fatness and looseness are violations of codes of feminine posture and behavior. Women of 'ill-repute' are described as loose, their bodies, especially their sexuality, seen as out of control. Fatness, of course, is an especially significant issue for women, and perhaps patriarchy nowhere inscribes itself more insidiously and viciously on female bodies than in the cult of thinness. Fat females are stigmatized as unfeminine, rebellious and sexually deviant (under or over-sexed). Women who are too fat or move too loosely appropriate too much space, and femininity is gauged by how little space women take up.[9] It is also gauged by the intrusiveness of women's utterances. As Henley notes, voices in any culture that are not mean to be heard are perceived as loud when they do speak, regardless of their decibel level ('shrill' feminists, for example). Farting, belching and nose-picking likewise betray a failure to restrain the body. Such 'extreme looseness of body-focused functions' is generally not available to women as an avenue of revolt but, as Nancy Henley suggests, 'if it should ever come into women's repertoire, it will carry great power'.[10]

Expanding that repertoire is entirely consistent with Roseanne's professed mission.[11] She writes of wanting 'to break every social norm ... and see that it is laughed at. I chuckle with glee if I know I have offended someone, because the people I intend to insult offend me horribly'.[12] In an interview in *People Weekly*, Roseanne describes how Matt Williams, a former producer on her show, tried to get her fired: 'He compiled a list of every offensive thing I did. And I do offensive things. ... *That's who I am. That's my act*. So Matt was in his office making a list of how gross I was, how many times I farted and belched – taking it to the network to show I was out of control' (my emphasis). Of course she was out of control – *his* control. He wanted to base the show on castration jokes, she says, recasting it from the point of view of the little boy. She wanted something else – something different from what she sees as the norm of television: a 'male point of view coming out of women's mouths ... particularly around families'.[13]

[...] There is much more to be said about Roseanne and the unruly woman: about her fights to maintain authorial control over (and credit for) her show; her use of the grotesque in the film *She Devil* (1989); her performance as a standup comic; the nature of her humour, which she calls 'funny womanness'; her identity as a Jew and the suppression of ethnicity in her series; the series' move toward melodrama and its treatment of social class. A more sweeping look at the unruly woman would find much of interest in the Hollywood screwball comedy as well as feminist avant-garde film and video. It would take up questions about the relation between gender, anger and Medusan laughter – about the links Hélène Cixous establishes between laughing, writing and the body and their implications for theories of female spectatorship. And while this article has emphasized the oppositional potential of female unruliness, it is equally important to expose its misogynistic uses, as in, for example, the Fox sitcom *Married ... With Children* (1988). Unlike Roseanne, who uses female unruliness to push at the limits of acceptable female behavior, Peg inhabits the unruly woman stereotype with little distance, embodying the 'male point of view' Roseanne sees in so much television about family.

Roseanne points to alternatives. Just as 'domestic goddess' can become a term of self-definition and rebellion, so can spectacle-making – when used to seize the visibility that is, after all, a precondition for existence in the public sphere. The ambivalence I've tried to explain regarding Roseanne is evoked above all, perhaps, because she demonstrates how the enormous apparatus of televisual star-making can be put to such a use.

Notes

1. The phrase 'slouching towards stardom' is Jeremy Butler's.
2. Janet Woollacott, 'Fictions and ideologies: the case of the situation comedy', in Tony Bennett, Colin Mercer and Janet Woollacott, *Popular Culture and Social Relations* (Philadelphia, Open University Press, 1986), pp. 196–218; Patricia Mellencamp, 'Situation comedy, feminism and Freud', in Tania Modleski (ed.), *Studies in Entertainment* (Bloomington, Indiana University Press, 1986), pp. 80–95.
3. Patricia Parker, *Literary Fat Ladies: Rhetoric, Gender, Property* (New York, Methuen, 1987).
4. Natalie Zemon Davis, *Society and Culture in Early Modern France* (Stanford, Stanford University Press, 1975), pp. 124–51.
5. Mary Russo, 'Female grotesques', in Teresa de Lauretis (ed.), *Feminist Studies, Critical Studies* (Bloomington, Indiana University Press, 1986), p. 217.
6. Teresa de Lauretis, *Technologies of Gender* (Bloomington, Indiana University Press, 1987), p. 109.
7. For example, 'Roseanne goes nuts!' in the *Enquirer*, 9 April 1989, and 'My insane year', in *People Weekly*, 9 October 1989, pp. 85–6. Like other labels of deviancy, madness is often attached to the unruly woman.
8. Mikhail Bakhtin, *Rabelais and His World*, trans. Helene Iswolsky (Bloomington, Indiana University Press, 1984).
9. Nancy M. Henley, *Body Politics: Power, Sex and Non-verbal Communication* (Englewood Cliffs, Prentice-Hall, 1977), p. 38.
10. *Ibid.* p. 91.
11. In 'What am I anyway, a Zoo?' *New York Times*, 31 July 1989, she enumerates the ways people have interpreted what she stands for – the regular housewife, the mother, the postfeminist, the 'Little Guy', fat people, the 'Queen of Tabloid America', 'the body politic', sex, 'angry womankind herself', 'the notorious and sensationalistic La Luna madness of an ovulating Abzugienne woman run wild' etc.
12. *Roseanne*, p. 51.
13. *People Weekly*, pp. 85–6.

11

A critical analysis of women's magazines

Ros Ballaster, Margaret Beetham, Elizabeth Frazer and Sandra Hebron

From their *Women's worlds: ideology, femininity and the woman's magazine* (Macmillan 1991)

The cover of *Cosmopolitan* for January 1988 advertises one of its leading features with the caption 'Men who hate women and the women who love them'. The world of the magazine is one in which men and women are eternally in opposition, always in struggle, but always in pursuit of each other; relations between them are beset by difficulty, frustration and failure. Yet, possible solutions like the dissolution of two exclusive and opposed gender categories, or the separation of women from men, or the dismantling of the power structures which now legitimate gender difference, have no place in the women's magazine. The heterogeneity of the magazine form, then, has its limits. Certain solutions and conclusions that might result from its representation of heterosexual relations are clearly not meant to be drawn. How does the women's magazine demarcate and delimit its own 'reading' of femininity?

In this section we introduce some of the central themes of women's magazines, as they have been identified by other analysts and our own examination of a sample of magazines from 1988. Critical analysts of the women's magazine attend to two kinds of issue. First, there are those which come under the heading of 'theme' proper, or subject-matter, such as gender opposition, domesticity, royalty, and so on. Second, issues come under the heading of 'formal textual features' to do with layout, the 'tone' of address to the reader, distribution of advertising, fiction, features, and so forth. Of course, formal and substantive features of magazines in practice affect and even positively shape one another.

Many analysts have been struck by the intimate tone employed to address the reader, the cosy invocation of a known commonality between 'we women' (Leman, 1980; Stewart, 1980; Hebron, 1983; Winship, 1978, 1987). Despite status, wealth, class and race distinctions, the magazine assumes a shared experience between women: 'It wouldn't matter if Jacqueline Onassis had a billion or a trillion dollars ... she is in exactly the same boat as you are when it comes to raising teenagers' (Lopate, 1978, p. 134). It is not only the editors and publishers who use this inclusive voice. A crucial feature of women's magazines is the readers' contributions in the form of letters, true life stories, the 'make-over'. The voice of the readers in all these contexts resonates with exactly the same register of intimacy as that of the professional producers of the magazine. It matters not at all whether this is because, as readers frequently suspect, all such contributions may be written by the professionals themselves. The *effect* is to make of producers and reader one group.

Such inclusivity is patently false. The 'ideal' or 'implied' reader of most women's magazines is self-evidently middle-class, white, and heterosexual. This inclusivity of address effectively marginalises or makes deviant black, working-class or lesbian women. Here, then, is an example of a formal, textual feature of the women's magazine – the intimacy of the editorial or journalistic 'we' – which works to define its content or theme, woman.

The construction of women as a homogeneous group, or even a group at all, is primarily achieved by the invocation of its supposedly 'natural' opposite – men. From the girl's magazine to the most popular women's magazines, such as *Woman*, there is an evident tension between the need to confirm the centrality and desirability of men in all women's lives and the equally insistent recognition of men as a problem for and threat to women. They are lazy, untidy, sometimes violent, require constant maintenance and upkeep both physically and psychically, are prone to faithlessness and heart attacks and, in recent years and registering the currency of a 'popular feminism', sexist and oppressive. This analysis of men as problematic is congruent, up to a point, with a feminist analysis of relations between men and women as quasi-class conflictual relations, relations of domination and oppression. But only up to a point. For, after all, magazines are part of an economic system as well as part of an ideological system by which gender difference is given meaning. They exist primarily as commodities and as the vehicle for advertisements of other commodities. If women are to continue to buy and consume commodities, not only for themselves, but for their families, they cannot also be sold feminist analyses of gender relations.

Defining women as 'not men', although it might be a necessary first step and a popular one with political philosophers and social theorists, is evidently not a sufficient one for the women's magazine. If women are to buy and to be, they cannot be defined solely in the negative; femininity has to be given particular content. The magazines' shared version of femininity varies, of course, from historical moment to moment. In what follows, as well as identifying shifts, we point to the instability and non-viability of the versions of female self-hood offered at different points in the history of the magazine. This instability holds both at the level of the components which make up the complex definition of womanhood available in the magazine at any one point and the relation between these components. For example, a dominant and consistent version of femininity offered by magazines, which still has currency in many of the more traditional titles, is that of woman as the repository of the nation's virtue. Virtue is here defined as essentially domestic and private, bound to 'family' ideals of affection, loyalty and obligation, to domestic production or housekeeping. Yet, by dint of their very posing of woman's existence as beset by 'problems' in need of resolution or attention through the medium of the magazine, women's magazines are forced to confront the undoubted realities of 'family' – domestic violence, poverty, illness – which directly conflict with the imaginary ideal

projected in such a construction of 'woman'. Moreover, when this definition of woman is one ingredient in an admixture which also includes the
representation of femininity as confident participation in the competitive
world of business, as it does in some magazines, its inviability becomes
even more glaring.

As well as the contradiction within magazines different magazines continually stress the qualities which distinguish them from their rivals. It is
in this light that we must read their own protestations of *exclusivity*, their
stress on the *difference* between '*Cosmo* girls' or '*Company* readers' and the
rest of the vast undifferentiated mass of (by implication) boring and conventional women (Braithwaite and Barrell, 1989, pp. 141–6). The *Cosmo* girl
and the *Company* reader is, in reality, distinguished from her sisters by her
consumption patterns or, as the industry terms it, 'lifestyle'. Publishers and
editors of British magazines can always identify their readers in terms of
the Registrar General's socio-economic classes which are demarcated by the
criterion of occupation (frequently, in the case of women, by husband's or
father's occupation). They are only, however, interested in occupation in so
far as it is a determinant of 'lifestyle'. The differentiation of the female
reader is then bound up with the exigencies of capitalist markets; collective
character is determined by what we (are able to) buy.

The 'lifestyles' portrayed in different magazines are not, of course, coterminous with the actual lifestyle, or consumption habits, of the majority of
readers of those magazines. It is a commonplace that *Jackie*, although
addressed to girls in their late teens is largely read by eleven- to thirteen-
year-olds. The clothes and cosmetics featured in the 'glossies' such as *Working Woman* are priced at a level which puts them beyond the means of the
typical reader; features present women who own their own business
empires, occupy top executive positions, convert country houses into
homes, while the magazine's readership consists mainly of women who
work for mediocre salaries in shops or offices (Glazer, 1980). Publishers and
editors recognise their readers as 'aspirational', aspiring to be older (in the
case of teenagers), richer, thinner, in a higher class or social bracket. Magazine editors know their audience to be largely from the C1–C2 British occupational groups (women with white-collar working husbands or fathers).
As one editor at the Oxford seminar which provided the origin for this book
put it, 'After all, they are the most numerous'. Magazines hold out to these
women the 'opportunity' to spend at A and B levels.

There are complex issues here. On the one hand, most women simply do
not have the opportunity to spend the amounts of money necessary to
acquire the goods featured. On the other, even if particular commodities are
bought, the whole 'lifestyle' may not be. A young woman might buy a wedding dress identical to the Duchess of York's without 'buying' the Duchess
of York's values. Yet again, women's magazines include features which
stress the message that it is much better to be poor and happy than royal
and hounded by photographers, or rich and hooked on drugs, drink or
divorce. The expensive commodities displayed in the magazine may, then,
not be appealing to aspiration at all, but rather to the realm of fantasy.

Either way, for our purposes several points are raised. First, a gap
emerges between the reader's social and economic reality and that projected

by the text she consumes. This gap vividly illustrates Simone de Beauvoir's famous observation that 'one is not born, but rather becomes a woman'. [...] Second, the 'femininity' we are invited to acquire in the process of consuming the magazine is not single, nor simple. The model of femininity extended by the magazine to the reader is severely contradictory, or rather, fragmentary. Perhaps instead of talking of contradiction, we should talk of multiplicity. Third, the woman who is addressed by the magazine text is addressed first and foremost as a consumer, of the message of the text *and* of the commodities which it presents as essential to the business of her 'becoming' or construction.

Notwithstanding the contradictions, tensions and difficulties involved in sustaining it as a coherent project, magazines which co-exist at any given historical moment do share a notion of femininity. Looking at the magazines of the late twentieth century, we can identify certain features which recur. A glance at almost any sample of magazines will suggest that whatever else femininity (and especially female sexuality) might be, it is certainly punishable (Gerbner, 1957; Sonnenschein, 1970). This is most evident in the fiction of 'True Romance' magazines, in which women who succumb to their sexual desires more often than not also succumb to severe psychological torment, illness, and even death, but it is also discernible in features such as the celebrity profile, the 'triumph over tragedy' true life experience, and that perennial favourite, the 'problem page'. The heroines of magazines suffer, appallingly and all the time. If they have positively sinned against the conformist sexual ideology of the magazine, their suffering may be brought to an end by repentance; if their only sin is that of being female then stoical resignation, passivity and 'goodness' will finally bring its reward.

Valerie Walkerdine, in analysing the fiction offered by the British girls' magazine *Bunty*, has pointed out the pattern of suffering at the hands of wicked step-parents, cruel teachers, or nasty bullying enemies inflicted on the magazine's heroines. In these stories the heroine's goodness through adversity is finally rewarded with the restoration of family and love (Walkerdine, 1984). Tania Modleski puts forward a strikingly similar analysis of the heroine's fate in Harlequin or Mills & Boon romances. Here the hero's cruelty and seeming contempt is finally transformed despite himself through the sheer passive virtue of the heroine (Modleski, 1984, p. 17). We might conclude, then, that in the romance structures shared by both popular fiction and the women's magazine femaleness is in itself punishable, but can only be transcended or transformed through the acquisition and display of an excessive femininity. Interestingly, Barbara Phillips argues that this theme is continued in the self-consciously feminist magazine *Ms*. Biographical articles in *Ms* feature a range of women in public life (trades-union organisers, compaigners against rape, etc.) who all 'succeed' because they put other people first and enjoy the intrinsic rewards of selfless devotion to duty and community (Phillips, 1978).

Women's magazines almost without exception situate women (all women) either firmly *in* the domestic sphere or in close proximity to it. Magazines vary between those that encourage women to work the double shift (run a home, raise children, reproduce husband and family on a daily basis, dress and groom spectacularly, climb a career ladder and maintain professional and emotional relationships outside the family circle) and those which encourage them to resist any pressure to leave the home. The latter 'reassert' the value of the domestic sphere, particularly that of maternity, and harp on the high cost to women of pursuing paid work. Thus, *Family Circle* tells its readers that the cost of broadcaster Barbara Walters' lifestyle has been high; she has lost a quantity of softness that other women may not be willing to sacrifice (Phillips, 1978, p. 120). Those magazines which do celebrate the 'independent' woman (*Cosmopolitan, Honey, Options*) nevertheless run regular features on cookery, interior decoration, parenting (otherwise known as motherhood).

Conspicuous by its absence and in contrast to the pervasiveness of the motif of domesticity is the theme of public and civic life, political progress or political institutions. This is not to say that subjects of a 'political' nature never feature in the magazines – they appear in three ways. First, discussion of 'issues' such as ecology, rape, incest, and homelessness invariably speaks to readers' 'personal' concerns about the quality of their family life or their children's future. Second, fairly frequent interviews with politicians, their wives, or leading public figures attend to their domestic setting and environment. Passions and convictions are discussed only in the context of an enquiry into the conflicting demands of job and family, a revelation of 'personality' through a discussion of taste in clothes, nightlife, friends. *Reality* is clearly the world of the family; that of civic virtue, the production of a collective life outside the family, political struggle, is quite unreal. To learn the truth about a politician is to learn the details of his or her domestic existence. Third, many of the weeklies now carry information about legal and political rights, more often than not presented as political goods for consumption. Policy, according to the magazine, is subject to the same laws of supply and demand as fashion. Laws on women and taxation are evaluated in the same manner as the respective merits of different kinds of washing-machine. Once again the forging of community cannot be understood as a public and civic process.

At the heart of the women's magazine lies the paradox that 'natural' femininity can be achieved only through hard labour. Most recently, this discourse of gender acquisition has had to negotiate with the problem of *feminism*. [...] Ours and others' readings of magazines crucially shows the discourse of gender that structures the genre to be intertwined with those of race, class, nation and age. Magazines acknowledge or construct social class differences in terms of 'lifestyle' or consumption, but consistently deny the existence of structured class or race conflict, offering only personal or moral resolutions to problems proceeding from these stratifications. Racial difference in particular is barely acknowledged in the contemporary British women's magazine. We are, to a woman, assumed to be white; when addressed at all, blackness is not understood as a political but an aesthetic category, taken on a par with the 'divisions' between women of dry and greasy hair, large and small breasts.

The feminine virtues of passive goodness, personal service to others and devotion to the domestic sphere by definition preclude women from productive activity in the public sphere. In the eighteenth century men read and circulated journals in the coffee-houses of London which also served as a distribution outlet for publishers. With the advent of magazines addressed to women, publishers developed means of distributing their product to the family home, to be read and circulated in the drawing-room. Women came to be conceived of as that phenomenon much beloved of the contemporary marketing man, the *final* consumer. The complete separation of coffee house from tea table, the public from the private is, of course, a myth. The writing of this myth continues throughout the nineteenth and twentieth centuries. Advertisers now conceive of women as primary consumers; their recyling of images of domestic bliss and eschewal of any civic or public values serves to maintain the continual circulation of that myth.

Any consumption is, undeniably, pleasurable. We must take care not to overdraw the picture of a population sated on pure consumption, the distopian nightmare of the theorist of mass culture of the post-war era, which we go on to discuss in the following section. The pleasure of consumption and that of the fantasy of possibilities of infinite consumption is central to the success of the magazine form and we cannot afford simply to reject it as cultural brainwashing.

[. . .] Feminist critics interpret the formal features of mass cultural forms addressed to women not only in terms of the meaning and construction of signification, but in terms of the way that different textual forms resonate, or not, with female desire, with the shape and texture of women's lives, with that difficult entity termed women's 'pleasure'. Michèle Mattelart, for example, comments on the congruence between the repetitive, open-ended form of women's popular culture (soap-opera and the magazine in particular) and the rhythmic, cyclical nature of women's lives. Cyclical temporalities are disparaged and devalued in masculinist cultures which privilege teleology and closure, thus alienating women from dominant culture; only in popular culture are feminised patterns of temporality and narrative indulged (Mattelart, 1986, p. 16). In an analogous argument, Tania Modleski identifies soap-opera's resistance to closure and privileging of 'private' domestic rhythms over public event as congruent with women's pleasure (Modleski, 1984, p. 111).

It is important to resist claiming that cyclical or open-ended form is *essentially* a female quality, rather than a culturally learned distinction of gender. However, we would argue that the formal elements of the women's magazine are fundamental to its commercial success and the kinds of pleasure it offers its reader. One of the most striking features of the magazine is its heterogeneity, juxtaposing different genres, mixing print and photography, offering a range of characterised 'voices'. It does not demand to be read from front to back, nor in any particular order, and its fragmentary nature is admirably suited to women's habitual experience in modern society of the impossibility of concentrated attention (distracted by calls on their time from men, children, the conflicting demands of work and home). The magazine's periodicity, its regular appearance once a month or once a week, allows both open-endedness (continuing series or features) and routinisation, confirming its readers in a way of life where leisure, like work, is regulated in time (Beetham, 1990).

We take seriously these arguments about the congruence of the magazine form with the nature of women's experience and the importance of exploring formal elements in order to explain the specific pleasures it offers its readers. Yet a recognition of this pleasure does not lessen, nor is it lessened by, an acknowledgement of the magazine's role in perpetuating women's oppression. An attention to the 'pleasure' of the magazine must, however, challenge and supplement the account offered by the theories of ideology and mass culture we outlined earlier. Psychoanalytic method has come to dominate accounts of textual pleasure in literary and cultural studies and with it the presumption that pleasure is always already sexual, that sexuality is the paradigmatic form of pleasure.

Roland Barthes's *The Pleasure of the Text* differentiates between what he terms the text of pleasure (*plaisir*) and that of bliss (*jouissance*). Barthes values reading pleasure in terms of the demands made upon the reader for *active* engagement with the text. Narrative pleasure is analogous to the pleasure of male orgasm, a journey that explores uncertainty and anxiety but is finally offered relief in the form of narrative closure. The agony and disruption of sexual excitement is embarked upon in order to reach satisfaction. In contrast, 'bliss', an unsatisfactory translation of the French term 'jouissance' with its wider connotations of an active, free, but crisis-ridden dissolution of subjectivity and ecstasy, might be understood as a peculiarly feminine form of pleasure/orgasm (Irigaray, ,1981, pp. 101ff). Free of narrative event as such, what 'happens' in the text of bliss happens in the reader's engagement with language itself, with indeterminacy of meaning, without crisis-point or closure (Barthes, 1976, pp. 11–13).

Clearly, Barthes's coinage and the focus of other psychoanalytic and semiotic theorists such as Julia Kristeva are directed toward disclosing the disruptive effects of the modernist literary text. If popular forms, such as the women's magazine, fit anywhere in this analysis it is in Barthes's category of the 'prattling text', employing an 'unweaned language: imperative, automatic, unaffectionate' (Barthes, 1983, p. 404). Barthes's characterisation of the prattling text is here reminiscent of Herbert Marcuse's dismissal of the texts of popular culture, which 'In [their] immediacy and directness ... impede conceptual thinking; thus, impede thinking' (Bennett, 1982, p. 44; Marcuse, 1968). Raymond Williams also comments, specifically with regard to women's magazines, on the imperative and didactic quality of popular culture: 'who can doubt ... that here, centrally, is *teaching*' (Williams, 1966, p. 15).

For Barthes, then, *jouissance* in reading stems from readerly *production* and cannot be generated by the prattling text of pleasure, where didacticism and imperatives impede the reader's participation and action. The paradigmatic form of pleasure here is, then, production. This raises two issues. First, we would point out with respect to magazines that 'reading' a magazine involves a number of pleasures of action and participation – reading ahead, reading back to front, creating one's own narrative. Second, the analysis of pleasure as production is unreasonably narrow, dismissing as 'inauthentic', or inherently conservative, the pleasure of consumption rather than production, of affirmation rather than negation. In contrast, Judith Williamson argues for the pleasures of consumption, specifically for women, although she is alive to the political limits of such pleasure. The pleasure of *choice* in consumption is evidently a partial illusion: 'we don't choose what is available for us to choose between in the first place' (Williamson, 1986, p. 230). However, she recognises that 'Consuming products does give a thrill, a sense of both belonging and being different, charging normality with the excitement of the unusual' (p. 13). Marx's analysis of the fetishism engendered in and from commodity production provides a framework for the understanding of such excitement in Williamson's work, but she insists that such pleasure should not be dismissed as simply a debilitating effect of capitalist culture. Williamson's account of popular culture captures what is obviously an important aspect of the pleasure of the magazine – not the *jouissance* of engagement with difficult language, nor the relief of narrative closure, but the excitement of consumption, both the actual consumption of the magazine as commodity and the potential consumption of the commodities it promotes in advertising (Lovell, 1987, p. 16).

Tania Modleski points to the proximity of pleasure and fantasy, complicating an interpretation of the satisfactions of popular culture as pure commodity fetishism. Romantic and gothic fiction, she suggests, resonate with feminine hysteria and paranoia. The manifest content of the Harlequin romance, the pursuit of heterosexual union, conceals and represses deep anxiety and ambivalence in relation to rape, validating the desire for power and revenge (Modleski, 1984, p. 48). Ultimately, we would argue, Modleski understands women's consumption of popular fiction as a form of addiction, the point at which pleasure dissolves into pain. Valerie Walkerdine's discussion of *Bunty* stories suggests that they speak to fantasies already present in the child's subconscious – the desire for the good parent in particular (Walkerdine, 1984, p. 168). In a different context, Frederic Jameson has challenged the Frankfurt School account of mass culture to claim that the texts of popular culture manage 'dangerous and protopolitical impulses .. . initially awakened within the very text that seeks to still them'. Despite their immediate ideological function these impulses 'resonate a universal value' in that they stem from deep unconscious structures (Jameson, 1981, pp. 287–8). Jameson's preoccupation here is with the management of class conflict in film but his attention to the political signification of unconscious desire is surely suggestive for a feminist reading of popular culture's management of gender conflict.

There is a paradox, however, in Jameson's attempt to incorporate a psychoanalytic and marxist perspective in relation to popular culture. For the psychoanalyst, the deep unconscious structures that generate desire and pleasure are pre-given and untransformable. By contrast, for materialist marxism and feminism, social and political transformation would enable the transformation of desire and pleasure. The theorists we have discussed in this section extend the possibility of producing new and differently structured fantasies which might negotiate desire and conflict without reconfirming gender inequity – fantasies which do not, for example, encourage little girls to displace their anger onto imaginary others ('bad people') or to direct it back upon themselves. We might use female desire to build an alternative feminist future and aesthetic. Nevertheless, the prospects for such psychic transformation seem slim, if the conflicts and desires in question are as deep-seated, the family drama as universal, as psychoanalytic theory would suggest.

In response to this preoccupation with negative ideological effect, which has spawned a large body of fault-finding political criticism of art, literature, popular culture, sexual practice and social relations, some theorists protest the radical and liberationist potential of pleasure itself. A feminist critique of patriarchy's control of women through sexuality must not be allowed to foreclose on a recognition of female sexual pleasure, despite its proximity to sexual danger (Vance, 1984; Weeks, 1985). Should feminists and left-wing critics attend to the progressive possibilities that inhere in a consumer culture? (Lovibond, 1989). Some might argue that a heterogeneity of style and culture enables the expression of alternative and multiple sexualities and subjectivities. [...]

Bibliography

BARTHES, R. 1972: Myth today. In *Mythologies* (trans. A. Lavers). London: Jonathan Cape.
— 1976: *The pleasure of the text* (trans. R. Miller). London: Jonathan Cape.
— 1983: *Selected writings* (ed. S. Sontag). London: Fontana.
BEETHAM, M. 1990: Towards a theory of the periodical as a publishing genre. In L. Brake, A. Jones and L. Madden (eds.), *Investigating Victorian journalism*. London: Macmillan.
BENNETT, T. 1982: Theories of the media, theories of society. In Gurevitch, Bennett, Curran and Woollacott (eds.), *Culture, society and the media*. London: Methuen.
BRAITHWAITE, B. and BARRELL J. 1979, 2nd edn. 1988: *The business of women's magazines: the agonies and ecstasies*. London: Associated Business Press.
GERBNER, G. 1957: The social role of the confession magazine. *Social Problems*.
GLAZER, N. 1980: Overworking the working woman: the double day in a mass magazine. *Women's Studies International Quarterly*, vol. 3.
HEBRON, S. 1983: *Jackie* and *Woman's Own*: Ideological work and social construction of gender identity. Occasional paper. Sheffield City Polytechnic.
IRIGARAY, L. 1981: This sex which is not one and When the goods get together. In E. Marks and I. de Courtivron (eds.), *New French feminisms*. Brighton: Harvester, pp. 99–110.
JAMESON, F. 1979: Reification and utopia in mass culture. *Social Text*, no. 1, pp. 130–48.
— 1981: *The political unconscious: narrative as a socially symbolic act*. London: Methuen.
LEMAN, J. 1980: The advice of a real friend: codes of intimacy and oppression in women's magazines 1937–55. In H. Baehr (ed.), *Women and media*, pp. 63–78.
LOPATE, C. 1978: Jackie! In Tuchman, Kaplan Daniels and Benèt (eds.), *Hearth and home*.
LOVELL, T. 1987: *Consuming fictions*. London: Verso.
LOVIBOND, S. 1989: Is feminism against pleasure?, unpublished paper, Oxford University.
MARCUSE, H. 1968: *One dimensional man: studies in the ideology of advanced industrial society*. London: Routledge & Kegan Paul, reprint 1986 Ark editions.
MATTELART, M. 1986: *Women, media, crisis: femininity and disorder*. London: Comedia.
MODLESKI, T. 1984: *Loving with a vengeance: mass produced fantasies for women*. New York and London: Methuen.

PHILLIPS, E. B. 1978: Magazine heroines: is ms. just another member of the family circle? In Tuchman, Kaplan Daniels and Benèt (eds.), *Hearth and home.*

SONNENSCHEIN, D. 1970: Love and sex in the romance magazines. *Journal of Popular Culture*, vol. 4.

— 1972: Process in the production of popular culture: the romance magazine. *Journal of Popular Culture*, vol. 6.

STEWART, P. 1980: He admits . . . but she confesses. In Baehr (ed.), *Women and media*, pp. 105–14.

VANCE, C. 1984: Pleasure and danger: towards a politics of sexuality. In Vance (ed.), *Pleasure and danger: exploring female sexuality*. Boston: Routledge & Kegan Paul, pp. 1–28.

WALKERDINE, V. 1984: Some day my prince will come: young girls and the preparation for adolescent sexuality. In McRobbie and Nava (eds.), *Gender and generation*, pp. 162–84.

WEEKS, J. 1985: *Sexuality and its discontents: meanings, myths and modern sexualities.* London: Routledge & Kegan Paul.

WILLIAMS, R. 1966: *Communications.* London: Chatto & Windus.

— 1977: *Marxism and literature.* Oxford: Oxford University Press.

WILLIAMSON, J. 1986: *Consuming passions: the dynamics of popular culture.* London: Marion Boyars.

WINSHIP, J. 1978: A woman's world: *Woman* – an ideology of femininity. In *Women take issue.* London: Hutchinson and Birmingham CCCS Women's Studies Group), pp. 133–45.

— 1987: *Inside women's magazines.* London and New York: Pandora Press.

12

The cover: window to the future self

Ellen McCracken

From her *Decoding women's magazines from Mademoiselle to Ms* (Macmillan 1993)

[...] The cover's role as primary advertisement for the magazine shapes the cover's cultural characteristics. As George Gerbner has noted with respect to romance magazines, the design and content of the cover reflect the distribution requirements and market relations of the magazine.[1] The competition engendered by the battle between magazines to deliver 'quality' groups of women to advertisers surfaces in the cover's cultural form. The distinct cultural identities of the nearly fifty magazines for women on US news-stands today cannot be explained simply as cultural developments. Whether we see a healthy young woman with the look of the outdoors, a professionally dressed business woman, or ornately decorated food on a cover depends on current market conditions in the magazine industry. [...]

The front cover, in addition to being the magazine's most important advertisement, is the vehicle by which we distinguish one magazine from another. Genre is an important initial element of the positionality a magazine offers readers and helps to shape the reading process. Just as we bring different expectations to the reading of detective novels and poems, so, too, do we respond to the generic differences the covers signal as we are about to begin reading. Angela McRobbie's research, for example, shows that young girls in Britain perceive that magazines address different age groups; one 15-year-old in her study noted: 'Well I buy *Jackie* and *Fab* now, but my sister, she's 17, buys *Honey* and *19* so I usually read them too. Once you go to work you start getting magazines with more on fashion than love stories.'[2] Such preconceptions about genre, which the magazines themselves foster as part of the encoding process, help to position readers as they buy and consume the publications. Genre does not predetermine who the readers will be; crossover readership occurs as McRobbie's interviewee indicates. However, the code of genre affects one's self-perception during the experience with a magazine; when one's use of the magazine enters the public sphere, the cover serves to label not only the magazine but the consumer who possesses it.

[...] Most covers try to create an idealized reader-image of the group advertisers seek to reach, by using the photo of a woman – usually a close-up of her smiling face. There is often an implied male presence, communicated through the woman's facial expression, make-up, body pose and clothing, as well as through the camera angle, lighting and color. Sometimes a man is explicitly present or the woman is pictured with a child. Often, an iconic sign, rich in secondary connotations accompanies the woman, or symbolically, represents her by itself. Invariably, the verbal text of the cover consists of the magazine's title in large type and a series of headlines designed to attract the reader to certain features inside.

Specific genres of magazines present variational encodings to attract the readers they seek. A special-interest magazine such as *BBW* (*Big Beautiful Woman*) follows the main traditions of the fashion and beauty genre, featuring a close-up shot of the model's face as the main pictorial message. *BBW*'s eyecatching transgression is to substitute a 'large-size' model for the traditional slender one. The *BBW* reader is to feel part of the discourse of the beauty-fashion magazine, yet recognize a message designed personally for her. Except for this departure from the normal generic rules, the *BBW* cover retains most of the previously established code for the beauty-fashion magazine.

The covers of *Woman's Day* and *Family Circle* reflect their special distribution requirements and define them as a subcategory of the women's service genre. Their extremely high circulations (approximately seven and eight million per issue respectively) are achieved primarily through supermarket and news-stand sales, allowing them to charge some of the highest advertising rates among women's magazines; large single-copy sales are especially desirable because they demonstrate the consumer's active decision to buy the magazine, instead of passively receiving it in the mail and perhaps not reading it. The generic encodings of the covers of these two magazines promote continued high sales of single issues.

[...] Sometimes a cover will more openly merge the characteristics of two genres. While *New Woman* is one of the new publications for women working outside the home, its cover format is similar to *Cosmopolitan*'s. Like *Cosmopolitan*, it uses a three-quarter or upper-body shot of the model instead of the usual close-up of the face common to beauty and fashion magazines. Headlines follow the *Cosmo* style in tone, the question-and-answer format, and the overuse of underlining and exclamation points. They are thematically similar to *Cosmopolitan*'s headlines, emphasizing relationships with men, marital life, and self-improvement. Overall, however, both in the photo and headlines, there is less of *Cosmo*'s emphasis on sex; a more subtle sex-symbol than the *Cosmo* model, the *New Woman* model wears less revealing clothes and more often has a closed-mouth smile and a less provocative head and body tilt. The *New Woman* cover model is a more businesslike 'Cosmo girl', and there is a material explanation for this.

New Woman wants to attract monied women working outside the home and claims to have 'the highest percentage of working women of any ABC [Audit Bureau of Circulation] magazine with over one million circulation – 89%.'[3] Each month its cover prominently boasts 'Over Four Million Readers' to encourage potential readers as well as advertisers. In effect, *New Woman* is aiming for both a 'class' and a 'mass' audience. By following the *Cosmopolitan* example, its cover will attract a large news-stand clientele, four times greater than its subscription numbers. Yet its cover also emphasizes the new woman worker, a 'quality' reader, whose spending power is especially attractive to advertisers. By mixing the cultural images of two genres, the *New Woman* cover aims to attract both quality readers and large numbers.

Genre identity is crucial to a magazine's sales and readership, and plays a role in the reader's sense of self as she consumes it. The cover's generic encodings often operate in the public sphere, so that when making a newsstand purchase, reading in a public place, or displaying the magazine on a coffee table, one identifies oneself to others as a Cosmo girl or a *Family Circle* reader. While the cover's encodings of genre are primarily designed to sell magazines, they offer readers ideological positionalities as well, helping to shape both the reading process that follows and readers' self-presentation to others.

[...] The photographic text of a magazine cover also extends meaning to the material inside. Usually a concrete representation of an idealized model of physical beauty, the cover photo whets the consumer's appetite for what is to follow. As a pleasurable visual representation, it invites us to enjoy further pleasure by consuming the magazine's contents visually, flipping through the pictures page by page. At the same time, it leads us necessarily to the verbal texts in the magazine, through which we will be given specific instructions for attaining the model of ideal beauty.

The covers that use the photo of a glamorous woman to represent physical perfection rely on readers' personal sense of inferiority, especially about their physical appearance. As Berger has noted, the consumer envies not only the glamorous model in an advertisement but herself as she will be in the future after having purchased the product advertised. According to Berger this relationship of envy 'explains the absent, unfocused look of so many glamour images. They look out *over* the looks of envy which sustain them.'[4] Sometimes the cover model appears to be looking directly at us, but a sense of superiority is still at work. Whether looking over us or directly at us, the model sustains our envy and feelings of insecurity, predisposing us to be receptive to the products advertised both overtly and covertly inside, as well as to the instructions for attaining beauty in the articles.

When covers represent women through the secondary significations of an iconic sign, feelings of insecurity and envy are also at work and carry through to the magazine's content. To achieve ideal womanhood, we must learn to prepare the ornately decorated food or make the crafts pictured on the covers of some magazines. In addition to framing our perception of the corresponding article and photo inside, these cover photos affect the meaning of apparently unrelated articles and photos in the magazine. Implicit is the notion that women's work in the home must always strive for the ornamental perfection of the cover photo. Many tasks are portrayed as unalienated labor in the ideal verbal and non-verbal representations which branch out from the cover photo to the magazine's contents. Just as we are to feel insecure about our failure to embody the image of physical beauty of the model on many fashion magazine covers, so, too, are we to idealize and envy the multitude of symbols of womanhood in the service magazines for which the cover signs set the stage.

The cover functions as an interpretive lens for what follows by offering us pre-embedded definitions through the magazine's title, the headlines, and the photo. Syntax, tone, color, visual images of ideal beauty and success, and covert images of consumption work to position us favorably to the magazine's content. Readers are not deterministically required to view the inside according to the cover frame, but a given model of interpretation is part of the cover's code and exerts strong influence.

The cover is the most important advertisement in the magazine, then, precisely through its roles as genre identifier, semiotic system, and frame. The interplay of the photographic, verbal, and chromatic texts on each cover creates a series of value-laden cultural significations but is primarily intended to attract revenues from advertisers and increase circulation. The cover's roles as a genre identifier, sign system, and frame are its means of achieving this revenue. Each role is closely connected to the commercial structure of the magazine industry and would be significantly different were the commercial goals of magazines to change.

Most of the 'ways of seeing' or windows to the future self that the covers of magazines create are also linked to these commercial goals. The ideal images on magazine covers that women see on news-stands, in waiting rooms, or concealing the faces of others who are reading them, attempt to integrate women further into the consumer economy. Hidden beneath the glamorous ideals are subtexts that play on anxieties and encourage feelings of inadequacy, while promising pleasure and the acceptance and love of others if we purchase. If the cover photo is, in Berger's words, 'a record of how x has seen y,' it is an image of how the contemporary consumer society [has] chosen to see women in order to sell more goods and services.

Notes

1. George Gerbner, 'The Social Anatomy of the Romance-Confession Cover Girl', *Journalism Quarterly* 35 (1958), p. 299.
2. See Angela McRobbie, 'Working Class Girls and the Culture of Femininity', in Women's Studies Group, *Women Take Issue: Aspects of Women's Subordination* (London, Hutchinson, 1978), p. 99.
3. Standard Rate and Data Service, *Consumer and Farm Publications* 63, No. 10 (27 October 1981), 515. (Hereafter referred to as SRDS.)
4. John Berger, *Ways of Seeing* (London, Penguin, 1972), pp. 132–3.

Section III

Audience: texts, subjects, contexts

Questions of audience are never far away from any feminist work on the media (Gray, 1987; Gamman and Marshment, 1988; Pibram, 1988; Press, 1990; Ang, 1991; Brown, 1994). This has often polarised into versions of the 'ideal' or 'implied' reader in the text compared with the 'real' readers, who may or may not inhabit or take up the subject positions offered. Strong arguments have been made against assuming the reader/viewer from textual analysis and calls for attention to actual readers have been numerous. But it is by no means a simple matter to explore these readers (Radway, 1984). Although the ideal and real reader polarity represents actual methodological differences within and between media and film studies, what they share is an acknowledgement of media forms as 'technologies of gender' (de Lauretis, 1987) operating as gendered media texts and in gendered media use (Ang and Hermes, 1991).

This section begins with **Tania Modleski**'s piece 'The rhythms of reception: daytime television and women's work' which seeks to connect the form of daytime television in the USA to the patterns of female domestic labour. Both, she argues, are based upon interruption and distraction. Furthermore, daytime programming such as soaps and quiz shows deal in traditional 'feminine' currency celebrating and confirming particular skills and competences, thus serving the demands of patriarchy. Modleski's analysis opens up some important questions around the context of reception and the constitutive role of media forms in daily life.

A similar insight emerged from the work carried out at the Centre for Contemporary Cultural Studies in Birmingham by women working at the centre in the mid- to late 1970s. However, this did not arise through a close study of the texts of broadcast media, but through qualitative research which sought to look at women in the home. **Dorothy Hobson**'s 'Housewives and the mass media' indicates the significance of media output in terms of imposing structure upon domestic work, of providing company and combating the isolation experienced by women at home. She also points towards the notion of gendered television output as described by the women in her study. Hobson employs the 'conversational' interview as her main research method, which has been an important device in later reception studies (Hobson, 1982) and insists on attention to domestic context in our understanding of women's media reception and use. This approach was adopted by **Ann Gray** in her study of the use of video cassette recorders (VCR). In 'Behind closed doors: video recorders in the home', Gray argues that attention should be paid to the many determining factors which shape women's domestic consumption of popular forms. These include domestic commitments, the significance of the VCR as technology, and the general denigration of women's genres. (For a full version of this study, see Gray, 1992; see also Spigel, 1992, which looks at the arrival of television in homes in the USA.)

It is true to say that television has been the dominant medium in reception studies, but there have been a number of important attempts to understand the readership of women's magazines (McRobbie, 1978; Hermes, 1995). Much of the early work on women's magazines used the concept of ideology, in common with other areas of media studies, in order to understand the role which magazines play in the construction of gendered identity. **Elizabeth Frazer** in 'Teenage girls reading *Jackie*' begins by taking issue with the concept and explores, through group discussions with young women, the ways in which they actively engage with the text, moving in and out of the dominant narratives of femininity offered through *Jackie*, a popular British magazine aimed at young women. She notes that the text's ideological effectiveness is 'undercut' by the readers' 'reflexivity and reflexiveness'.

This same 'undercutting' is noted by **Ellen Seiter**, **Hans Borchers**, **Gabriele Kreutzner** and **Eva-Maria Warth** in their 'Don't treat us like we're so stupid and naive' – towards an ethnography of soap opera viewers', a study of soap opera viewers in Oregon. Drawing on existing audience studies, they use ethnographic methods to investigate the meanings of soap opera and the significance of these programmes for a predominantly white working class sample of men and women. Thus, the research involves an understanding of social use of a specific genre, but also readings and interpretations which the respondents bring to soap operas. Assumptions of the 'ideal reader' made from textual analysis are directly challenged by recalcitrant readings described by the viewers in the Oregon study. The authors refer to their research as an 'ethnography', but their reflection on this approach provides us with an example of a more general tendency towards reflexivity and questions of the employment of particular kinds of research methods (Walkerdine, 1987; Seiter, 1990).

Qualitative audience research has presented complex versions of the female viewer, but in the studies done to date she is almost always exclusively 'white'. Seiter *et al.* acknowledge this as a major shortcoming in the Oregon study. One significant exception to this state of affairs is preliminary research carried out by **Evelyn Cauleta Reid** in 'Viewdata: the television viewing habits of young black women in London'. She seeks to explore and reveal the differences of viewing practices and attitudes towards television by young black women, thus challenging an assumed unified or homogenous black perspective. Her study is a reminder of the often unacknowledged 'whiteness' of much media audience work and of the necessity for further empirical studies which would explore difference and diversity in media reception and use.

References and further reading

ANG, I. 1991: *Desperately seeking the audience*. London/New York: Routledge.

ANG, I. and HERMES, J. 1991: 'Gender and/in media consumption'. In Curran, J. and Gurevitch, M. (eds.), *Mass media and society*. London: Edward Arnold.

BROWN, M.E. 1994: *Soap opera and women's talk: the pleasures of resistance*. Thousand Oaks/London/New Delhi: Sage.

DE LAURETIS, T. 1987: *Technologies of gender: essays on theory, film and fiction*. Bloomington: Indiana University Press.

GAMMAN, L. and MARSHMENT, M. (eds.) 1988: *The female gaze: women as viewers of popular culture*. London: The Women's Press.

GRAY, A. 1987: 'Reading the audience'. *Screen* 28, 24–35.

— 1992: *Video playtime: the gendering of a leisure technology*. London: Routledge.

HERMES, J. 1995: *Reading women's magazines: an analysis of everyday media use*. Cambridge: Polity.

HOBSON, D. 1982: *'Crossroads'* – the drama of a soap opera. London: Methuen.

McROBBIE, A. 1978: *'Jackie*: an ideology of adolescent femininity'. Occasional paper, Birmingham CCCS.

PIBRAM, E.D. (ed.) 1988: *Female spectators*. London: Verso.

PRESS, A.L. 1990: *Women watching television: gender, class and generation in the American television experience*. Philadelphia: University of Pennsylvania Press.

RADWAY, J. 1984: *Reading the romance – women, patriarchy, and popular literature*. Chapel Hill/London: The University of North Carolina Press.

SEITER, E. 1990: 'Making distinctions in television audience research'. *Cultural Studies* 4, 61–84.

SPIGEL, L. 1992: *Make room for TV: television and the family ideal in post-war America*. Chicago: University of Chicago Press.

WALKERDINE, V. 1987: 'Video replay: families, films and fantasy'. In Donald, J. and Kaplan, C. (eds.), *Formations of fantasy*. London: Methuen.

13

The rhythms of reception: daytime television and women's work

Tania Modleski

From E. Ann Kaplan (ed.), *Regarding television: critical approaches – an anthology* (The American Film Institute 1983)

In his book *Television: Technology and Cultural Form* Raymond Williams suggests that the shifts in television programming from one type of show to another and from part of a show to a commercial should be seen not as 'interruptions' – of a mood, of a story – but as parts of a whole. What at first appear to be discrete programming units in fact interrelate in profound and complex ways. Williams uses the term 'flow' to describe this interaction of various programs with each other and with commercials. 'The fact of flow,' he says, 'defines the central television experience.'[1]

Here I would like to examine the flow of daytime television, particularly the way soap operas, quiz shows, and commercials interrelate. More specifically, I want to look at how the flow of these programs connects to the work of women in the home. As the ladies' magazines never tire of telling us, this work involves a variety of tasks and requires a wide range of abilities. Moreover, this work tends to be very different from men's work. As Nancy Chodorow describes it:

> Women's activities in the home involve continuous connection to and concern about children and attunement to adult masculine needs, both of which require connection to, rather than separateness from, others. The work of maintenance and reproduction is ... repetitive and routine ... and does not involve specified sequence or progression. By contrast, work in the labor force – 'men's work' – is more likely to be contractual, to be more specifically delimited and to contain a notion of defined progression and product.[2]

Apparently, women's work itself is a kind of flow, so my task would seem to be especially pertinent.

One of the chief differences between daytime television and nighttime programming is that the former appears to be participatory in a way that the latter almost never is: it stresses, in other words, 'connection to, rather than separateness from, others'. This is obviously the case with quiz shows and talk shows [...], but it is also true of soap operas. For example, on soap operas, action is less important than *re*action and *inter*action, which is one reason why fans keep insisting on soap opera's 'realism,' although critics continually delight in pointing out the absurdity of its content. Despite the numerous murders, kidnappings, blackmail attempts, emergency operations, amnesia attacks, etc., which are routine occurrences on soap operas, anyone who has followed one, for however brief a time, knows that these events are not important in themselves; they merely serve as occasions for characters to get together and have prolonged, involved, intensely emotional discussions with each other.

Furthermore, audiences are much more likely to become intimately involved with soap opera characters and to experience them as equals than they are with the characters on nighttime programs. A comparison with *Dallas*, the popular nighttime serial, is instructive. There the characters are highly glamorized, the difference between their world and that of the average viewer could not be greater, and the difference is continually emphasized. On soap operas, in contrast, glamor and wealth are played down. Characters are just attractive *enough* so that their looks are not distracting, well-off *enough* so that [...] they can worry about more exciting problems than inflation at the supermarket. But glamor and wealth are *not* preoccupations as they are on *Dallas*. Obviously, the soap opera world is in *reality* no more like the average spectator's than the world of *Dallas*; yet the characters and the settings all connote, to use a Barthesian neologism, 'averageness.' This accounts for the fans' frequent contention that soap opera characters are just like them – whereas no one is likely to make such a claim about the Ewing family. The consequent blurring of the boundaries between fantasy and life which sometimes occurs (for example, when fans write letters to the 'characters,' giving them advice about their problems) suggests that the psychological fusion which Chodorow says is experienced by the wife/mother applies in these instances to the *viewer's* experience of the characters.

This last observation would seem to lend support to Luce Irigaray's thesis that identification is an inadequate term for describing women's pleasure. As film critics have recently been pointing out: 'Cinematic identification presupposes the security of the modality "as if." '[3] Soap operas tend, more than any other form, to break down the distance required for the proper working of identification. But rather than seeing these cases as pathological instances of *over*-identification [...], I would argue that they point to a different *kind* of relationship between spectator and characters, one which can be described in the words of Irigaray as 'nearness' – 'a nearness so close that any identification of one or the other is impossible.'[4] The viewer does not *become* the characters [...] but rather relates to them as intimates, as extensions of her world. Speaking of woman's rediscovery of herself, Irigaray writes, 'It is a sort of universe in expansion for which no limits could be fixed and which, for all that, would not be incoherent.'[5] I need not belabor the similarities between this description and soap opera as a form. But I mention it because I believe it is crucial to understand how women's popular culture speaks to women's pleasure at the same time that it puts it in the service of patriarchy, keeps it working for the good of the family.

Television also plays on women's fears that they are not near enough to those around them. Consider the happy ending of a well-known television commercial: Wife: 'Why didn't you *tell* me you like Stove-Top Stuffing with chicken?' Husband: 'You never asked me.' So, it seems, women must play guessing games, be mind readers. Is it then merely accidental that several popular television quiz shows emphasize mind reading over the possession of correct answers? I am referring to programs which have contestants guess the responses of a studio audience or a poll of people, programs like *The Match Game, Card Sharks* and *Family Feud*. In a perceptive article in *Screen Education*, John Tulloch argues that quiz shows on British television present a reified view of knowledge which is current in the culture at large.[6] Increasingly, daytime quiz shows on American television relate not so much to any particular view of knowledge as to a desire to overcome one's *exclusion* from knowledge, from the thoughts and feelings of others. Answers are no longer right or wrong in any 'objective' sense; contestants are rewarded when they correctly guess what *other people* think.

Questions about what is on other people's minds provide many of the enigmas of soap operas as well as of other popular feminine narratives. In gothic romances, for example, the solution to the mystery lies less in the intellectual process of detection – following external clues to determine who provided the corpse, how, and with what motive – than guessing what the aloof, attractive, enigmatic male is thinking and feeling. In soap operas, characters spend an inordinate amount of time trying to find out what is 'bothering' another character. Soap operas may be excessively wordy, as Horace Newcomb has pointed out, but this wordiness is built around deep silences.[7] Characters talk, speculate endlessly about why other characters are *not* talking.

Furthermore, not only are the characters on soap operas impelled to fathom the secrets of other people's minds; the constant, even claustrophobic use of close-up shots stimulates the audience to do likewise. Often *only* the audience is privileged to witness characters' expressions, which are complex and intricately coded, signifying triumph, bitterness, despair, confusion – the entire emotional register, in fact. Soap operas contrast sharply with other popular forms aimed at masculine visual pleasure, which is often centered on the fragmentation and fetishization of the female body. In the most popular feminine visual art, it is easy to forget that characters even have bodies, so insistently are close-ups of faces employed. One critic significantly remarks, 'A face in close-up is what before the age of film only a lover or a mother ever saw.'[8] Soap operas appear to be the one visual art which activates the gaze of the mother – but in order to provoke anxiety (an anxiety never allayed by narrative closure) about the welfare of others. Close-ups provide the spectator with training in 'reading' other people, in being sensitive to their (unspoken) feelings at any given moment.

This openness to the needs and desires of others is, of course, one of the primary functions of the woman in the home. The wife and mother, who is excluded from participation in the larger world in which her husband and children move, must nevertheless be attuned to the effects of this world upon her family. Moreover, although her family cannot be bothered with the details of *her* world, with making such 'trivial' decisions as whether to have stuffing or potatoes with dinner, such decisions nevertheless affect her family's attitudes and moods, and it is well for her to be able to anticipate desires which remain unuttered, perhaps even unthought. Thus, the enigmas of a significant number of commercials, as in the one quoted above, center around the wife's anxiety about what her husband or children will think of one of her little changes in the menu or the running of the household. She waits in suspense as her husband takes the first forkful of his meal, or breathlessly looks on as he selects a clean shirt, wondering if he will notice just how clean and fresh it is. Of course, he *does* notice, as she ecstatically exclaims. This last example seems to come very close to subverting its own project – the project of many commercials – of showing the immense rewards involved in being a housewife. To me, it announces a little too clearly how extraordinary it is when family members pay the least attention to all the work the woman in the home does for them. It is worth noting that in the commercials in which a male tests a female (for example, gives her a new medicine to reduce tension) there is never any anxiety involved. He is absolutely certain what brand will please her. Men, it appears, don't have to try to 'read' women; they already know them and fully understand their needs.

Not only is it the responsibility of the woman in the home to be sensitive to the feelings of her family, her job is further complicated by the fact that she must often deal with several people who have different, perhaps conflicting moods; and further, she must be prepared to drop what she is doing in order to cope with various conflicts and problems the moment they arise. Unlike most workers in the labor force, the housewife must beware of concentrating her energies exclusively on one task – otherwise the dinner could burn, or the baby could crack its skull (as happened once on a soap opera when a villainess became so absorbed in a love encounter that she forgot to keep an eye on her child). The housewife functions, as many creative women have sadly realized, by distraction. Tillie Olsen writes in *Silences*:

> More than in any human relationship, overwhelmingly more, motherhood means being instantly interruptable, responsive, responsible. ... It is distraction, not meditation, that becomes habitual; interruption, not continuity; spasmodic, not constant toil.[9]

Daytime television plays a part in habituating women to interruption, distraction, and spasmodic toil. Here I must take issue with Raymond Williams, who rejects the notion that television programs and commercials may be seen as interruptions. Indeed, I would argue that the flow of daytime television reinforces the very principle of interruptability crucial to the proper functioning of women in the home. In other words, what Williams calls 'the central television experience' is a profoundly de-centering experience.

'The art of being off center,' wrote Walter Benjamin in an essay on Baudelaire, 'in which the little man could acquire training in places like the Fun Fair, flourished concomitantly with unemployment.'[10] Daytime television programs, most obviously soap operas, also provide training in 'the art of being off center' (and we should note in passing that it is probably no accident that the nighttime soap opera *Dallas* and its offshoots and imitators are flourishing in a period of economic crisis and rising unemployment). The housewife, of course, is, in one sense, like the little man at the fun fair, unemployed, but in another sense she is perpetually employed – her work, like a soap opera, is never done. Moreover, as I have said, her duties are split among a variety of domestic and familial tasks, and her television programs keep her from desiring a focused existence by involving her in the pleasures of a fragmented life.

The multiple plot lines of soap operas, for example, keep women interested in a number of characters and their various fates simultaneously. When one plot threatens to become too absorbing, it is interrupted, and another story line resumed, or a commercial is aired. Interruptions within the soap opera diegesis are both annoying and pleasurable: if we are torn away from one absorbing story, we at least have the relief of picking up the thread of an unfinished one. Commericals, of course, present the housewife with mini-problems and their resolutions, so after witnessing all the agonizingly hopeless dilemmas presented on soap operas, the spectator has the satisfaction of seeing *something* cleaned up, if only a stained shirt or a dirty floor.

Although daytime commercials and soap operas are set overwhelmingly within the home, the two views of the home seem antithetical, for the chief concerns of commercials are precisely the ones soap operas censor out. The soggy diapers, yellow wax buildup and carpet smells constituting the world of daytime television ads are rejected by soap operas in favor of Another World, as the very title of one soap opera announces, a world in which characters deal only with the 'large' problems of human existence: crime, love, death and dying. But this antithesis embodies a deep truth about the way women function in (or, more accurately, around) culture: as both moral and spiritual guides and household drudges – now one, now the other, moving back and forth between the extremes, but obviously finding them difficult to reconcile.

Similarly, the violent mood swings the spectator undergoes in switching from quiz shows to soap operas also constitute a kind of interruption, just as the housewife is required not only to endure monotonous, repetitive work but also to be able to switch instantly and on demand from her role as a kind of bedmaking, dishwashing automaton to a large sympathizing consciousness. It must be stressed that while nighttime television certainly offers shifts in mood, notably from comedy to drama, these shifts are not nearly as extreme as in daytime programming. Quiz shows present the spectator with the same game, played and replayed frenetically day after day, with each game a self-contained unit, crowned by climactic success or failure. Soap operas, by contrast, endlessly defer resolutions and climaxes and undercut the very notion of success by continually demonstrating that happiness for all is an unattainable goal: one person's triumph is another person's bitter disappointment.

Not only this, but the pacing of these two types of programs are at opposite extremes. On quiz shows contestants invariably operate under severe time pressure. If the answer is not given in 30 seconds, a most unpleasant-sounding buzzer, rather like an alarm clock or an oven timer, forces the issue: 'Time is up, your answer please.' Whereas quiz shows operate on the speed-up principle, compressing time into tight limits, soap operas slow down the action and expand time to an extent never seen on nighttime television (not even on shows like *Dallas*). Soap opera time coincides with or is actually slower than 'real' time, and, moreover, throughout the years, the lengths of the programs themselves have been expanding. If the two kinds of time embodied by these two types of programs reflect the fact that the housewife must both race *against* time (in completing her daily chores) and *make time* (to be receptive to the demands on her attention made by her family), on a deeper level they are not as divergent as they appear. Speaking of games of chance, in which 'starting all over again is the regulative idea,' Benjamin related the gambler's psychological experience of time to that of the man who works for wages. For both, it is 'time in hell, the province of those who are not allowed to complete anything they have started.'[11] The desire for instant gratification, says Benjamin, is the result of modern man's having been cheated out of his experience. But gratification instantaneously awarded (as in games of chance), or gratification infinitely postponed (as in soap operas) both suggest the deprivation of experience, a deprivation suffered not only by those who work for wages, but obviously also pertaining to those who work at repetitive tasks for *no* tangible rewards, but rather for the gratification of others.

The formal properties of daytime television thus accord closely with the rhythms of women's work in the home. Individual programs like soap operas as well as the flow of various programs and commercials tend to make repetition, interruption and distraction pleasurable. But we can go even further and note that for women viewers reception itself often takes place in a state of distraction. According to Benjamin, 'reception in a state of distraction ... finds in the film its true means of exercise.'[12] But now that we have television we can see that it goes beyond film in this respect, or at least the daytime programs do. For the consumption of most films as well as nighttime programs in some ways recapitulates the work situation in the factory or office: the viewer is physically passive, immobilized, and all his or her attention is focused on the screen. Even the most allegedly 'mindless' program requires a fairly strong degree of concentration if its plot is to make sense. But since the housewife's 'leisure' time is not so strongly demarcated, her entertainment must often be consumed on the job. As the authors of *The Complete Soap Opera Book* tell us:

> The typical fan was assumed to be trotting about her daily chores with her mop in one hand, duster in the other, cooking, tending babies, answering telephones. Thus occupied, she might not be able to bring her full powers of concentration to bear on *Backstage Wife*.[13]

This accounts, in part, for the 'realistic' feel of soap operas. The script writers, anticipating the housewife's distracted state, are careful to repeat important elements of the story several times. Thus, if two characters are involved in a confrontation which is supposed to mark a final break in their relationship, that same confrontation must be repeated, with minor variations, a few times in order to make sure the viewer gets the point. 'Clean breaks' – surely a supreme fiction – are impossible on soap operas. Quiz shows, too, are obviously aimed at the distracted viewer, who, if she misses one game because she is cleaning out the bathroom sink, can easily pick up on the next one ten minutes later.

Benjamin, writing of film, invoked architecture as the traditional art most closely resembling the new one in the kinds of response they elicit. Both are mastered to some extent in a state of distraction; that is, both are appropriated 'not so much by attention as by habit.'[14] It is interesting to recall in this connection the Dadaist Eric Satie's concept of furniture music, which would be absorbed while people went about their business or chatted with each other. Television is the literalization of the metaphor of furniture art, but it must be stressed that this art is more than simply background noise in the way, for example, that muzak is; daytime programs, especially soap operas, are intensely meaningful to many women, as a conversation with any fan will immediately confirm. Moreover, as I have tried to show, their rhythms interact in complex ways with the rhythms of women's life and work in the home.

Ironically, critics of television untiringly accuse its viewers of indulging in escapism. In other words, both high art critics and politically oriented critics, though motivated by vastly different concerns, unite in condemning daytime television for *distracting* the housewife from her real situation. My point is that a distracted or distractable frame of mind is crucial to the housewife's efficient functioning *in* her real situation, and at *this* level television and its so-called distractions, along with the particular forms they take, are intimately bound up with women's work.

Notes

1. Raymond Williams, *Television: Technology and Cultural Form* (New York, Schocken Books, 1975), p. 95.
2. Nancy Chodorow, *The Reproduction of Mothering: Psychoanalysis and the Sociology of Gender* (Berkeley, CA, University of California Press, 1978), p. 179.
3. Mary Ann Doane, 'Misrecognition and Identity', *Ciné-Tracts* Vol. 3 No. 3 (Fall 1980), p. 25.
4. Luce Irigaray, 'When the goods get together' (from *Ce sexe qui n'en est pas un* [Paris, Minuit, 1977]), in *New French Feminisms*, ed. Elaine Marks and Isabelle de-Courtivron (Amherst, MA, University of Massachusetts Press, 1980), pp. 104–105.
5. Ibid, p. 104.
6. John Tulloch, 'Gradgrind's Heirs: The Quiz and the Presentation of "Knowledge" by British Television', *Screen Education* No. 19 (Summer 1976), pp. 3–13.
7. Horace Newcomb, *TV: The Most Popular Art* (New York, Doubleday/Anchor Books, 1974), pp. 168–169.
8. Dennis Porter, 'Soap Time: Thoughts on a Commodity Art Form', *College English* Vol. 38 No. 8 (April 1977), p. 786.
9. Tillie Olsen, *Silences* (New York, Dell Publishing, 1979), pp. 18–19.
10. Walter Benjamin, 'On Some Motifs in Baudelaire', in *Illuminations*, trans. Harry Zohn (New York, Schocken Books, 1969), p. 176.
11. Ibid, p. 179.
12. Benjamin, 'The Work of Art in the Age of Mechanical Reproduction', in *Illuminations*, p. 240.
13. Madeleine Edmondson and David Rounds, *From Mary Nobie to Mary Hartman: The Complete Soap Opera Book* (New York, Stein and Day, 1976), pp. 46–47.
14. Benjamin, 'The Work of Art', pp. 239–240.

14

Housewives and the mass media

Dorothy Hobson

From S. Hall, D. Hobson, A. Lowe and P. Willis (eds.), *Culture, media, language* (Hutchinson 1980)

[...] Television and radio are never mentioned as spare-time or leisure activities but are located by the women as integral parts of their day. (The exception to this is the television viewing which is done after the children are in bed, but even then the period is not completely free for the woman because she still has to provide drinks or food if her husband wants them.) There is a separation between the consumption of radio and television, but both provide crucial elements in the experience and management of their lives.

Radio

[...] The predominance of presenters or DJs [...] can be seen from various aspects. First, it is necessary for the personality of the disc jockey to be a prominent feature in the programme, since all the records which are played throughout the day on Radio 1 are the same; the only variation which exists is in the chatter between records which the disc jockeys provide. Inevitably, then, it is their ability to form a relationship with their audience which gives the disc jockeys their appeal. The disc jockeys have become personalities in their own right, as have the presenters of television current affairs programmes, and the increasing professionalism and development of the necessary features and components of the successful disc jockey could be seen as analogous with the professionalization of other television presenters. As early as the first year of the existence of Radio 1, which began in November 1967, the following point was noted: 'It soon became clear that Radio 1 DJs were going to be accorded almost as much attention by the media as the Royal Family.' (BBC/Everest 1977) The disc jockeys are prominent as a structural feature of the production process of these programmes, and it is they who direct the discourse of the radio programmes towards their known audience – in this case the housewives. Secondly, the women respond to that notion of themselves as 'feminine domestic subjects' of radio discourse which is presented by the disc jockeys. In this study I have concentrated on the reactions of the women to the disc jockeys rather than on the production process of the media messages.

Within the overall picture of isolation which has emerged in the lives of the women in this study, the disc jockey can be seen as having the function of providing the missing 'company' of another person in the lives of the women. As well as helping to combat isolation, it is not too far fetched to see the DJ as also playing the role of a sexual fantasy-figure in the lives of the women who listen. [One woman's] comments about Noel Edmonds [...] are certainly not limited to his role as someone who breaks the isolation in her life; they include references to his attractiveness and physical appearance, although she does not make this explicit. Nevertheless, my *reading* of the role of the DJs is that they play the role of a safe, though definitely sexually attractive man, in the lives of the women. The responses to other DJs confirm this assumption. Tony Blackburn is talked about more in terms of the content of his programme and his manner of presentation than in terms of endearment or enthusiasm. However, Blackburn himself obviously realizes the potential for fantasy relationships with his audience. When he was suffering from a throat infection, which made his voice sound rather husky, he said: 'I hope I am not turning you ladies on too much. I know your husbands have left for work, it's you and I together, kids.' (Recorded from Radio 1, autumn 1977)

Blackburn is a disc jockey whom it is impossible to ignore. Rather like *Crossroads*, the women either like him or hate him, but rarely do they remain indifferent to him. Blackburn himself provides interesting comments on his own views on radio and pop music, describing his show as 'a pleasant bit of entertainment in the background if you like – inane chatter. I think there's room for a station that comes on and is full of a lot of people talking a load of nonsense'. (*Guardian*, 9 January 1976)

Fortunately for him, he does not have to listen to his own programme for, as he says, 'It would drive me mad if I had to physically sit down and listen to David Hamilton's show, or mine, for that matter.' (ibid) And fortunately for the women in this study, they do not have to sit and listen either; they can treat the programme as background chatter. But if by chance they happen to listen to what Tony Blackburn has to say, they will be subjected to an onslaught of chatter which definitely reinforces the ideology of the sexual division of labour and places women firmly in their 'correct' place – in the home. It is in the direct comments which he makes about the records and current topics of interest that Blackburn reveals the depth of his conservatism. The 'working man', strikers, punk rockers, women involved in divorce actions, (in the wake of his own recent divorce) all warrant criticism from him. Women who are playing their traditional role as housewives and mothers constantly earn praise from him. In one programme he was promoting a record by Nancy Wilson (which was supposedly sung by a woman who had enjoyed a 'liberal' life, yet still yearned for the love and security of a husband and family and wanted to tell her 'sisters' of the truth of her misspent life), Blackburn fervently 'plugged' the record and consistently reminded his listeners of the 'truth' of the theme, saying, 'If you understand this, ladies, you understand everything.' In case his listeners did not fully get the message of the song, he took the trouble to explain it, using his own interpretation: 'I hope you understood these lyrics. Nothing is more important, no matter what the press and the media tell you, there is nothing more wonderful than bringing up a child, nothing more difficult either.' (Recorded from Radio 1, autumn, 1977)

Perhaps Tony Blackburn does represent an extreme form of the reinforcement of the ideology of domesticity of the housebound listeners of Radio 1, but far from providing background chatter which can be ignored, he obviously intends his comments to be heard by his audience – and he knows who his audience is. The reinforcement of the dominant ideology of domesticity is definitely a function of the encoded media messages emanating from Radio 1.

The disc jockey, as well as providing relief from isolation, links the isolated individual woman with the knowledge that there are others in the same position. Similarly, this can be seen as a functional effect of 'phone-in' programmes. One of the women says: 'I like listening to the people that phone in. I like the conversations ... I suppose it's 'cos I'm on me own.' These programmes not only provide contact with the 'outside' world; they also reinforce the privatized isolation by reaffirming the consensual position – there are thousands of other women in the same situation, in a sort of 'collective isolation'.

Radio can be seen, then, as providing women with a musical reminder of their leisure activities before they married. It also, as they say, keeps them up to date with new records. Since they do not have any spare money to buy records, this is an important way in which they can listen to music. Since listening to music and dancing are the leisure activities which they would most like to pursue, radio is also a substitute for the real world of music and discos which they have lost. Also, it provides a crucial relief from their isolation. The chatter of the disc jockey may appear inane and trivial, but the popularity of radio, both in national and local terms and in the responses of the women in this study, would appear to suggest that it fulfils certain functions in providing music to keep them 'happy and on the move'. Radio creates its own audience through its constant reference to forthcoming programmes and items within programmes. [...] The women in this study do appear to regard Radio 1 as a friend, and they certainly view the disc jockeys as important means of negotiating or managing the tensions caused by the isolation in their lives.

Television – 'two worlds'

Linda   No, I never watch the news, never!

The ideology of a masculine and a feminine world of activities and interests and the separation of those gender-specific interests is never more explicitly expressed than in the women's reactions and responses to television programmes. Here both class- and gender-specific differences are of vital importance, in terms of both which programmes the women choose to watch or reject and their definition and selection of what are appropriately masculine and feminine programmes and topics. Also, they select television programmes much more consciously than radio programmes. This must partly be a consequence of the fact that they have more freedom during the evenings, and they can make active choices because they are no longer subject to constant interruptions caused by their responsibility for domestic labour and child care. This is in contrast to their listening to the radio during the day, when radio programmes are selected primarily as 'easy listening', a background while they do their housework or look after the children.

There is an *active* choice of programmes which are understood to constitute the 'woman's world', coupled with a complete *rejection* of programmes which are presenting the 'man's world'. However, there is also an acceptance that the 'real' or 'man's world' is important, and the 'right' of their husbands to watch these programmes is respected: but it is not a world with which the women in this study wanted to concern themselves. In fact, the 'world', in terms of what is constructed as of 'news' value, is seen as both alien and hostile to the values of the women. For them television programmes appear to fall into two distinct categories. The programmes which they watch and enjoy are: comedy series [...]; soap operas [...]; American television films [...]; light entertainment and quiz shows [...] and films. All these programmes could be broadly termed as 'entertaining' rather than 'educational and informative'. The programmes which are actively rejected deal with what the women designate the 'real world' or 'man's world', and these predominantly cluster around the news, current affairs programmes [...], scientific programmes [...], the subject-matter of politics or war, including films about war, and, to a lesser extent, documentary programmes. Selected documentaries will be viewed as long as the *subject-matter* is identified as of feminine interest.

[...] It is clear that the news, current affairs, political programmes and scientific programmes, together with portrayals of war (real or in the guise of war films) are actively rejected by the women. They will leave the room rather than sit there while the news is on. The world as revealed through the news is seen to be (a) depressing, (b) boring, but (c) important. The 'news values', as realized in agendas, are 'accepted', but they have *alternative* values which the women recognize but do not suggest should form an alternative coverage. In fact, the importance of accepted 'news values' is recognized, and although their own world is seen as more interesting and relevant to them, it is also seen as secondary in rank to the 'real' or 'masculine' world. In terms of what the news is seen to present, they only select items which they *do not wish to see*. Comments or judgements are made in terms not only of what the items are but also of the effect which they have on the individual. Thus the items are not judged solely for their 'news value' but also for the way they affect the individual. There would appear to be a model for the programmes which are discussed and then rejected.

The news

Content	Conceptualization of value of content	Effects on individual
Politics	Boring	Depressing
War	Male-orientated	Causing nightmares
Industrial troubles		and sleeplessness

The women's interpretation of news and current affairs programmes is an accurate reflection of the news items which are contained in these programmes. They may mis-identify the foci of some news reports, but this perhaps reinforces their claim not to watch these programmes. [...]

The grouping together of the news and current affairs programmes by the women is a response to the circularity of these programmes, which is determined by the interrelation between the news and current events programmes and the prior selection of news items for their news value. A news 'story' becomes a 'current events topic', and the selection of news items according to the hierarchy of 'news value' puts political and military concerns, industrial relations and economic affairs at the head of topics for inclusion. The editorial selection of these items is premised on their 'news value', and this also reflects a masculine bias in terms of the ideology of the subjects of the items included. The women find little of interest for them in the news except for any 'human interest' items, which are necessarily low in news value and rarely occur. When domestic affairs do reach the news it is often in terms of deviation or murder, and this in turn reinforces the accepted absence of these items from 'normal' news bulletins. [...]

The ideology of femininity and feminine values over-determines the structures of what interests women. It is topics which can be regarded as of 'domestic' interest which they see as important or interesting, and it is also significant that 'domestic affairs', constructed in terms of 'news values' to include the economy and industrial relations, are not defined as 'domestic' in the categories which the women construct for themselves. 'Domestic' clearly relates to their own interests and not to the definition which is constructed through the hierarchy of 'news values'. It can be said that the majority of items which are included in news, current affairs and documentary programmes have a content which has little or no intrinsic interest for these women, and the way that they are presented means that they exclude these women from 'participation' at the point of identification with the items included. At the same time, the women accept that these are *important*, and this reinforces the split between the masculine values, which are interpreted as being important, and the interests which they see as representing their own feminine values.

D. Do you like programmes that are like your life or that are entirely different?

R. I think I like things different really, 'cos if it's like me life, it's not very exciting 'cos there's nothing much really ever happens. Something exciting, different. I like watching detectives, anything creepy like ghost stories, I love ghost stories, anything creepy like that.

First, in conjunction with the programmes which women reject, there are programmes which they choose to watch and to which they obviously relate. These can be defined as those which are related to their own lives, the programmes which can loosely be termed 'realistic' – *Coronation Street*, [...] *Emmerdale Farm* [...]. Secondly, the programmes which can be described as having 'fantasy content' (horror movies, or American movies or television movies), although not seen as representing 'real life' in the women's own terms, are seen as an alternative to the reality of their own lives. Finally, there are the programmes which can be categorized as light entertainment (quizzes, or competitions which often have an 'everyday' or 'domestic' theme, either because the contestants are seen as ordinary people or because of the subject-matter. In *Whose Baby?*, for example, the children of celebrity guests appear and the panel has to guess who is the famous father or mother – a direct link of parenthood between the 'famous' and the 'ordinary' viewer (in this case, the woman).

The programmes which are interpreted by the women as portraying 'everyday' or 'family' life are, in fact, far from portraying anything which has a point of *real* identification with the women's own lives. The programmes may not relate to the everyday lives of the women in the study. Within the programmes which are seen as 'realistic' there are common elements of identification. Many of the characters in [soaps] are women who themselves have to confront the 'problems' in their 'everyday' lives, and the resolution or negotiation of these problems within the drama provides points of recognition and identification for the women viewers. It is in the 'living out' of problem areas that much of the appeal of the series is located. However, the resolution of areas of conflict, contradiction or confusion within a dramatic situation is double-edged. The woman can be confronted with the problems and also informed of the different elements which have to be considered in any 'living out' or resolution of problems. It is in the forms that the resolutions are made within programmes that the ideological basis of consensual femininity is *reproduced* and *reinforced* for women. As with the problems that are discussed in phone-in programmes and in the chatter of DJs, the very fact of recognition and *seeming* discussion or consideration by some 'outside' or 'independent' authority gives an impression that the problems have been aired. The outcome remains the same. The resolutions within either the soap opera series or the telephone conversations or talks are not revolutionary; what emerges is the reinforcement of the fatality or inevitability of the situation, without the need to change it.

It is impossible to attempt a detailed analysis of the decoding of the programmes which is made by the women because at this stage this would be only supposition. What is clear, however, is that the programmes which the women watch are differentiated specifically in terms of both class and gender. Overall the programmes fall into the categories of popular drama and light entertainment, and although it is obvious that the women reject news and the political content of current affairs programmes, it would be wrong to contend that they do not have access or exposure to news or politics. Within comedy programmes, news and current affairs topics are presented in a mediated form – and often in a more easily accessible or even 'joking' or parodying manner. The news on Radio 1, which is transmitted every hour, is relatively accessible; it is also introduced by music which is unrecognizable, bright and repetitive and demanding of attention. The women in this study are exposed to news in this form, but they do not mention finding that unacceptable. Clearly, what is important is the definition of specifically feminine interests which women select from media output and the rejection of items which they see as specifically of masculine interest. They combat their own isolation through their interest in radio programmes during the day, and they see television programmes as a form of 'leisure' or relaxation. Radio is integral to their working day, but early-evening television is secondary to the domestic labour which they perform. The programmes which the women watch and listen to, together with the programmes which they reject, reinforce the sexual division of spheres of interest, which is determined both by their location in the home and by the structures of femininity that ensure that feminine values are secondary (or less 'real') than those of the masculine world of work and politics, which the women regard as *alien*, yet *important*.

15

Behind closed doors: video recorders in the home

Ann Gray

From H. Baehr and G. Dyer (eds.), *Boxed in: women and television* (Pandora 1987)

The video cassette recorder is arguably the major innovation in home entertainment in Britain since television. When we address questions of how women watch television and video we inevitably raise a complex set of issues which relate to women and their everyday lives. In talking to women about home video cassette recorders (VCR) and television use, I have identified some of the determining factors surrounding these activities which take place within the domestic environment.[1] With the development of VCRs and other products such as home computers and cable services, [there is an] ever increasing trend towards home-centred leisure and entertainment. New technology in the home has to be understood within a context of structures of power and authority relationships between household members, with gender emerging as one of the most significant differentiations. This far from neutral environment influences the ways in which women use popular texts in general and television and video in particular, and the pleasures and meanings which these have for them.

The video revolution

Although it is a relatively recent phenomenon, home video arrived as long ago as 1972 with Philips VCR and Sony U-matic. But it wasn't until Sony Betamax and VHS (video home system), both of which use 19 mm tape, brought the cost down significantly, that the stage was set for a consumer boom. In 1983 15 per cent of households in the United Kingdom had access to a VCR, by 1986 the figure had reached 40 per cent. An important factor in the British VCR experience is that the distribution of recorders operates through the already existing television rental networks, thereby making it possible to rent a VCR on a monthly basis, without the necessity for large capital investment. This results in video recorders being made available to a much wider range of socio-economic groups than might at first be imagined. We are not, in the British case, considering a 'luxury' item which graces the affluent household, rather, a widely available home entertainment facility which has rapidly become an accepted and essential part of everyday life, cutting across economic and class boundaries.

The development and marketing of entertainment consumer hardware can often outpace the provision of 'software' or 'content'. Raymond Williams points out that when domestic radio receivers were first marketed there was very little to receive in terms of programming content, 'It is not only that the supply of broadcasting facilities preceded the demand; it is that the means of communication preceded their content' (Williams, 1974, p. 25).

There are two major uses for VCRs: time-shift, which involves recording off-broadcast television in order to view at a different time, and the playing of pre-recorded tapes.[2] These can be purchased, though the majority are hired through video rental 'libraries'. Although off-air recording is an attractive proposition, it has become obvious to a few entrepreneurs that there is a large potential market for the hiring of pre-recorded tape. In Britain during the early 1980s one feature of almost every high street was a new phenomenon known as the 'video library'. These were often hastily converted small shops offering tapes, mainly of movies, for hire. In these early days, in order to finance their purchase of new material, the libraries demanded a membership fee, often as high as £40, as well as a nightly fee for the hiring of tapes. Nowadays, it is possible to join a video library free of charge, with a nightly rental fee of £1.00–£1.50 per tape. There are now upwards of 6,500 movies[3] available for hire on video tape and at a rough estimate four million tapes are hired a week. Indeed, 97 per cent of film watching is now done outside the cinema, mainly on broadcast television, but the hiring of films accounts for a significant proportion of this viewership (Howkins, 1983).

The video library industry – and I use this term to describe the distributors and retailers of pre-recorded tapes for purchase or hire – has experienced major change. Many of the smaller retail outlets have gone by the board, forced out by the larger and well-established distributors who moved in once the market had been tested. The industry has established its own quasi-professional organisations in order to protect itself against 'video piracy' and to professionalise and improve its image, which has not been good. The 'moral panic' which resulted in the Video Recordings Bill of 1984, providing for every film on hire to be censored for home viewing, had a devastating effect on the public image of the video libraries. This was fuelled enthusiastically by the popular press (Petley, 1984; Kuhn, 1984a; Barker, 1984). On 1 September 1982 the *Sun* carried the headline 'Fury over video nasties' and referred to the video distributors and retailers as 'the merchants of menace' who were threatening the well-being of our children. This kind of response to a new development in mass cultural production is similar to those precipitated by the novel in the nineteenth century, cinema in the 1920s and television in the 1950s. The moral reformers were then, as now, fearful for the effects of these new mass-produced cultural forms on those 'weaker' members of society – women, children and the 'lower orders' in general – whom they sought to protect.

Video and family life

Although there are many aspects of the video phenomenon which are worthy of study, my research initially focuses on the potential choice which the VCR offers for viewing within the domestic and family context. The major reason for this is that, until recently, attention to the context of viewing seems to have been largely neglected in media and cultural studies.[4] The relationship between the viewer and television, the reader and text, is often a relationship which has to be negotiated, struggled for, won or lost, in the dynamic and often chaotic processes of family life. As video recorders offer, above all, extended choice of content and time management for viewing within the home, research into its use has to be focused within that very context. The context of 'the family' is, for my purposes, conceived of as a site of constant social negotiation within a highly routinised framework of material dependency and normative constraint,[5] and all these elements enter into the negotiations which surround viewing decisions. This family setting, with its power relationships and authority structures across gender, is an extremely important factor in thinking more generally of 'leisure' and, specifically, home-based leisure. The home has increasingly become the site for entertainment, and we can see VCRs as yet one more commodity which reduces the necessity for household members to seek entertainment outside the home, a situation reinforced by the present economic climate in Britain:

> JS: Well, we can't really afford to go out to the pictures, not any more. If we all go and have ice-creams, you're talking about eight or nine pounds. It's a lot of money.

What is especially important for women is that the domestic sphere is increasingly becoming defined as their only leisure space. Many married women are in paid work outside the home, but women are still largely responsible for the domestic labour in the home. Childcare, food provision, laundry, shopping and cleaning the living space, are ultimately women's responsibility even if their male partners help. While men in paid employment come home to a non-work environment, women who either work in the home all day or go out to paid employment still have to work at home in the evenings and at weekends:

> AS: Him? Oh, he sits on his backside all night, from coming in from work to going to bed.

Indeed, many women do not consider themselves as having any leisure at all (Deem, 1984). And many certainly would not allow themselves the luxury of sitting down to watch television until the children are fed and put to bed and the household chores have been completed:

> JK: I'd feel guilty, I'd feel I was cheating. It's my job and if I'm sat, I'm not doing my job.

This is a context which, at the most basic and practical level, positions women in relation to the whole area of leisure, but particularly in relation to television and video viewing:

> AS: Like, if he comes in and he's rented a video, straight after tea he

wants to put it on. I say 'well let me finish the washing-up first'. I mean, I just wouldn't enjoy it if I knew it was all to do.

Video as technology

Women and men have differential access to technology in general and to domestic technology in particular. The relations between domestic technology and gender are relatively unexplored,[6] though there is more work on gender and technology in the workplace where, as Jan Zimmerman notes, new technology is entering existing and traditional sets of relations. Old values in this way become encoded in new technologies (Zimmerman, 1981; Cockburn, 1983, 1985). It is interesting to note that American researchers discovered that in the early 1970s the full-time housewife was spending as much time on housework as her grandmother had done fifty years earlier. Domestic technology may be labour-saving, replacing the drudgery of household work, but it is time-consuming in that each piece of equipment requires work if it is to fulfil its advertised potential. Rothschild argues that far from liberating women from housework, new technology, embedded as it is in ideological assumptions about the sexual division of labour, has further entrenched women in the home and in the role of housewife (Rothschild, 1983).

When a new piece of technology is purchased or rented, it is often already inscribed with gender expectations. The gender specificity of pieces of domestic technology is deeply implanted in the 'commonsense' of households, operating almost at an unconscious level. As such it is difficult for the researcher to unearth. One strategy I have employed which throws the gender of domestic technology into high relief is to ask the women to imagine pieces of equipment as coloured either pink or blue.[7] This produces almost uniformly pink irons and blue electric drills, with many interesting mixtures along the spectrum. The washing maching, for example, is most usually pink on the outside, but the motor is almost always blue. VCRs and, indeed, all home entertainment technology would seem to be a potentially lilac area, but my research has shown that we must break down the VCR into its different modes in our colour-coding. The 'record', 'rewind' and 'play' modes are usually lilac, but the timer switch is nearly always blue, with women having to depend on their male partners or their children to set the timer for them. The blueness of the timer is exceeded only by the deep indigo of the remote control switch which in all cases is held by the man:

SW: Oh, yes, that's definitely blue in our house. He flicks from channel to channel, I never know what I'm watching – it drives me mad.

It does appear that the male of the household is generally assumed to have knowledge of this kind of technology when it enters the household, or at least he will quickly gain the knowledge. And certain knowledges can, of course, be withheld and used to maintain authority and control:

AS: Well, at first he was the only one who knew how to record things, but then me and my young son sat down one day and worked it out.

> That meant we didn't have to keep asking him to record something
> for us.

Although women routinely operate extremely sophisticated pieces of domestic technology, often requiring, in the first instance, the study and application of a manual of instructions, they often feel alienated from operating the VCR. The reasons for this are manifold and have been brought about by positioning within the family, the education system and the institutionalised sexism with regard to the division of appropriate activities and knowledges in terms of gender. Or there may be, as I discovered, 'calculated ignorance':

> CH: If I learnt how to do the video it would become my job just like everything else.

If women do not feel confident or easy in approaching and operating the recorders, let alone in setting the timer for advance recording, they are at an immediate and real disadvantage in terms of exercising the apparent choices which the VCR offers. This, combined with constraints in the hiring of video tapes, either financial or simply normative, means that for women the idea of increased freedom and choice of viewing may well be spurious.

Genre and gender

If women are 'positioned' within the context of consumption, it seems that they are also positioned, or even structured in absence, by the video industry itself in terms of the kind of audience it seems to be addressing. To enter a video library is to be visually bombarded by 'covers' depicting scenes of horror, action adventure, war, westerns and 'soft' pornography, traditionally considered to be 'male' genres.[8] Is it therefore mainly men who are hiring video tapes, and if so, what do women feel about the kinds of tapes they are watching at home? Do women ever hire tapes themselves, or do they feel alienated from both the outlets and what they have to offer? In other words, what are the circumstances surrounding the use of video libraries and what is the sexual division of labour associated with the hiring and viewing of tapes? I have already made reference to the so-called 'male' genres which imply that certain kinds of films address themselves to and are enjoyed by a male audience and the same, of course, could be said for 'female' genres. But why do certain kinds of texts or genres appeal to women and not to men and *vice versa* and how should we conceive of the audience for these texts made up of women and men?

The 'gendered audience' has a theoretical history which, as Annette Kuhn usefully points out, has developed within two different perspectives, one emerging from media studies and the other from film theory (Kuhn, 1984b). This has resulted in two quite different notions of the gendered audience. The sociological emphasis of media studies has tended to conceive of a 'social audience', that is, an audience made up of already constituted male and female persons who bring (among other things) maleness or femaleness to a text, and who decode the text within that particular frame of reference. Film theory on the other hand, has conceived of a 'psychological audience', a collection of individual spectators who do not read the text, but rather the text 'reads' them. In other words, the film offers a masculine or feminine subject position and the spectator occupies that position. Of course, this is not automatic and there is nothing to prevent, for example, a female spectator taking up a masculine subject position. However, the construction of masculinity and femininity across the institutions within society is so powerfully aligned to the social categories 'male' and 'female' that the two usually coincide apparently seamlessly. But, as Kuhn points out, what is suggested by these two perspectives is a distinction between femaleness as a social gender and femininity as a subject position. The problem here is that neither of these two perspectives is sufficient in themselves to gain a full understanding of what happens when men and women watch films. In the former case, context is emphasised over text and in the latter text over context. The spectator-text relationship suggested by the psychoanalytic models used in film theory tend to disregard those important factors of social context involved in film and TV watching. Also, they find it difficult to allow for the subject constituted outside the text, across other discourses, such as class, race, age and general social environment. The social audience approach, conversely, sees the response to texts as a socially predetermined one, and in this way does not allow for consideration of how the texts themselves work on the viewers/readers.

There have been some attempts to link text with context by examining the particular features of 'women's genres'. Soap operas, for example, have been looked at in terms of their distinctive narrative pattern, which is open-ended and continuous; their concern with so-called 'female' skills; their scheduling on television which fits into the rhythm of women's work at home, all of which can be seen as specifically addressing a social audience of women (Brunsdon, 1981; Modleski, 1982). However, this would still seem to stress context over text and in this area the film theory perspective has certainly been limited by its implicit assumption of an intense and concentrated relationship between spectator and text in a darkened cinema. For television this relationship is more likely to be characterised by distinction and diversion. As Kuhn points out:

> This would suggest that each medium constructs sexual difference through spectatorship in rather different ways: cinema through the look and spectacle, and TV – perhaps less evidently – through a capacity to insert its flow, its characteristic modes of address and the textual operations of different kinds of programmes into the rhythms and routines of domestic activities and sexual divisions of labour in the household at various times of day. (Kuhn, 1984b, p. 25)

This distinction is important and useful, but when thinking about the use of VCRs the two media are viewed in the same context. Movies have long been a part of television's nightly 'flow' as well as part of daytime viewing. But in video recording movies off television for watching at a later date, and in hiring movies, we have a discrete 'event' which disrupts the flow of television and its insertive scheduling:

> AC: Oh yes, we all sit down and watch – 'we've got a video, let's sit down' – TV's different, that's just on.

Concepts of the psychological audience and the social audience are not sufficient in themselves to explore the whole complexity of text, subject and context and the ways in which they intersect. But both are necessary, representing as they do different instances within the process of consumption of popular texts. While the psychological model posits an unacceptably homogeneous and 'universal' audience, it does allow us to consider the importance of how texts work, not only in terms of subject positioning and interpellation, but also in terms of pleasure and desire. The social model demands that the audience is heterogeneous and requires us to explore those other differences and contexts which, to a greater or lesser extent, determine the ways in which women and men read those texts. It seems clear that the problem of the relationship between text and gendered audience cannot be resolved at the theoretical level, but rather must be kept in play and, if possible, problematised throughout the research enterprise.

Viewing contexts

It would seem that women do have certain preconceptions about what constitutes a 'film for men' as against a 'film for women', and furthermore, a typology of viewing contexts is beginning to emerge, along with appropriate associated texts (see Table 15.1).

I wish to focus mainly on Context (Female alone), but before I do it is worth mentioning the difference between the negotiations around Contexts (Male alone) and (Female alone). For the latter to exist, the male partner must normally be out of the house, either at work or at leisure, whereas, Context (Male alone) would be likely to exist when both male and female were in the house together. The women simply wouldn't watch:

Table 15.1   Typology of viewing contexts[9]

Context	Film	TV
1 Family together	*Superman*	Children's TV
	Walt Disney	Quiz shows
	Jaws	Comedy
	Comedy	*EastEnders*
2 Male and female partners together	*An Officer and a Gentleman*	*Aufweidersehen Pet*
	Kramer v. Kramer	*Minder*
	The Rockys	Shows
	Any Clint Eastwood	*Coronation Street*
		EastEnders
3 Male alone	War	Sport
	Action Adventure*	News
	Horror*	Documentaries
	Adults*	
4 Female alone	*Who Will Love My Children?*	*Coronation Street*
	Evergreen	*Crossroads*
	Romance	*Dallas*
		Dynasty
		A Woman of Substance
		Princess Daisy

*These are the category headings used by many video libraries

BA: If he's watching something I'm not enjoying, I'll either knit or read.

JS: Well, I can read when the telly's on if it's something I don't like.

DS: I usually go to bed with a book, or sometimes I'll watch the portable in the kitchen, but it's damned uncomfortable in there.

CH: Well, when he's in, Father has priority over what's on. Yes, he does, but I can go in the other room if I don't want to watch it.

Women only

For women who are at home all day, either with very small children or children of school age, and whose husbands are out at work, there are obvious opportunities for them to view alone. However, most of the women I have talked to are constrained by guilt, often referring to daytime viewing as some kind of drug:

SW: No, I've got too many things to do during the daytime, I couldn't do it to myself, I'd be a total addict.

JK: Well, I watch *Falcon Crest* – it's a treat, when I've done my work, then I sit down and it's my treat. But I'm not one to get videos during the day because I think you can get really addicted, then everything else suffers.

The second woman quoted indicates what is a fairly common strategy – that of using daytime television programmes to establish some time for herself as a reward to which completion of household tasks will lead. This assuages the guilt to a certain extent and the pleasure afforded by this particular viewing context seems to go far beyond the pleasures of the text itself. What it represents is a breathing space when the busy mother can resist the demands of her children and domestic labour for a brief period of time. One of the most popular daytime programmes cited was *Sons & Daughters*, an Australian imported soap opera, transmitted three afternoons a week in the Yorkshire region. Most of the women preferred to watch this alone, some taking the telephone off the hook to ensure uninterrupted concentration, but they would watch it with a friend if they happened to be in each other's houses at the time. Janice Radway in her study of women and romantic fiction talks with regret of the isolated context within which popular romances are consumed by women (Radway, 1984). The next viewing context I wish to discuss reveals a more optimistic state of affairs for women.

This context is again female only, but is one in which several women get together to watch a video which they have hired jointly. This would normally happen during the day when their children are at school. Far from being instrumental in isolating women, it would seem that there is a tendency to communal use of hired videos, mainly on economic grounds, but also on the grounds that the women can watch what they want together without the guilt or the distraction of children:

BS: There are three of us, and we hire two or three films a week and watch them together, usually at Joyce's house when the kids are at school. We can choose what we want then.

JK: Yes, if there's something we want to see we wait 'til the kids have gone back to school so's we can sit and watch it without them coming in saying 'can I have... can I have...' it makes it difficult.

The idea of viewing together during the day for this particular network of women living on the same street came when one of them found herself continually returning the video tapes which her husband had hired the night before. She discovered that there were films which she would like to watch but which her husband never hired. A good relationship was established with the woman who worked in the video library who would look out for good films:

BS: She comes into the shop where I work and I go 'have any new videos come out?' She tells me. She knows what we like.

One favoured form for this viewing network is that of the long family saga, often running to two or three tapes:

JK: We like something in two or three parts; something with a really good story to it so's you can get involved.

BS: Mm... the other week we had a Clint Eastwood and Burt Reynolds film because she [MD] likes Clint Eastwood but we talked all the way through that, didn't we?

When the group views sagas which extend over two or three tapes there is obvious pleasure in anticipating both the outcome of the narrative and the viewing of the following tape. A considerable amount of discussion and speculation ensues and a day for the next viewing is fixed:

MD: We like to spread them out – every other day, it helps to break the week up. Sometimes we have them on an evening, if our husbands are away or out. We'll have a bottle of wine then, then we don't even have to get up to make a cup of tea.

These women are also devotees of the American soap operas and operate a 'failsafe' network of video recording for each other, refusing to discuss each episode until they have all seen it. These popular texts form an important part of their friendship and association in their everyday lives and give a focus to an almost separate female culture which they can share together within the constraints of their positions as wives and mothers. Furthermore, they are able to take up the feminine subject positions offered by these texts comfortably and pleasurably. In contrast, the films which their husbands hire for viewing Context (Male & female partners together) mainly offer a masculine subject position which the women seem to take up through their male partners, who in turn give their approval to such texts.

The major impetus for a viewing group like this is that films which women enjoy watching are rarely, if ever, hired by their male partners for viewing together because they consider such films to be 'trivial' and 'silly' and women are laughed at for enjoying them:

BA: I sit there with tears running down my face and he comes in and says 'you daft thing'.

This derision also applies to soap operas, and is reproduced in male children:

JK: Oh, my son thinks I'm stupid because I won't miss *Dallas* – perhaps I am.

It is the most powerful member within the household who defines this hierarchy of 'serious' and 'silly', 'important' and 'trivial'. This leaves women and their pleasures in films downgraded, objects and subjects of fun and derision, having to consume them almost in secret. But the kinds of films and television soap operas which women enjoy watching alone deal with things of importance to them, highlighting so-called 'female' concerns – care of children, concern for members of one's own family, consideration for one's own sexual partner, selflessness in characters – all of which are the skills of competence, the thought and caring which husbands and children expect of women and assume as a matter of natural course.[10] This is a deeply contradictory position for women, lying between the realities of their day to day lives and the pleasures and gratifications that they seek to find in texts that their partners and very often their children, look upon as so much rubbish:

JS: I think a lot of storylines in soap operas are very weak and I think a man needs something to keep his interest more than a woman. That makes a man sound more intelligent, but that's not what I mean. It's got to be something worth watching before he'll sit down and actually watch it, but I'd watch anything. I think he thinks it's unmanly to watch them.

SW: All the soap operas are rubbish for men, fantasy for women.

AG: *Do you think men need fantasy?*

SW: They need fantasy in a different way, detectives and wars, that's their fantasy world, and science fiction, a tough, strong world. Not sloppy, who's fallen in love with who, who's shot JR – it's rubbish. Men know it's rubbish, that's the difference.

Here are two women talking about a genre they love in relation to their male partners, giving us a sense of the 'power of definition' within the partnerships, but also the ways in which the women themselves think of their own pleasures.

Conclusion

Theories of the gendered audience as they have been developed are useful, but when women and men watch movies and television they become that hybrid, the *social spectator* (Kuhn, *ibid.*) and, in understanding the subject-text-context relationship, the social and psychological have to be kept in play to a proportionately greater or lesser degree. This allows us to consider how texts and contexts (both the specific and the wider social context) combine together in producing the gendered reading subject. Charlotte Brunsdon, writing on *Crossroads*, has attempted to resolve this dualism and suggests that, 'The relation of the audience to the text will not be determined solely by that text, but also by positionalities in relation to a whole range of other discourses – discourses of motherhood, romance and sexuality for example' (Brunsdon, 1981, p. 32).

This enables us to think of the subject in the social context occupying different positions in relation to different discourses which change across time. As particular discourses become central issues, they will affect the ways in which the social subject occupies, or resists, the subject position contructed by a text.

The viewing and reading of texts takes place, for the majority of people, within the domestic context. However, this is a context which is not singular and unchanging, but plural and open to different permutations, dependent upon the negotiations between members of the household and the particular texts involved. The VCR offers the potential for extended choice of viewing in terms of text and context. But in order to explore how this potential is being used the particular conditions of its consumption must be addressed. The viewing contexts and their associated texts which I have outlined here have emerged from my discussions with women who occupy different social positions and there are remarkable similarities in the ways in which all the women have spoken about their domestic viewing practices. However, it is simply not sufficient to have identified these similarities, and my analysis of the interview 'texts' continues in an attempt to make visible the important differences between the women's accounts and these practices. These differences must be seen in relation to their particular social positioning and the various specific discourses which they inhabit. The interview material I have gathered demands a framework of analysis which uses theories and concepts developed within different disciplines and will, I am sure, test their relative strengths and weaknesses in revealing the complexity of how women relate to television and video in their everyday lives.

Notes

1. This research was initially funded by the Economic and Social Research Council and has taken the form of long, open-ended discussions with women whose age, social position, employment and family circumstances differ (race is a variable which has not been introduced). Part of my strategy has been to encourage open discussion and allow the women themselves to introduce topics which are of importance to them. By keeping the discussions open they can take pleasure in having the opportunity to explore and express their own ideas and feelings on these matters. For discussions on feminist research methods see Roberts, 1981; Stanley and Wise, 1983; Bell and Roberts, 1984.
2. VCRs can also be used in conjunction with a video camera to produce home video tapes.
3. 'Movies' in this context include films made specially for video distribution, films made for TV, both British and American, as well as 'feature' films which are produced primarily for the cinema.
4. There are notable exceptions (Hobson, 1981, 1982; Morley, 1986; Collett, 1986).
5. I am grateful to Elizabeth Shove and Andrew Tudor for this working definition.
6. However a recent publication by W. Faulkner and E. Arnold (eds), *Smothered by Invention Technology in Women's Lives* (Pluto Press, 1985) does address issues of domestic technology and gender.
7. These were ideas discussed at a seminar given by Cynthia Cockburn at York University, June 1985. See also Cockburn, 1985.
8. It is interesting to note that video tapes are now being distributed which are

specifically aimed at a female audience; IPC and Videospace combined magazine and video to market their *Woman's Own Selection,* along with their more recent label *Images of Love,* while Polygram Video are offering a label, *Women's Choice.* However, in the North of England certainly, these have a very limited distribution.

9. These are the names which the women themselves gave to the different texts and genres.
10. Charlotte Brunsdon has made this point in relation to *Crossroads,* but we can see that it can apply to other 'women's genres' (Brunsdon, 1981).

References

BARKER, M. (ed.) 1984: *The video nasties.* London: Pluto Press.

BELL, C and ROBERTS, H. (eds.) 1984: *Social researching.* London: Routledge & Kegan Paul.

BRUNSDON, C. 1981: Crossroads: notes on a soap opera. *Screen* 22 (4), 32–37.

COCKBURN, C. 1983: *Brothers.* London: Pluto Press.

COCKBURN, C. 1985: *Machinery of dominance.* London: Pluto Press.

COLLETT, P. 1986: Watching the TV audience. Paper presented to International Television Studies Conference 1986.

DEEM, R. 1984: Paid work, leisure and non-employment: shifting boundaries and gender differences. Paper presented to British Sociological Association Conference 1984.

FAULKNER, W. and ARNOLD, E. (eds.) 1985: *Smothered by invention.* London: Pluto Press.

HOBSON, D. 1981: Housewives and the mass media. In Hall, S. *et al.* (eds.), *Culture, media, language.* London: Hutchinson.

HOBSON, D. 1982: *'Crossroads': The drama of a soap opera.* London: Methuen.

HOWKINS, J. 1983: Mr Baker: a challenge. *Sight & Sound,* autumn, 227–29.

KUHN, A. 1984a: Reply to Julian Petley. *Screen* 25 (3), May/June, 116–17.

KUHN, A. 1984b: Women's genres. *Screen* 25 (1), 18–28.

MODLESKI, T. 1982: *Loving with a vengeance.* Hamden: Connecticut, Shoe String Press.

MORLEY, D. 1986: *Family television: cultural power and domestic leisure.* London: Comedia.

PETLEY, J. 1984: A nasty story. *Screen* 25 (2), March/April, 68–74.

RADWAY, J. A. 1984: *Reading the romance.* Chapel Hill: University of North Carolina Press.

ROBERTS, H. (ed.) 1981: *Doing feminist research.* London: Routledge & Kegan Paul.

ROTHSCHILD, J. 1983: *Machina ex Dea.* New York: Pergamon Press.

STANLEY, L and WISE, S. 1983: *Breaking out.* London: Routledge & Kegan Paul.

WILLIAMS, R. 1974: *Television technology and cultural form.* London: Fontana.

ZIMMERMAN, J. 1981: Technology and the future of women: haven't we met somewhere before? *Women's Studies International Quarterly* 4 (3), 355.

16

Teenage girls reading *Jackie*

Elizabeth Frazer

From *Media, Culture and Society* 9, 407–25 (1987)

[. . .] The research with girls about reading *Jackie* is part of a wider enquiry into the acquisition of a feminine gender and sexual identity, and about the role of 'ideology' in this process. In recent years social and cultural researchers have taken feminine heterosexuality as peculiarly 'ideological'. Girls seem to suffer from what we might call 'false consciousness' in sexual matters; the social organization of sexuality benefits men and boys and disbenefits women and girls; sexual meanings and definitions uphold the valorization of masculinity and the oppression of females; behaviour, values and ideals which to radicals look highly artificial and political are widely perceived as 'natural', and so on (for example: Barrett, 1980; Griffin, 1985; Hebron, 1983; Lees, 1986; McRobbie, 1978a, 1978b; Sharpe, 1976; Wilson, 1978; Winship, 1978). Sociologists have studied sexist beliefs and attitudes. Cultural analysis has paid attention to texts which are said to be bearers of the ideology of feminine sexuality: pornography, romantic fiction, girls' and women's magazines, sex education materials. One text which has received a considerable amount of this sort of attention is *Jackie* (Griffin, 1982; Hebron, 1983, McRobbie, 1978b). However, I could not discover any research in which readers were asked about the magazine.

In my fieldwork I had prolonged and regular contact with seven groups of teenage girls. One was a racially mixed working-class group who regularly go to a youth project in Inner London. I have used conventional sociologists' occupational status criteria for determining class; typical parental occupations from among this group are kitchen assistant, factory worker, shop assistant, cleaner. On the other hand, for racial identity I have used the girls' own self-ascriptions; this group is mainly black British, but included two white girls and one Turkish. They attend a variety of schools (mixed, or single-sex comprehensives, or single-sex convents) and range in age from thirteen to seventeen. There were also two groups of fourth formers (fourteen-year-olds), and a group of upper sixth formers from the Oxfordshire single-sex comprehensive. The parental occupations of these girls included secretaries, plumber, police officer, nurse, master butcher, cabinet maker, night porter. They were more homogeneous racially – one fourth former was Afro-Caribbean, and one sixth former was a black

African. There were also two groups of sixth formers (one upper, one lower), and a group of third formers (thirteen years) in an Oxfordshire headmistresses' conference public school for girls. The parental occupations of these girls included barrister, managing director, solicitor, stud manager, stockbroker, landowner, army officer. They were all white.

In the *Jackie* session I gave the girls a photocopy of the story to read, and then just asked them to talk about it.[1] They were not surprised to be asked to do this as we had talked a lot about TV, books, advertising and so on before, and they knew what my research was about. Discussion about the story generally lasted about twenty minutes. After this the talk drifted off, different ways, depending on the group. The comprehensive fourth years, and the public school upper sixth began to talk about problem pages, with interesting results which I discuss later in this article.

To begin with, though, I want to discuss some philosophical and conceptual problems with 'ideology'. These problems are invariably overlooked, or ignored, by social theorists and researchers, but they have serious implications for the use of 'ideology' as the powerful explanation of social phenomena that it is often taken to be.

[...] The social origin of ideology is, in ordinary language contexts, taken to imply falsity (although of course, arguments about *why* people believe what they believe are quite irrelevant to the truth-value of those beliefs). Nevertheless, in much political and social theory, 'ideology' is set against something like 'science'; this obviously means we do have to have a means of judging what is true in the social realm if we are to recognize the non-ideological and this raises complex philosophical difficulties. Second, there is a problem with exactly specifying the content of a 'coherent set of ideas'. When researchers 'look' inside people's heads, they rarely find 'coherent' ideas, and it is normally taken that this is because people are only partially subject to ideology, or are subject to multiple, and conflicting, ideologies. (This is to ignore other methodological difficulties with the project of 'measuring attitudes' or discovering opinion or belief.) In any case, most theorists take it that ideology is not properly a category of 'the mental', but of 'the social', and therefore 'exists' in the public realm, in 'texts', taking that in its broadest sense.

But this, also, raises difficulties: *which* texts are to be taken to be representative of, for example, liberal ideology? In addition, theorists normally take it that 'ideology' is in fact analytically distinct from the ideas expressed in the texts themselves. It is that which determines those ideas, or constructs the meanings of the text; it is logically prior to the text itself. For theorists who still consider 'ideology' to be to do with 'belief', the same sort of argument applies – ideology is logically prior to the formation of the beliefs themselves. But it can easily be seen that this makes 'ideology' a very difficult thing to research.

Of course, that a concept is of an unobservable does not condemn it out of hand. Many perfectly respectable scientific concepts fall into this category, and they fulfil the necessary function of explaining what we *do* observe. 'Ideology', in this tradition explains 'false consciousness' or the fact that people seem to have contradictory beliefs about the social world; or the maintenance of the class system; or the meanings of keywords, or texts;

or (crucially for the purposes of this article) the positioning of 'subjects' in an 'objective' social order. But, it is the argument of this paper that the con-cept of 'ideology' is overly theoretical, in the sense that it is explanatorily unnecessary. The legitimation of social orders, what texts means – all of these things must be explained by social theorists; I argue that we can explain them with concepts which are more concrete with 'ideology'.

Paradoxically, I shall also go on to argue that the concept is too mono-lithic, and, as it stands, predicts that people will be more, or differently, affected by 'ideology' than evidence actually shows they are. For there is no doubt that the ordinary language notion of ideology carries with it an implication of 'normativity' and of efficacy – ideology makes people do things. Although it is rarely spelt out as such, researchers and theorists work with an implicit model as follows:

$$
\left.\begin{array}{l}\text{Ideology}\\ \text{unitary or}\\ \text{multiple}\end{array}\right\} \rightarrow \left.\begin{array}{l}\text{meanings}\\ \text{'culture'}\\ \text{representation}\end{array}\right\} \rightarrow \left.\begin{array}{l}\text{belief}\\ \text{attitude}\\ \text{opinion}\end{array}\right\} \rightarrow \text{behaviour}
$$

Much empirical research has focused on the third element in this chain, i.e. subjects' beliefs and attitudes. This work tends to take 'attitude' or 'opin-ion', or 'belief' to be measurable, and fixed. I believe that this in itself is an unwarrantable assumption. In this article, though, I want to concentrate on the work which attends to the second element – the meanings and repre-sentations of the culture which are encoded in texts of various sorts. Espe-cially significant are semiotic, and other contents analyses of texts, which carry the implication that from the analysis we can infer the content of ideology, and predict or explain the beliefs and behaviour of readers. [...]

All too often theorists commit the fallacy of reading 'the' meaning of a text and inferring the ideological effect the text 'must' have on the readers (other than the theorists themselves, of course!). We may oppose this strat-egy at two points. First, we may dispute that there is one valid and unitary meaning of a text. Second, we may care to check whether, even if we grant that there is one meaning, it does have this, or an ideological effect on the reader (see Richardson and Corner, 1986). In this article I am mainly con-cerned with the second of these two queries.

When we had the discussions about the story I knew the girls in the groups fairly well, as I had had at least half a dozen intensive sessions with each, discussing topics loosely connected with 'femininity', and doing group work exercises, playing communication games and so on. They knew I was interested in what they watched, read and listened to, and that if possible I wanted to find out how these things affected them. A crucial part of my fieldwork methodology is feeding the analysis and concepts *I* use back into the groups, so in previous sessions we had discussed concepts like 'stereo-types', 'roles', 'alternative meanings' and so on. They were not, therefore, in the least bit surprised to be asked to read and discuss the photo-story. I gave them enough time to read it once from start to finish, and then said something like: 'OK, what do you think of that story then?'

[...] It seems to be generally assumed that *Jackie* and publications like it are read ordinarily in a superficial and lazy fashion, and judging by the number of 'It's OK's' my eager youth worker's questions have elicited in time, I suppose I'm inclined to agree. But I see no way of discovering the *effect* of this sort of reading in the 'objective' way.

In fact, for what it's worth, my data lend credence to the hypothesis that *Jackie* is read lazily. Several of the girls didn't follow the story on one reading:

Zara	he's got a different jersey on, like different jersey, different trousers
Claire	well, it happens to be a different day, he changes
Zara	yes, but he meets her on that day doesn't he?
Dawn	he says, but I like you, I like that, your jealousy means you really care for me
Liz	that's Mike
Dawn	oh, is it? oh well...
(laughter)	

The discussion about the story generally lasted about twenty minutes – I worked quite hard to keep them on the subject (it is a very boring story) – and in the end the talk moved off, in the case of the comprehensive sixth formers into a general discussion on sexism, the double standard and gender stereotypes; in the case of the fourth formers into talk on books, magazines, and how what you read changes as you get older; and the public school third years got on to a very long discussion of class. Their reading of the story itself highlighted class issues too:

Claire	I like his jersey
(laughter)	
Sophie	I've been looking at his jumper
(laughter)	
Liz	d'you know boys who wear jumpers like that?
several	yes
Claire	I'd say most of Eton
...	
Liz	so you like the way he dresses, right?
Claire	I don't know what he's got on his feet though
(laughter)	
Claire	it's really annoying you know
Sophie	probably Adidas trainers or something
Claire	I wouldn't go out with him if he was wearing those
...	
Sophie	and then you know trousers that you know only come to about here then long white socks under
Claire	oh long *white* socks
...	
Liz	what, whether you'd like him or not?
Claire	well, it depends what kind of school he goes to, what kind of I mean that sounds really awful but I'm
Lucy	his classical background (laughs)
Claire	yes, no

| Lucy | yes, but Latin and classical background |
| (laughter) | |

...

| Claire | I don't like the jeans, I don't I don't like the way she dresses so I mean if he goes with people like her then I mean... |

Above all, though, they read the story as a work of fiction:

Claire	it needs to be a bit dramatic though to get there
Liz	and there wasn't much drama in this one apart from would he or would he not turn up in the cafe
Claire	and that only took one picture in the thing so it wasn't particularly...
Lucy	and it was all a bit of an anti-climax in the end you know, it seems quite good at the beginning, but 'It's my nasty mind', I mean that's not much of a story...

(It was Claire who introduced this thought about the dramatic structure of the story, not me.)

| Katherine | well there isn't a basic there isn't a sort of start and middle and end sort of things, there isn't a real story to it, she just thinks that was wrong and found out that it's wrong in the end but it wasn't really, I don't know there wasn't much to it |

| Liz | OK, what do you think of that story then? |
| Nannette | well, I thought it was a bit obvious that Ben lives next door to the cafe |

Although there were other reactions which suggested that the reader was evaluating the characters as if they were real people:

Liz	OK, what d'you think of that story then?
Claire	I've read better ones
Lucy	I think she's quite vain, the girl's quite...

(Note that Claire is doing literacy criticism from the first, while Lucy is not.)

| Liz | right, what d'you think of that story then? |
| Helen | I don't know, she was just an insecure little person who had to keep shouting down these blokes and he found that attractive, there you go, that's it |

Shifts from first- to second-order discourse occurred throughout the discussions, but on the whole, second-order talk is dominant; and the discussion tended to focus on why the story was or was not realistic when measured against the girls' own lives and experience. [...]

On the whole then, it seems that the girls I asked to read the photo-story do not coincide with the implied reader constructed by the text, who we can take to be a sympathetic confidante of Julie, the narrator and heroine. The pretence that Julie is a sixteen-year-old talking to a friend didn't come off at all with any of the teenage girls I talked to (including those who were closest to the fictional heroine in socio-economic status and age – the comprehensive school fourth years). This failure occurred first because, as we have seen, the girls were overwhelmingly reading the story as a fiction, with all that entails. Second, none of them identified with Julie's actions, thoughts, or attitudes. That is, these real readers were freer of the text than much theory implies.

However, there was one very significant exception – they could understand her being attracted to Ben because:

Lucy	he's sort of strong, silent
Sam	yeah, caring, yeah
several	yeah
Helen	big old beefy jumpers
Sam	that's it, it's the jumper more than anything and the little shirt coming out the top
Lorna	hands in pockets

We've already seen the attraction of the jumper to the public school girls! And:

Lucy	well, it's not that he's goodlooking, he's got you know
Sophie	he's quite a hunk
Claire	well he's not you know
Claire	wimpish or anything like that
. . .	
Lucy	he's so gentlemanly
Zara	yes
Claire	he's quite gentle

But one group thought he was a creep:

Jo	you wouldn't feel offended, you would feel that he's creepin a bit an he's it's not he's not, oh it doesn't show that he's creepin all the time but it's related in a way
Liz	mm
Alison	yeah but it's creepy the way he um...
Jo	in that picture there he's got his arms around her like y'know that shows...

This straightforward attraction to the hero, though, was understood as an ingredient of fantasy:

Jo	cos they're a bit like this you know fairy tales aren't they?
Alison	yes it's all like one of those dream things
Nannette	it all goes so well, it's always like he lives next door to the cafe, she goes walking a dog, her dog runs off
(laughter)	
Jo	all of a sudden there's the boy, exciting eh?
Alison	it's just a dream innit?

[...] My preliminary analysis of the transcripts of these discussions, then, strongly suggests that a self-conscious and reflexive approach to texts is a natural approach for teenage girls. Further, they demonstrated a level of understanding, not only of the fiction, but of the genre of publications for girls of which *Jackie* is an example. They were even curious about the production of the text, which is entirely obscure in the magazine:

Claire	I wonder who takes all these pictures, and who are the people?

So far then, this empirical evidence suggests that the kinds of meanings which are encoded in texts and which we might want to call ideological, fail to get a grip on readers in the way the notion of ideology generally suggests. Ideology is undercut, that is, by these readers' reflexivity and reflectiveness.

[...] The concept of ideology is unsatisfactory in two main ways, as I have argued. On the one hand real people don't seem to be 'in the grip of' ideology, as the theory (and especially much theory which is based on the analysis of texts) implies. On the other hand, 'ideology' is of altogether too ethereal a nature to be properly researched. Its existence is only and always inferred; we can never examine it directly.

However, I suggest that we take seriously the power of concrete conventions and registers of discourse to constrain and determine what is said and how it is said. Registers are material, and directly researchable. We can compare how real people speak with institutional discourse, for example the discourse of cultural artefacts like *Jackie*, the tabloid press, and with institutional practices like that of the 'discussion group'. We can pay attention to the forums in which people learn different registers, for example, girls in girls' groups learning the appropriate register; what registers are acceptable in school; the influence of popular culture. But we should not take it that people are unselfconscious about these registers, as do theories of ideology.

Note

1. The story is entitled 'It's My Nasty Mind'. Julie, the heroine, tells off her boyfriend, Mike, in no uncertain terms when he arrives late to meet her, accusing him of having been with another girl. He tells her that she has a 'nasty and suspicious mind', but that her jealousy proves she really cares. In response to this she says 'Goodbye Mike, if I never see you again it'll be too soon'. This altercation is overheard by Ben, who admires her spirit: 'That was a great performance', and takes her to a nearby cafe for a Knickerbocker Glory. When he leaves he says 'Next time you're giving some guy the big heave, let me know, I'd love to see you in action again'. Julie hangs around the cafe hoping to see Ben; when she does bump into him he repeats his admiration: 'Is some other guy about to get it in the neck?' Rather than admit she wants to see him, Julie says that she is going to 'have a showdown' on the following evening and invites him to watch. She then has to find a boy to play the opposite part, but fails. When she arrives at the assignation she admits to Ben that she had treated Mike badly, and that she had made up the boyfriend: 'Do you think I'm dreadful? I don't think I'm a very nice kind of person' to which Ben says, among other things: 'You're insecure, and you've got a strong sense of justice' and 'You're too self critical' and he invites her to go out with him, and to go for another Knickerbocker Glory.

References

BARRETT, M. 1980: *Women's oppression today – Problems in Marxist feminist analysis.* London: Verso/NLB.

GRIFFIN, C. 1982: *Cultures of femininity: romance revisited*. Birmingham: CCCS Occasional Paper.
— 1985: *Typical girls? Young women from school to the job market*. London: Routledge and Kegan Paul.
HEBRON, S. 1983: *'Jackie' and 'Woman's Own': ideological work and the social construction of gender identity*. Sheffield: City Polytechnic.
LEES, S. 1986: *Losing out: sexuality and adolescent girls*. London: Hutchinson.
McROBBIE, A. 1978a: Working class girls and the culture of femininity. In CCCS Women's Studies Group, *Women take issue*. London: Hutchinson.
— 1978b. *'Jackie': an ideology of adolescent femininity*. Birmingham: CCCS Occasional Paper.
RICHARDSON, K. and CORNER, J. 1986: Reading reception: mediation and transparency in viewers' accounts of a TV programme. *Media Culture and Society* 8, 4.
SHARPE, S. 1976: *'Just like a girl': how girls learn to be women*. Harmondsworth: Penguin.
WILSON, D. 1978. 'Sexual codes and conduct – a study of teenage girls', in Smart, C. and Smart, B. (eds.) *Women, sexuality and social control*. London: Routledge and Kegan Paul.
WINSHIP, J. 1978. A woman's world: *Woman*, an ideology of femininity. In CCCS Women's Studies Group, *Women take issue*. London: Hutchinson.

17

'Don't treat us like we're so stupid and naive' — towards an ethnography of soap opera viewers

Ellen Seiter, Hans Borchers, Gabriele Kreutzner and Eva-Maria Warth

From their *Remote control: television, audiences and cultural power* (Routledge 1989)

[...] Our study of Oregon soap opera viewers is indebted to recent work in the 'ethnography' of reading that has been done by David Morley and Janice Radway. In *The 'Nationwide' Audience*, Morley proposes a model for the interaction of viewer and television text which challenges both the uses and gratifications model, with its unlimited possibilities for individual responses to the media, and the hypodermic needle theory of mass culture, with its ideological overdetermination.[1] In 'A Critical Postscript' to *The 'Nationwide' Audience*, published in 1981, Morley raises a number of issues pertinent to our own study.[2] Whereas the *'Nationwide'* study emphasized the influence of class as a parameter of cultural decodings, the postscript draws attention to the investigation of sex/gender as a crucial aspect in the production of meaning. As the work of Charlotte Brunsdon suggests, the social category of gender is essential to an understanding of the specific relationship between a generic form and gender-specific cultural competences of viewers.[3] Morley's critical reassessment of *'Nationwide'* also points to theoretical problems raised by fictional texts. The concept of 'preferred reading,' which has been developed in the context of news and current affairs television, raises a number of problems when applied to fictional forms. The hierarchy of discourses in television's fictional texts tends to be more ambiguous, preventing narrative closure on all levels of the text, and thus rendering the text more open to divergent meanings.

Another point of departure from *Nationwide* lies in Morley's reformulation of the notion of decoding, which is no longer conceived of as a single act of reading, but also as 'a set of processes – of attentiveness, recognition of relevance, of comprehension, and of interpretation and response.'[4] This conceptual shift is closely related to a stronger emphasis on respondents' actual interlocutions as primary 'data' rather than, as in *Nationwide*, dealing only with the substance of the viewers' responses. Morley suggests that specific meaning constructions can only be accounted for by close attention to the linguistic form in which they are expressed. In conclusion, Morley proposes an 'ethnography of reading' which would account for the cultural rules organizing individual diversities of a basically social phenomenon.[5]

Janice Radway's study of forty-two American women who are avid readers of romances, *Reading the Romance: Women, Patriarchy, and Popular Literature*, starts from the premise that the popular appeal of a fictional text depends on the recognition of its genre attributes. Radway sets out to 'represent schematically the geography of the genre as it is surveyed, articulated, and described by the women themselves.'[6] By relying on empirical work – questionnaire responses and intensive interviews – Radway avoids the pitfalls both of an older type of formula criticism developed within popular culture studies and of the theoretical assumption of the implied reader as used in models of reader-response criticism. The value of this approach lies in its capacity to account for the affinities and correspondences between a certain narrative style and the cultural competences of a particular group of readers.

Conceived of as an ethnography, Radway's book is not limited to the exploration of text and genre. Locating her findings within the theoretical frameworks furnished by feminist sociologist Nancy Chodorow and Marxist critic Fredric Jameson, she concludes that women who purchase and read romances use the act of reading to create their own space in the confining routines of their daily lives as wives and mothers. Thus, reading romances provides the women relief from the seemingly endless demands on them as nurturers. In more general terms, the reading of romances implies a gesture of protest against the strictures of their everyday lives within a patriarchal society. Radway's decision to shift the emphasis of inquiry from the text itself to the social event of reading, and to investigate this event through the application of ethnographic methods, were influential on the design of our own research project. Like David Morley's recent work on television in the familial context, *Family Television*, Radway offers the insight that in order to understand the meaning of popular culture, one has to ask what it is that people are doing when they read or watch, and how they themselves understand these activities.

In adapting Morley's and Radway's work to a study of the soap opera, our work focuses on a privileged object within television research. The genre's special status has a number of rather different sources. Thus the first empirical broadcast media audience study, Herta Herzog's pioneer article 'On Borrowed Experience,' investigated soap opera listeners.[7] Textual analyses have frequently centered on soap operas, which attract scholarly interest because of their comparatively long history, their proliferation, and the special problems posed by seriality and melodrama. Because they are broadcast daily, soap operas lend themselves to an investigation of television in the context of the everyday. Since the genre has been associated with an audience of women, it has attracted the attention of feminist critics. This body of work has attempted to theorize the construction of gender within the text and within the audience. Finally, prime-time serials such as *Dallas* and *Dynasty* have become symbols of US cultural imperialism, and the subject of study outside the United States. Within the context of the problematic of culture and ideology, empirical audience studies on US prime-time soap operas in other countries have attempted to come to terms with cross-cultural readings of these shows.

The Oregon audience study

All of the interviews took place in the Eugene/Springfield metropolitan area of western Oregon. The area is characterized by high unemployment (9.5 per cent during the summer of 1986), relatively low per capita income ($7,302 per year), and a predominantly white population (blacks making up only 1,618 of a county population of 275,226; other minorities, mostly Chicanos (Hispanic-Americans), Asians, and Indians, make up about 3 per cent of the total population). The largest employer in Eugene is the University of Oregon; in Springfield it is the Weyerhauser lumber mill, where the workers were on strike during most of the interview period (a strike which ended with the workers giving up about $4 an hour in wages and fringe benefits). Like the entire state of Oregon, Eugene/Springfield has suffered from serious economic depression since the 1970s, due to its reliance on the lumber industry (which suffered from a drastic fall in housing starts) and tourism (which suffered from the rise in gasoline prices).

Between July 21 and August 16, 1986, we conducted a total of twenty-six interviews. Each interview was carried out by two scholars of whom at least one was German. Fifteen all-women groups were visited by a female research team. All of our informants were white. Among the sixty-four participants were fifteen men. Eleven informants were unemployed at the time of the interview. The large number of unemployed men and women in our pool reflects our technique for contacting informants – to run an ad. in the Help Wanted section of the Eugene newspaper – and also reflects the economic depression which characterizes the region. Because of the tendency in this kind of academic research to deal predominantly with middle-class informants, and because of our interest in working-class readings of soap operas, we welcomed this composition of our informant pool. We judge our failure to contact any women or men of color for the interviews, however, as a serious limitation of the study.

The text of our ad. ran, under the bold print headline **SOAP OPERAS**, as follows: 'We are writing a book and need to talk to people about soap operas. If you and your family/friends watch them, we would like to interview you as a group at your home ($5/hour per person). Please contact us at. ...' The advertisement ran for three days; we were flooded with telephone calls. We asked the callers what programs they were interested in, where they lived, and how many friends or family members were available for an interview. Appointments were arranged with callers, giving preference to those who could promise large groups for the interview, to older respondents, and to callers who lived outside the university area.

The groups ranged in size from two to nine participants. The interviews took place at one informant's home and in the company of friends and family members she had chosen for the purpose of the interview. While some audience studies hire interviewers who are not involved later in the analysis of the transcripts and tapes, we remained within the boundaries of the ethnographic method in that all of the interviews were carried out by the four primary researchers on the project.

The informants impressed us as remarkably open and secure in the uncontested and undisparaged status of their knowledge about soap operas. The location of the interviews – the home of the informant who initially answered our advertisement in the newspaper – added to the sense of comfort. This also allowed us to gather more information about the informants by observing the domestic surroundings, which were carefully noted immediately after the interview. The ethnographic concern with speech was facilitated by the cultural difference between informants and interviewers (since at least one of the two interviewers was German). The definition of slang expressions, the identity of characters and actors, the description of the shows, and reviews of past plot events could be elicited from a believable (and often factual) non-initiate position that created less defensiveness from the informants, who were in a position, as members of the culture and authorities on US television, to speak to the 'foreigners' with competence and expertise.

In the first minutes of each interview we explained that US prime-time shows such as *Dallas* or *Dynasty*, but no daytime soap operas, are shown on German television, and that the goal for the German members of the team was to learn about soap operas while visiting the United States. The informants usually were not at all surprised to hear about the success of *Dallas* or *Dynasty* in West Germany, but frequently expressed some pity for German viewers deprived of daytime soap operas.[8] Most of our informants assumed from our ad. that we were interested in talking about daytime programs, and hesitated to discuss prime-time serials until they were assured of our interest.

Questions of methodology

The author of the leading textbook on ethnographic methods defines ethnography as 'the work of describing a culture.'[9] Ethnographers working within anthropology emphasize 'the native point of view' or the 'ideational orientation,' that is 'the importance of understanding any given group's lifeways by discovering the learned systems of meaning by which it is structured.'[10]

Television audience studies, even when they use ethnographic or qualitative methods, have not satisfied the requirements of ethnography proper, and our own study is no exception. White ethnographies are based on long-term and in-depth field work, most television audience studies have involved only brief periods of contact, in some cases less than one hour, with the informants. Also, while ethnographic methods have traditionally been used to study culture as a whole, television researchers study only one aspect of a culture when using this method and attempt to relate it to social identity.[11] Ethnographic audience studies share, however, ethnography's basic interest in an empirical investigation of cultural practices as lived experiences.

Recently, hermeneutic and discursive approaches to the study of culture have led to a fundamental critique of the epistemological, theoretical, and political assumptions implied in the concept of ethnography as 'the work of describing a culture.' As the title of James Clifford's seminal article indicates, 'ethnographic authority' has increasingly come under scrutiny.[12] Of particular importance in our context is the critical challenge to traditional ethnography's implicit insistence on scholarly experience as an unproblematic source and ultimate guarantee of knowledge about a specific culture or cultural process. Today, there is an increasing tendency within ethnography to reject 'colonial representations,' i.e. 'discourses that portray the cultural reality of other peoples without placing their own reality into jeopardy.'[13] Such a position does not only apply to ethnographic accounts of 'other' cultures, but is also significant on an intracultural level. Audience studies are carried out by academics with specific social and cultural backgrounds, who 'go out in the field' to learn about the uses and understandings of groups of viewers with social and (sub)cultural backgrounds usually different from their own. This means that the differences and similarities between participants and scholars in terms of class, gender, race, culture or subculture, educational background, age, etc. have to be reflected. These aspects will inevitably be at work in the exchange between interviewer and interviewee, and, as we shall try to show, they will shape the understandings and meanings produced in this situation.[14]

The following sections of our chapter present preliminary reports on our analyses of the interviews.[15] In the first section, 'Soap operas and everyday life,' Eva-Maria Warth describes the way soap operas serve to organize time in the context of everyday life, especially housework. In the second section, 'Text and genre,' Hans Borchers discusses the various ways in which viewers define and describe the soap opera as text and as genre. Ellen Seiter and Gabriele Kreutzner, in 'Resisting the place of the ideal mother,' compare women's readings of the soap opera with the feminine subject position which critics see 'inscribed' in the soap opera text.

It was above all the work performed at the Centre for Contemporary Cultural Studies at Birmingham and by Hermann Bausinger at the Department for Empirical Cultural Studies at the University of Tübingen which drew attention to the necessity of analysing media experience in its social context. According to this approach, the construction of the meaning of television and its programs is a social process that occurs within the everyday interactions of the home and the workplace. The question of how the media take part in structuring and organizing everyday life is inextricably related to the question of what meaning viewers give to a certain media product, in our case, the soap opera. What is important here, however, is the relationship between the levels of the general and the concrete: while soap operas certainly do belong to everyday life for those who watch them, individual routines differ remarkably according to class, gender, and age.

This section concentrates on the ways in which soap operas intersect with the everyday lives of women working in the home. While our study turned out to be rich in material on the interrelationship between the social condition of housewives and the soap opera discourse, this section focuses mainly on how our informants describe the ways in which media schedules influence and intersect with the temporal organization of their work. We will begin with a brief historical outline of the mass media's implications for the organization of time in the domestic sphere. The media's function in the context of the rationalization of housework will then serve as a backdrop for our informants' accounts of how their viewing is fitted in between the demands of housework and their need for leisure.

In his influential study 'Time, Work-Discipline, and Industrial Capitalism,' E. P. Thompson proposes that temporal organization must be analysed historically in terms of its relation to the production process.[16] His study shows that the revolution in the experience of time in the nineteenth century was not limited to the production process proper, but rather influenced all aspects of life. Training in time discipline was reinforced by rationalization efforts in the industry at the beginning of this century, which also produced changes in the time organization of the domestic sphere. The subjugation of the sphere of reproduction to time patterns similar to those of the production sphere resulted in a rigidity typical of the workplace.

These changes were of special importance for women, for whom the home primarily represents a place of work rather than a sphere of leisure, as it usually is for men. Despite the interdependency of the spheres of production and reproduction, housework is still surrounded by a discourse of naturalness, which renders it universal and timeless. In this context, housework is theorized as determined by natural time cycles, as a sphere of autonomy which resists industrial time economy.

It is the achievement of Gisela Bock and Barbara Duden to have countered such ideologies of naturalness by theorizing housework in economic and historical terms.[17] They show how Taylorism, which initiated the rationalization process in the US in the 1920s, grew to encompass the sphere of reproduction as well. This extension of rationalization to the home was seen as a prerequisite for workplace efficiency. According to the new principles of scientific management, housework appeared irrational and unstructured. The separation of planning and execution of daily work was seen as the most important requirement in the process of restructuring. Housework was no longer theorized as relying on the natural skills of women, but was conceived of as a 'science' which needed to be studied. If on the one hand this implied an upgrading of housework, it simultaneously surrendered housework to a male discourse, which from then on was assigned final authority in questions of child rearing and household management. Radio, and especially daytime soap operas, which were designed for a specifically female audience in the 1930s, played a vital part in this process. Informative programs on household management as well as other women's programs such as the soap opera dealt, respectively, with practical and emotional problems encountered by women working in the home. In addition, the regularity of the broadcast supported the efforts toward efficiency and rationalization which were introduced via daily schedules, e.g. distinct time structures which were modelled in accordance with the production process. The schedules of radio and television were not arbitrary, but were designed in accordance with certain structures created by housework itself. The schedules thereby became synchronized and tied into a well-defined and 'universal' schedule. Lesley Johnson describes this process:

> In the promotion of radio as the constant companion to the housewife, pro-
> grammers had adapted their timetables to the imagined patterns of a woman's
> life. Through this process radio stations set out to regulate the work and
> rhythms of daily life of all women to this pattern. So similarly did radio strive
> to control the domestic lives of all members of the community in the attempt
> to time-table their listening according to strict, reliable schedules.[18]

Although the hour or two of soap opera watching represents a fixed point in the daily schedule for most of our informants, there were significant differences in the way women reconciled this fixed pattern to their obligations and needs.

Soap opera viewing raises the problem of female pleasure and its place in women's lives. Housewives especially are not usually granted a right to relaxation, since housework is constructed as a potentially endless task. Nancy Chodorow has drawn attention to the 'fundamental asymmetry in daily reproduction. Men are socially and psychologically reproduced by women, but women are reproduced (or not) largely by themselves.'[19] The problem of women's reproduction is aggravated by the fact, noted by Ann Gray, that 'the domestic sphere is increasingly becoming defined as their only leisure space.'[20] The lack of a clear spatial demarcation between work and leisure therefore makes it even more complicated for women to assign a comfortable space for themselves and to reconcile their own needs with the needs of others.

For women in the home, leisure activities such as watching television must be viewed as complementary to work. The practices of soap opera viewing and their evaluation may be seen as women's attempts to resolve contradictions inherent in domestic work. In this context, television reveals the constraints of housework as unpaid labor (which accounts for the absence of regulated leisure time).

In our study we observed significant differences in our informants' patterns of soap opera engagement and their evaluation of viewing as a habit. These differences seem to be closely connected to the way in which the organization of their work allows for or excludes the possibility of leisure time. These organizational patterns correspond closely to Ann Oakley's findings in her seminal study, *The Sociology of Housework*.[21] Oakley differentiates between women who perform their household duties according to set standards and routines and those who do not. The work patterns of the first group show the effects of the industrialization of 'domestic' time in the attempt to impose a sense of rationality, efficiency, and security on a potentially endless and typically frustrating activity. Those of our informants who fit this first category used soap operas as a fixed point in time around which daily tasks are organized: 'I schedule all my activities in the morning so that I'm home in the afternoon to watch my shows.' Household duties are planned and timed according to the television schedule: 'I go out and fix casseroles for supper and throw them in the oven between two and three o'clock, you know, so I don't miss them [the soaps].'

In the context of this kind of household management, which is subjected to norms of efficiency and rational organization, soap operas may be more easily regarded as a reward, as a well-earned moment of leisure which is enjoyed without guilt:

> SS   What I try to do is get everything I want to do done before that time. Then I don't feel guilty if I sit down and watch them ... I like to get up in the morning and get done what I figure I should do and then that's my relaxing time. It's just to sit down for a few hours.

One woman in her fifties very self-confidently described the way she defends her soap opera pleasure against social obligations and the needs of others:

> MD   People know not to call me between 12.30 and 3.00 unless it's a dire emergency. If it's really something, they can call me at 1.30. Cause *Capitol* is on and I don't really watch it ... All of my friends know, do not call at that time. My husband ... if he comes in he's very quiet and just goes right on out.

The pleasure of undistracted and concentrated viewing, which Charlotte Brunsdon has described as a mode of viewing associated with power (and thus with male viewing patterns) is made possible for these women by adapting their work to principles associated with the sphere of production and thus paid for by a submission to the norms of male discourse.

While most of our informants would consider undivided viewing the ideal mode of soap opera reception, the women who belong to the second group – those who do not adhere to a strict routine – experience this pleasure only as a rare luxury. One of these informants could afford a soap opera 'treat' only during a time which for many women is associated with guilt-free indulgence: 'I used to sit, especially when I was pregnant, to sit three hours and watch TV ... I can't do that any more.' The women who do not tightly structure their housework, either because domestic circumstances do not allow it (e.g. the presence of small children in the household) or because it is not their style, must constantly struggle to reconcile their need for leisure with conflicting obligations: 'I turn it on when I can, if I'm in the kitchen, I turn the TV on ... I'm usually cooking dinner or making the kids' lunch or something.'

If soap operas cannot be aligned with special household chores demanding little concentration, the soap opera text becomes reduced to what can be heard while working in different parts of the house: 'I *listen* to them, honest to God, I never sit! The voices ... I keep it punched [keep the volume up].' Viewing in this case becomes highly selective and is restricted to moments of high dramatic impact, as the following quote from another viewer suggests:

> RG   I'll clean, but I'll have the TV on so I can hear it ... if you can hear what's going on ... like, you know, if there is a good fight or something going on, I always run in here and turn off the water and then sit in here and watch what's going on.

The conflict between household demands and the pleasures of soap opera viewing is one aspect which may account for the ambivalent attitude some of these women have toward their habit of viewing. The underlying sense of guilt ('I realized that I'm not getting anything done') which accompanies viewing for women in the second group may have contributed to the different kinds of relationships they established with us as interviewers compared to the first group. Those women who presented themselves as untroubled by conflicts over housework tended to remain rather formal and distant in the interview situation and tended to address us mainly in terms of our roles as academics. In contrast to this attitude, the informants belonging to the second group often quickly transformed the interview into the scenario of an intimate confession. We were frequently treated as confidantes, with the expectation that we would be sympathetic to the pleasures of soap opera viewing and understanding of the troublesome consequences these pleasures were reported to have in terms of neglected household work.

These differences in viewing behavior suggest that the conditions under which soap operas are watched differ even for women in similar situations, i.e. those working in the home, and they have considerable influence over selectivity, attention, and involvement with soap opera programs.

[. . .] Generally speaking, we found that viewers have a strong sense of the constructedness of soap operas, of the essential artificiality of their favorite program. Not only did viewers frequently talk about and criticize the people who make soap operas (especially writers), they also commented on the conventions that rule and structure the shows. Their genre competence comes in many disguises. It was apparent in the complaint that writers cancel and replace characters too facilely, in the sober assessment of the cycles soap opera plots go through in the course of a year relative to the ratings sweeps weeks, as well as in the often-reported practice of predicting future plot developments – what Charlotte Brunsdon has called, 'the pleasure of hermeneutic speculation.'[22]

Another aspect of their generic competence was the informed and mostly negative opinion the majority of our interviewees expressed about prime-time soap operas. Since we encouraged them to talk about prime-time television, they offered a whole assortment of critiques of *Dallas, Dynasty, Knots Landing*, and other prime-time shows. With the exception of a few viewers who voiced their impatience with a certain dragging on of storylines on daytime soaps, the large majority expressed their preference for the daytime variety of the genre. Prime-time soap operas were judged as too glittery and expensive-looking; our informants complained that they don't deal with 'the normalcy of people.' Others resented the rich veneer of prime-time soaps, their 'mega-buck characters', especially the actress Joan Collins ('She makes more in one day than I've made in my whole life'). For many, prime-time soap operas belong to a different category altogether. One viewer said he likes 'the soaps better than *Dallas* and *Falcon Crest*'; another told us that 'the soaps are more laid back, they're not made for nights,' and a third viewer remarked that although she watches daytime and prime-time soaps, the prime-time variety is 'not as hooky.' Most of our viewers expressed their loyalty to the daytime soaps and tended to be very conscious of the differences between the original thing and the spin-off.

Alongside their generic expertise, their discrimination and critical distance, our informants also evinced the seemingly contradictory impulse to permit the fiction to spill over into their real lives and social worlds. Most of them told us they were bound to the characters on their show by feelings of intimacy. [...]

The pleasure our viewers derive from their appreciation of the text's fictionality does not prevent them from getting personally involved in the text – and, by extension, from experiencing soap operas as texts which are relevant to social reality. [...]

It seems, then, that the soap opera text, not least because of the strong need it creates for collaborative readings, has considerable potential for reaching out into the real world of the viewers. It enables them to evaluate their own experiences as well as the norms and values they live by in terms of the relationship patterns and social blueprints the show presents. It is important to remember, however, that this is only one side of the text's appeal. Our women informants appreciated the notorious Erica Kane of *All My Children* because of the remarkable success she enjoys in her personal life and her career, and it became clear that they tend to see her as a model applicable to their own private situations and to the social roles they were themselves involved in. At the same time, they took great pleasure in the very unreality and fictional constructedness of the storylines Erica was often a part of. When a particularly outlandish turn in the plot required Erica to walk through the jungle for three days, they commented: 'It's unreal that she would look like that after three days of not washing her hair and.... But they had her that way so...it was kind of funny! That's part of it, that it's fun to watch that!'

Our viewers' appreciation of both aspects of the Erica Kane character points to the divergent ways in which the soap opera text may elicit gratification. It also testifies to the ability of experienced viewers to commute with considerable ease between a referential and a purely fictional reading – even if these readings appear to be mutually exclusive. The evidence our interview material contains leads us to conclude that, while the text has the potential of addressing its readers on a level of social engagement, its principal appeal is undoubtedly to their genre competence, sense of critical distance, and enjoyment of the sheer playfulness of fiction.

In her influential analysis of the daytime soap opera, Tania Modleski describes the woman's position as a reader inscribed in the text in these terms:

> The subject/spectator of soap operas, it could be said, is constituted as a sort of ideal mother, a person who possesses greater wisdom than all her children, whose sympathy is large enough to encompass the conflicting claims of her family (she identifies with them all), and who has no demands or claims of her own (she identifies with no one character exclusively).[23]

The soap opera villainess may make it difficult for viewers to assume this female position comfortably, for they may find that she acts out their own, largely hidden, desires for power although at the same time they feel they must condemn and despise her. The model Modleski uses is Freudian: 'The extreme delight viewers apparently take in despising the villainess testifies to the enormous amount of energy involved in the spectator's repression and to her (albeit unconscious) resentment at being constituted as an egoless receptacle for the suffering of others.'[24]

Modleski offers no possibility for *conscious* resistance to the soap opera text: the spectator position is conceived of in terms of a perfectly 'successful' gender socialization entirely in keeping with a middle-class (and white) feminine ideal. The desire to watch soap operas comes from a kind of repetition compulsion brought about by the conflict between the ideal mother position of feminine passivity and the villainess's expression of real but hidden fantasies of power. Robert C. Allen has suggested that this work poses a problem in that 'although Modleski seems to present the mother/reader as a textually inscribed position to be taken up by whoever the actual reader happens to be, she comes close at times to conflating the two.'[25]

In our description of those Oregon interviews conducted within all-female groups, we would like to take Modleski's concept of the textual position offered by the soap operas as a starting point. While this position was partially taken up by some of our middle-class, college-educated informants, it was consciously resisted and vehemently rejected by most of the women we interviewed, especially by working-class women. The relationship between viewer and character more typically involved hostility – in the case of some of the presumably sympathetic characters – as well as fond admiration – for the supposedly despised villainesses.

Strongly held preferences for individual characters and dislikes for others prevented the ideal mother position as Modleski describes it from ever being fully taken up. Sympathy for characters was mentioned only rarely, while outrage, anger, criticism, or a refusal to accept a character's problems was frequently expressed. The women we interviewed showed a conscious, full-fledged refusal of the narrative's demand for sympathy and understanding. This refusal was fueled by the recognition of a gaping class difference between the comfortable professional lives of the television characters and the difficult financial situations in which many of our informants often find themselves. The fact that women characters on soap operas usually bear no visible responsibility for childcare and housework increased this resentment. It is not the villainess whom these working-class informants despise – it is the woman who suffers despite her middle-class privileges, a character type they call the 'whiner,' or the 'wimpy woman.'

The 'whiner' came up repeatedly in our interviews with a group of six women, the mother MP, her three daughters, and their female room-mates, all of whom lived next door to each other in Springfield, worked at minimum-wage jobs (newspaper delivery, bartending) and helped operate M's home telephone answering service. What is most irritating and infuriating about the 'whiner' is her passivity, her dependence on men, her failure to take care of herself. While reconstructing the storyline around the character of Rick Webber, one of *General Hospital*'s doctors, his wife, television journalist Jeannie Webber, was discussed by the group:

DI   And now he married Jeannie and all she does is cry and whimper, that's all she does.

MT   I don't like her either!

DI   She don't do nothing! I mean she cries about her son, she cries about her job, she cries about her baby, she cries about everything.

MT   She cries when she makes love, I think.

DI   She cries all the time! She's a wimpy woman!

Both   They can take her off! She's a wimpy woman!

Among a group of middle-class women in their fifties who worked at home, we found another hostile rejection of a sympathetic character who herself acts like an ideal mother:

MD   Like Karen on *Knots Landing*, the neighbor that you'd like to choke. I mean she's a little busybody. She's always going around and telling everyone what to do and what they should do. And sympathizing.

This remark is especially interesting because Karen comes under attack specifically for her feminine qualities, such as sympathizing with others.

In a group consisting of a woman in her thirties, JS, and her mother-in-law, two foster-daughters, a cousin, and a friend and neighbor, the women discussed their feelings for the villainesses on their favorite shows. All of the women commented on their preference of strong villainesses; the younger respondents expressed their pleasure in and admiration for the powerful female characters who were also discussed in terms of transgressing the boundaries of a traditional pattern of resistance for women within patriarchy. The pattern here of finishing each other's sentences was typical of many of our interviews with all-female groups:

LD   Yeah, they can be very vicious [Laughs] – the females can be very vicious...
JS   Seems like females have more of an impact than the males.
SW   ...and they have such a...
TM   ...conniving...
SW   ...brain! Yeah! [Laughter]
LD   They're sneaky!!! Yeah!
SW   They use their brain more...[Laughter] instead of their body! They manipulate, you know!

Tania Modleski's work suggests that the only outlet for female aggression and anger on the soap opera is the character of the villainess. Drawing on psychoanalytic theory, Modleski argues that female aggression is repressed and is symbolically taken up, played out, and neutralized in the character of the villainess. Our respondents, however, expressed love and admiration for these powerful female transgressors. For them, one of the pleasures of soap opera viewing consists in targeting certain characters as objects of their own verbal aggressions. KK and JH, two college-educated women sharing a house and making their living from organizing adult education courses, put it this way:

JH   A lot of times we just get caught up in it, and [we go] 'Oh you bitch' or something...
KK   Yeah, it's a good cathartic kind of thing, you know, because, we can just kind...one creep Waide comes on, you know, and we go: 'Yeah, I hate you, this is stupid,' you know, so we get out a lot of stuff...

These women explained their own viewing in terms of their interest in eastern philosophy and psychotherapeutic work. The pleasure in working out aggressions, however, seemed to be extremely important for many of our viewers. In another interview, KH, a 35-year-old woman employed doing clerical work for a cottage-industry record business expressed her enjoyment in taking unrestricted aggression toward a male character:

KH   We should have Jodie here, she's fourteen years old, and she and I just get so excited talking about *One Life to Live* . . .

DH   Yeah, Jodie yells at them, I don't. [Turns to KH] You sit there and yell at them!

KH   Oh, I do! . . . Especially when that ugly guy was on *General Hospital*, and he played two parts . . .

DH   Oh, Grant!

KH   Grant and somebody . . . who was his own twin . . .

DH   She hated Grant!

KH   And I hated him! I hated him, the original one, and then when they came up with a twin, and I had to see him again, in another part, I just screamed at him: 'Where's your forehead', you know, I just hated him!

DH   . . . and he was . . . he was in Eugene, and a friend of hers saw him and she wanted to run out and say: 'Please, can I have your autograph, my friend hates you!' I love that! Isn't that great?

Aggression was not limited to the actors, but extended to the scriptwriters as well, for slowing down the storylines and underestimating the viewer's intelligence, as MT expressed it: 'just don't drag them out and don't treat us like we're so stupid and naïve, you know! Like I said: I don't like to figure out stuff myself: keep me hanging, too.'

Most women have an ambivalent relationship to the narratives: enjoying the suspense but conscious of being manipulated by the story, made to wait for plot developments. And while some women enjoyed successfully predicting plot developments, for MT (who works for minimum wage), scriptwriters have a job to do, one they get paid a lot of money for, and they should be better at it than she is, i.e. able to provide her with surprises. Like MT, a number of women felt they could write soap operas themselves, if given a chance.

In our interviews, female anger was far less repressed than the Freudian model of the feminine subject or Modleski's textual position allows for. In their interaction with the fictional world of the soap opera, women openly and enthusiastically admitted their delight in following soap operas as stories of female transgressions which destroy the ideological nucleus of the text – the sacredness of the family. In a follow-up interview with JS and SW, both expressed their partisanship for female transgressions of the holy law of marriage in cases where the (fictitious) situation seemed to become unbearable for the female character. Both said their husbands disapproved of this attitude:

SW   But there's lots of times where you want the person to dump the husband and go on with this . . .

JS   Oh, Bruce [her husband] gets so angry with me when I'm watching the show and they're married and I'm all for the affair. [Laughter] It's like, it's like (Voice changes to imitate Bruce): 'I don't like this, I don't know about you' [Laughter] . . . [and I say] 'Dump him!!!'

Both women explained to us that they strongly favored the breakup of soap opera marriages in cases where the husband neglected the wife, and drew explicit connections to their own situations:

SW   He gets mad at me, but . . . it does justify the reason for her [if the hus-

band neglects the wife], I'm all for it ... think where you're saying: pay
more attention!

JW   Right! See, this happens to you if you don't pay attention to me!

These quotations indicate a vast gap between the model of the passive feminine subject inscribed in the text and our women viewers who fail to assume the position of the all-understanding (and therefore powerless) spectators of textual construction. The 'successful' production of the (abstract and 'ideal') feminine subject is restricted and altered by the contradictions of women's own experiences. Class, among other factors, plays a major role in how our respondents make sense of the text. The experience of working-class women clearly conflicts in substantial ways with the soap opera's representation of a woman's problems, problems some women identified as upper or middle-class. This makes the limitless sympathy that Modleski's textual position demands impossible for them. The class discrepancy between textual representation and their personal experience constituted the primary criticism of the programs. Let's return to our conversation with MP and her daughters:

MP   The one thing I guess I don't really care about in the soaps is that ...
       they're playing all the women as being career-oriented and, ah, making lots of money, they are not ... they are not bringing other people .
       . . you know, not every woman is making a good income.

DI   Asa's wife doesn't. Asa's wife, she's not ...

MP   Yeah, but she's not working, she's a staying-home wife. They need to
       bring in a few single mothers that are trying to ...

DI   Make and take on five an hour.

MP   Yeah, right, trying to juggle the books and find a baby sitter ...

MT   ... deliver newspapers at one o'clock in the morning, working there
       until ...

MP   They don't need too many of them, 'cause there is a lot of women that,
       you know, don't want that, they need escape to what it would be like
       when they're rich, but once in a while they should bring that in, 'cause
       ... it shows: 'Hey, this is what it's really like!'

DI   Say, wake up and ...

MT   That's why you want them to escape, cause after three hours you turn
       them off and you might return to your three thirty-five job.

MP   Yeah, I know, but if that's all you see, then, it'll ... you'll lose your
       interest.

One of the problems with the spectator position described by Modleski is that the 'ideal mother' implies a specific social identity – that of a middleclass woman, most likely with a husband who earns a family wage. This textual position is not easily accessible to working-class women, who often formulate criticism of the soap opera on these grounds. But criticism is expressed only in terms of realism and escapism, as in the quote above, where a complaint about class norms (having only career women or staying-home wives as characters) is answered by a validation of their function as escapism on these very same grounds (characters whose lives are different from those of the viewers). Any alternative version of the text is impossible for these women to imagine because it is so far beyond the horizon of reasonable expectation.

Recent audience studies conducted by David Morley and Ann Gray in Great Britain have found women to speak 'defensively and self-depreciatingly about their choices and preferences' with regard to television programs.[26] Charlotte Brunsdon argues that these studies confirm the 'extremely contradictory position that female viewers seem to occupy in relation to their pleasures'.[27] In comparison, our interviews show no such explicitly apologetic overtones. Moreover, they are considerably less informed by what Ien Ang calls 'the ideology of mass culture.'[28] This non-defensive position about television viewing was held most strongly in interviews conducted in groups where all the participants (informants and interviewers) were women – fifteen of the twenty-six interviews. In part, this suggests significant differences between the United States and Europe in what we might call the social construction of femininity.[29] But it also indicates the importance of situating the decoding of television programs within the context of concrete social exchanges, among subjects whose histories determine the interaction and the kind of discourses which will be used.

To use Benveniste's definition of discourse, the meanings given to soap operas in our interviews depended on the 'Is' and 'Yous' engaged in a given communicative exchange.[30] Although recent audience studies try to address the discursive 'Yous' as historical subjects (rather than as scientific objects), they tend to exclude (as is the academic norm) any systematic account of the researcher's own subjectivity. But discourse analysis focuses on the practices of all participants (including the interviewers) as social and historical beings. This is especially important when dealing with interviews, which unlike 'natural' conversations, are, from the beginning, the researcher's creation. Because of the way we initially identified ourselves in the newspaper advertisement ('writing a book'), the discourse of the interviews was to some extent predetermined by our roles and status as: 1) employers, 2) foreigners, 3) academics, and 4) women. The interviewers' initial identification as academics and employers means that a social hierachy is already at work in the interactions. In order adequately to understand the meanings of soap operas produced in our interviews, we have to recognize the asymmetrical, power-laden nature of the discourse in which they are produced and, more specifically, the significance of the researchers' subjectivities therein.

In retrospect, our communicative strategy was to de-emphasize our role as academics and employers. The position of relatively ignorant but interested 'non-initiates' into soap operas and of non-native speakers helped Kreutzner and Warth to counterbalance the initially asymmetrical discursive arrangement.[31] However, in analysing the interview tapes and transcripts, our status as women and our activation of specific patterns of gendered communication emerge as the most decisive factors for the developing interlocutions. These gendered patterns include both what we talked about – fashion, housework, heterosexual relationships, fantasy, sexism – and the way we talked. The interviews evidence what sociolinguists have found to be

> recurring patterns which distinguish talk among women from that in mixed-sex and all-male groups: mutuality of 'interaction work' (active listening, building on the utterances of others), collaboration rather than competition,

flexible leadership rather than the strong dominance patterns found in all-male groups.[32]

If our identification as academics, foreigners, and employers placed us in the category of 'other', gender provided a position of 'sameness' in relation to the informants.

In his reflections on ethnographic interviews, James Clifford points to the necessity of an intersubjective ground in any attempt to interact. According to Clifford, such a shared experimental world is 'precisely what is missing or problematic for an ethnographer entering an "alien culture"'[33] But ethnographic audience studies significantly differ from classic ethnography's attempt to understand 'other' cultures. Coming from western, late capitalist, and patriarchal societies, both interviewers and informants spontaneously relied on such a 'common sphere,' a shared experiential world according to which 'sameness' in terms of gender provides specific possibilities to interact. That is, the intersubjective relations between the discursive 'Is' and 'Yous' were predominantly constructed according to the historical subjects' gendered identities. In retrospect, our motives for subordinating other social positions to the gendered one can be explained by three factors: 1) the existence of what a German ethnographer has called the researcher's *Angst* created by the transition from the relatively secure and well-known academic (sub)culture to the 'unknown' field situation;[34] 2) our own (varying) gender-specific ambivalences concerning our positions as academics;[35] and 3) the fact that such a communicative repertoire is an integral part of female subjectivity practiced since we learned to talk. Indeed, these communicative patterns seem to be so 'natural' and 'transparent,' so much a part of ourselves, that they go unnoticed in everyday activities, and we were scarcely conscious of using them in the interviews.

Our informants, on the other hand, were provided with few other social positions which they could take up discursively. As Susanne Sackstetter points out, ethnographic interviews in which researchers and informants are men can rely on a broad repertoire of possible discursive relations in terms of shared social positions.[36] Except for a gendered one, women have few social positions at their disposal which can be taken up communicatively.

The discursive formation of women talking to women in a domestic setting suggests the construction of a distinctly female space. Such a discursive space corresponds to the one in which most of our female informants reportedly engage with the soap opera text – a private, domestic space which is often characterized by the absence of men. In this social context, the focus is on the women: they are the protagonists, whereas men play supportive, if not subordinate parts. The metaphor of performance illustrates a particular 'fit' between women's understanding of their immediate social environment and of the soap opera texts (as both were expressed in the interviews). Here and there, female characters are of absolute priority. The male characters/subjects will add problems, pleasures, and 'spice' (e.g. in terms of romance), but they are placed second – the emphasis is on the women who perform and perceive themselves as strong and active subjects. In critical retrospect, the context provided by feminist ethnographic work confirms that such understandings have to be contextualized: interpretations based on this kind of self-perception tend to be expressed only in discursive formations characterized by a collectively shared female identity and by the absence of men. It is significant that the ongoing discourse in the female group interviews was always at some point defined in terms of differing from an 'other' one – usually identified as the male perspective on soap operas or in terms of the ideology of mass culture. Some women mentioned their male partner's deprecatory attitude toward the genre, yet such deprecation was not represented as leading to conflict.

This suggests that the opportunity to produce meanings and pleasures by engaging with a discriminated popular text is 'paid for' by women's willingness to conceal these pleasures and meanings whenever the dominant discourse is spoken in a social situation. There, women tend to remain silent or describe their own meanings and pleasures from a position which discriminates against itself. If we perceive women's social contexts in terms of a set of interrelating speech practices, the relationship between the gendered and the dominant discourse(s) on soap operas is a monological, unreciprocal one. Within the framework of social relations under patriarchy, women create a gendered, oppositional space to produce their own meanings and pleasures. The closing off of these meanings and pleasures can be seen as a strategy to avoid confrontation and conflict.

By relating differing discourses on soap operas produced in varying social contexts to each other, we can begin to trace the 'working' of social power in the cultural production of meaning. Therefore, our future work will address the production of meanings (and pleasures) by historical subjects in at least two interrelating frameworks: 1) one which is constituted by the historical subjects' social practices (in which other discourses on the text are prominent); and 2) one established by the textual determinacy executed by the television program or genre. Both interactions – between a historical subject and a television text and between a historical subject and her social environment – have to be understood as a site of social struggle fought out on the terrain of language and speech practices.

Notes

1. David Morley, *The 'Nationwide' Audience: Structure and Decoding* (London, British Film Institute, 1980).
2. David Morley, '"The Nationwide Audience" – A Critical Postscript,' *Screen Education* 39 (1981), pp. 3–15.
3. Charlotte Brunsdon, '*Crossroads*: Notes on Soap Opera,' *Screen* 22, no. 4 (1981), pp. 32–37.
4. Morley, 'A Critical Postscript,' p. 5.
5. In this context see also Morley's *Family Television: Cultural Power and Domestic Leisure* (London, Comedia, 1986).
6. Janice Radway, *Reading the Romance: Women, Patriarchy, and Popular Literature* (Chapel Hill and London, University of North Carolina Press, 1984), p. 13.
7. Herta Herzog, 'On Borrowed Experience. An Analysis of Listening to Daytime Sketches,' *Studies in Philosophy and Social Science* 9, no. 1 (1941), pp. 65–95.
8. While German viewers are familiar with US prime-time serials such as *Dallas, Dynasty,* and most recently *Flamingo Road, Knots Landing* and *Falcon Crest* which

are broadcast by West Germany's public broadcast stations ARD and ZDF, it was only with the advent of commercial television that German viewers became acquainted with daytime soap operas like *Guiding Light* and *Santa Barbara* in 1987. US daytime serials had already been adopted by commercial stations in other European countries such as Italy and France, and the expected opening of West German television to these programs was one of the motivations for the Tübingen Soap Opera Project to investigate the genre.

9. James P. Spradley, *The Ethnographic Interview* (New York, Holt, Rinehart & Winston, 1979), p. 2.
10. John L. Caughey, 'The Ethnography of Everyday Life: Theories and Methods for American Culture Studies,' *American Quarterly* 34, no. 3 (1982), p. 226.
11. See David Morley, *The 'Nationwide' Audience*; Elihu Katz and Tamar Liebes, 'Once Upon a Time in *Dallas*,' *Intermedia* 12, no. 3 (1984), pp. 28–32; and James Lull, 'How Families Select TV Programs; A Mass-Observational Study,' *Journal of Broadcasting* 26, no. 4 (1982), pp. 801–11.
12. James Clifford, 'On Ethnographic Authority,' *Representations* 1, no. 2 (1983), p. 128.
13. James Clifford, 'On Ethnographic Authority,' p. 133.
14. See also James Clifford, 'Introduction: Partial Truths,' in James Clifford and George E. Marcus, eds., *Writing Culture. The Poetics and Politics of Ethnography* (Berkeley, California, The University of California Press, 1986), pp. 1–26.
15. In-depth analyses will be presented in the forthcoming book: Hans Borchers, Gabriele Kreutzner, and Eva-Maria Warth, *Never-Ending Stories: American Soap Operas and the Cultural Production of Meaning. CROSSROADS: Studies in American Culture* (Trier, Wissenschaftlicher Verlag Trier).
16. E. P. Thompson, 'Time, Work-Discipline and Industrial Capitalism,' *Past and Present* 38 (1967), pp. 56–97.
17. Gisela Bock and Barbara Duden, 'Arbeit aus Liebe – Liebe aus Arbeit. Zur Entstehung der Hausarbeit im Kapitalismus,' in their *Frauen und Wissenschaft. Beiträge zur Berliner Sommeruniversität der Frauen* (Berlin, 1977), pp. 118–99.
18. Lesley Johnson, 'Radio and Everyday Life. The Early Years of Broadcasting in Australia, 1922–1945,' *Media, Culture and Society* 3, no. 2 (1981), pp. 167–78.
19. Nancy Chodorow, *The Reproduction of Mothering: Psychoanalysis and the Sociology of Gender* (Berkeley, California, University of California Press, 1978), p. 36.
20. Ann Gray, 'Behind Closed Doors: Video Recorders in the Home,' in Helen Baehr and Gillian Dyer, eds., *Boxed In: Women and Television* (London, Pandora Press, 1986), p. 41.
21. Ann Oakley, *The Sociology of Housework* (London, Martin Robertson, 1974).
22. Charlotte Brunsdon, 'Writing about Soap Opera,' in Len Masterman, ed., *Television Mythologies: Stars, Shows, and Signs* (London, Comedia, 1986), p. 83.
23. Tania Modleski, *Loving With a Vengeance: Mass-Produced Fantasies for Women* (Hamden, Connecticut, Archon Books, 1982), p. 92.
24. Ibid., p. 94.
25. Robert C. Allen, *Speaking of soap operas* (Chapel Hill and London, University of North Carolina Press, 1985) p. 94.
26. Charlotte Brunsdon's review of Morley and Gray's work in 'Women Watching Television,' *MedieKultur* 4 (1986) p. 105.
27. Ibid., p. 109.
28. Ang, *Watching "Dallas," Soap Opera and the Melodramatic Imagination* (London and New York, Methuen, 1985), pp. 86–116.
29. The importance of this difference was called to our attention by Charlotte Brunsdon.
30. 'Discourse, in Benveniste's classic discussion, is a mode of communication where the presence of the speaking subject and of the immediate situation of

communication are intrinsic' (Clifford, 'On Ethnographic Authority,' p. 131).

31. Our roles as 'students' of soap operas and, for Kreutzner and Warth, as non-native speakers operated on two levels: we could apply them as 'strategic devices,' e.g. to interrogate particular descriptions and concepts ('What is a "hunk"?') and to motivate character descriptions or narration of plotlines. However, such a strategic use did not contradict our sincerity as communicative partners (which is essential to intersubjective exchange), since our familiarity with the soap texts was indeed a limited one.

32. Barrie Thorne, Cheris Kramarae, and Nancy Henley, 'Language, Gender and Society: A Second Decade of Research,' in Barrie Thorne , Cheris Kramarae, and Nancy Henley, eds.; *Language, Gender and Society* (Rowley, Mass., Newbury, 1983), p. 18.

33. Clifford, 'On Ethnographic Authority,' p. 128.

34. Rolf Lindner, 'Die Angst des Forschers vor dem Feld,' *Zeitschrift für Volkskunde* 77 (1981) 1, pp. 51–65.

35. In her theoretical reflections on ethnographic interviews on women's lives, Susanne Sackstetter points out that the psychological discomfort caused by the entrance into an 'unknown field' must be experienced even more strongly by female scholars whose 'space' within academia is much less established than that of men. Moreover, to 'go out into the world' may produce conflicts with gendered social norms, both individually and socially. This is especially true in West Germany, where women's public positions are significantly less well established than in the United States. See Susanne Sackstetter. '"Wir sind doch alles Weiber." Gespräche unter Frauen und weibliche Lebensbedingungen,' in Utz Jeggle, ed., *Feldforschung: Qualitative Methoden in der Kulturanalyse* (Tübingen: Tübinger Vereinigung für Volkskunde, 1984), pp. 159–76.

36. Sackstetter points to Utz Jeggle's account of an ethnographic interview which he calls 'Honoratioren unter sich' ('The intimacy of people of rank'). Jeggle argues that in his interview the discursive relationship between ethnographer and informant was constructed via a shared social position as 'men of rank' (the interviewer as a university professor and his male informant as a village celebrity); Utz Jeggle, 'Geheimnisse der Feldforschung,' in *Europäische Ethnologie: Theorie und Methodendiskussion aus ethnologischer und volkskundlicher Sicht* (Berlin, Veröffentlichung des Museums für Völkerkunde Berlin, Staatliche Museen Preussischer Kulturbesitz, 1982).

18

Viewdata: the television viewing habits of young black women in London

Evelyn Cauleta Reid

From *Screen* 30, 114–21 (1989)

A series of interviews with young black women in London forms the first stage of what will build into a detailed comparative survey of television viewing habits. This article suggests some tentative conclusions, but is mainly intended to provide an indication of the material on which the survey will be based. Most analyses of blacks are based on the assumption that there is a relatively homogeneous black perspective, most blacks have similar views on political and social issues. However, I shall aim to isolate the factors that lead to *differences* in attitudes toward television among young black women. In the same way, while research often focuses upon the effects of the media on attitudes and behaviour, the degree to which orientation *toward* the media is itself a function of attitudes, behaviours and socio-economic characteristics is seldom examined: I shall consider this relatively ignored aspect, primarily in relation to race.

Respondents were asked which programmes they watched and why, which ones they were less likely to watch and why, and their opinions of the portrayal of black people and programmes aimed at ethnic minorities. I recorded the interviews and analysed the material.

This raised a number of issues. The first of these concerned the notion of watching television from a particular socio-cultural position. The second involved the nature of television messages and mode of address – how much do the aesthetic codes of television affect viewing orientation? The third examined the ways in which variables such as race, age, education, gender, or religion themselves influence viewing, and the fourth, the effects of their interrelationships. The evidence suggest that people view television from a multiplicity of positions of identity in any one day. John Fiske and John Hartley argue that:

> Social mobility, changed historical conditions and changes in what Marx (1968, p. 117) calls the **entire superstructure of distinct and peculiarly formed sentiments, illusions, modes of thought and views of life** have produced among all groups in our culture a complex set of interrelations with other groups, a pervasive intersubjectivity whereby clear-cut distinctions between them are difficult to discern. The same applies to individuals – each one of us holds mutually contradictory beliefs about our position in society, and we respond to our condition in different ways at the same time.[1]

The questions to ask, therefore, are: Which of these bases of identity are salient? Which of them is (or ought to be) served by television? How do they operate in combination? What are the effects upon the spectator?

The sample of those interviewed was as follows: I interviewed twenty-three black women between the ages of fifteen and twenty-five. Five were pupils at a mixed comprehensive school; three were media workers; two were students, one on a media degree course, the other on a B TECH National Diploma course; three were unemployed; there were six office workers; a library assistant; a fashion house sample machinist; a doctor's receptionist and part-time youth worker; and a crèche worker. Among the twenty-three interviewed, four were single mothers, and four were active members of the Pentecostal church.

The interviews consisted of group discussions and individual interviews. Certain groups were no doubt privileged by this method. The media workers and the student on the media course were more informed about media ownership and structure as well as programme form and content. In group discussions some respondents tended to be overshadowed by more dominant members. The questions were:

Do you watch television?
How much do you watch?
What are your favourite programmes?
Why do you like them? What don't you like about them?
What programmes would you make a special effort to watch? Why?
What don't you like watching? Why?
Do you watch programmes specifically about women/black people?
Are all channels on television the same?
What kinds of programmes would you like to see on TV?
What do you think of the portrayal of black people on TV?

It must be stressed that these questions only formed the famework of the interviews. Many other issues arose in discussion as a result of the response of particular interviewees – for instance, discussions frequently spilled over to include the print media, especially the *Sun* newspaper, the police, responsibilities of black actors and artists and the 'struggles' of black people in general.

The media workers questioned were critical of the approach of this research and projects like it because, they argued, emphasis should be placed on the development of black aesthetics which they see taking place in small video workshops. This comment from one of them sums up the sentiment:

> I believe the premise of your paper is wrong. The very structure of your paper is in a way endorsing the society we live in and the structure of television by asking us to comment on it. What would be more positive, in my opinion, is if you were asking me or trying to find black women generally who are doing something to counter and to redress the situation.

As expected, viewing was constrained by a number of factors. Fourth-formers were more involved with outside entertainment and school activities such as games and rehearsals. Media workers were 'activists' and said they would rather be 'doing than watching' and argued that the bulk of television programmes made people less sensitive to the world around them. Women actively involved with religion said they often attend meetings on weekdays, and Sundays were mainly taken up with church activities. Mothers complained that interesting programmes often came on late at night when they were too tired to stay up and watch them after looking after their children most of the day; they, however, were the group most likely to watch daytime television.

Of those questioned, apart from the three media workers, most of the women's available television viewing time was spent watching soap operas. The fourth-formers, the unemployed, and some of the clerical workers were those most likely to make a point of watching them. The others, particularly the 'educated' group tended only to watch soap operas if they happened to be on. *EastEnders* and *Neighbours* were the most popular soaps. Those women who were at home during the day said they also watched programmes like *Falcon Crest*, and *The Young Doctors*. All respondents were critical of the black actors in these programmes and the realism of the shows:

> I watch soaps like **Neighours**, all soaps really. **Coronation Street**, now, that's got interesting because of the black and white relationship. I used to be an avid fan of **EastEnders**: now that the black family is moved off I'll only watch it if I'm in.
>
> – clerk typist, aged 22

> They made it seem as if it was a broken home, as if to say all black people have those sorts of problems all the time. They didn't make it seem as if it was a happy relationship.
>
> – receptionist, aged 25

> They were just put there to say, **yeah, we've got a black family**, but other than that, they're not really too interested in them. I don't know any black family that go on like they did; I'm not saying there aren't any, but I don't know any. I'm a black person and I couldn't relate to anything in there. Maybe it's because I don't know any family like that.
>
> – doctor's receptionist, aged 20

Brookside was less popular.

> I've lost interest in **Brookside**. I used to watch it, it's down to earth but the issues they do are too serious. And I think **EastEnders** was advertised more at the beginning, and **Brookside** came on when Channel Four started and people didn't catch on to it, and people can't be bothered to start watching it now, because they're not into it. Considering that Liverpool is supposed to have a lot of black people, you've only had one black girl in the programme, and they killed her off.
>
> – student, aged 21

> **EastEnders** is more gossipy, it's more about what's going to happen to him, what's going to happen to her and although they're true to life, they go a bit over the top, whereas **Brookside** is dead serious.
>
> – clerk, aged 21

The next most popular programme was the *Cosby Show* with ten saying that they would try hard to watch it or would video it. Four respondents said that they used to make a special effort to watch it when it first came out, but wouldn't now. The media workers, the two students and the library assistant said they would not go out of their way to see it, or any other television programme, as they often had other things to do. All had seen the programme at some time but were critical of it:

> Some people say it's boring because it's like they are the perfect family, but for me because black people are portrayed so negatively in all other aspects I don't care. I mean, why can't black families be portrayed as good, why should they put on more negative things when that's been chucked at us every day? I think they should come out with positive things and give other black people something to stand up for.
>
> – doctor's receptionist, aged 20

> I don't find it so funny now, it's kind of repeating itself. It's got a bit boring, it's not as good as it used to be. I don't really make an effort to stay in and watch anything any more.
>
> – student, aged 21

> I think it's a bit extreme; they could have had somebody who's a bit in-between. I mean, he's really rich, he lives in a big house with all his kids, and I just think that it's a bit unrealistic. There's no in-between.
>
> – library assistant, aged 24

> Cosby, he's an upper-class doctor, big house, lots of money and five kids. Now, there's no way that kids like that could grow up in a black family and act the way they do. The children – they listen to their parents, but they're not exactly disciplined, I mean, they get away with murder. There's no discipline in the family whatsoever because they just do what they want to do.
>
> – clerk, aged 22

Amen, another comedy from America was most popular, not surprisingly among the church-goers, as were gospel programmes such as *People Get Ready, Everybody Say Yea* also from the States, which they said they would make an effort to watch or video. Ten of the respondents had not watched *Amen* but had heard about it. The least favourite kind of programmes among all respondents was sitcoms – one person said that she did not watch them at all. The consensus was that comedy shows were boring, racist and old-fashioned. Three respondents said that *French and Saunders* was one of their favourites. *The Young Ones*, Jasper Carrott and Russ Abbot were thought to be exceptions to the run of the mill. There was a mixed reaction to comic Lenny Henry. Four interviewees thought he was as bad as white comedians because he was overly preoccupied with the negative aspects of black culture:

> In a way I don't like him, because he still portrays stereotyped images of black people.
>
> – receptionist, aged 25

> Lenny Henry – he reminds me of a white person. He acts really stupid; it just don't suit a black person. His jokes are more geared to white people than black people.
>
> – sample machinist, aged 18

However, the majority thought that his jokes weren't derogatory, and that he was just a good comedian:

> Lenny Henry's depiction is good because you feel you've met someone or you

know someone that he's depicting. He's speaking as a black person who's been in a situation and knows what he's talking about. If a white person makes those sorts of jokes you think they are getting at black people for not saying things properly, because what they do isn't how black people speak.

– library assistant, aged 24

[...] There was a consensus about the way documentaries about black people are presented: they were useless to black people. They reinforced negative imagery, they were voyeuristic, they were only useful when they told black people what they could do about a particular situation, they were often taken out of context. Most said that they felt depressed while the programmes were on, but that they made them more determined to succeed in life. Some said they didn't watch documentaries about South Africa because they found them too depressing and that they didn't show the whole picture:

The problem with these kinds of programmes is that journalists think that they are just there to raise the problem. Now I'm saying that the media are there to do a lot more. If they wanted to, they could use TV to eliminate racism. You can't use laws, but you can use the media to challenge the way people think, because you're telling them what to think through it. And so the whole notion that it's enough to just explore a problem is redundant, defunct and invalid. The whole idea that journalists are neutral and objective is invalid. Now programmes that address racism should address it from the point of view that they can actually be part of the process of stopping it.

– media worker, aged 24

If the programme approached the issue with a view to arriving at some conclusions as to what black people can do about the situation, fine, but all they do is show – as if to say this is it, it's a *fait accompli*; we have no resources to challenge this. They present us as hapless victims again and again.

– media worker, aged 25

All the time they just show Africa and the famine. They never show any part where they've improved it, for the amount of millions that's gone over there. That's the most hurtful part of it. If it's any programme where black people are concerned they always show you the worst part.

– sample machinist, aged 18

You've got this white camera crew and this white presenter and they go to find out things that you know, as a black person, exist already – so sometimes they're not really saying much you don't know. They see black people as the problem. They don't see it from a black person's point of view that it's the white people who've got the problem and black people are just reacting to the way they are treated.

– library assistant, aged 24

[...] Programmes aimed at ethnic minorities like *Ebony, Black on Black* and the *Bandung File* were considered important viewing. However, some respondents felt that there was a danger of ghettoisation and that these programmes should appeal to a wider audience, that there should be more black people in mainstream programmes. The term 'ethnic minorities' was offensive to the media workers who said it implied pagans and heathens.

All respondents were critical of their seasonal scheduling because they could never be sure when one was going to be shown.

> The whole idea of having separate programmes and departments for black people is one way of the BBC getting itself off the hook. I want them to integrate, to find a different approach and not call it ethnic minorities anything. I want a total change. I accept that to an extent there might be a complementary need in addition to the thorough reappraisal of their approach on programme policies. I mean, you can still justify the instance of a separate unit specifically to address certain issues, but on its own it's just a little speck in a whole sea of racism.
>
> – media worker, aged 24

[...]

> What happens on programmes like **Ebony** is that they run out of ideas and then it starts getting repetitive, and they look at the same thing from one angle and then another angle. The problem is format – the magazine framework is too restricting. They are trying to cover everything; they can't be very in-depth, they haven't got the space.
>
> – media worker, aged 25

Films of any genre were popular with all respondents. But there was a preference for US films among younger viewers, the unemployed, and some clerical workers, because they had 'a lot of action' and they were 'fast moving', and there was a preference for foreign and experimental films by media workers. *LA Law* and *Cagney and Lacey* were frequently mentioned as being 'really good programmes'. But, again the portrayal of black people was problematic, especially in old films. This comment was typical:

> One thing I really hate are those stupid black nurses with their eyes popping out and their lips are highlighted and they speak funny, or people portrayed as slaves.
>
> – fourth-former, aged 15

Game shows and quizzes provoked little reaction except from the media workers who thought they were the sort of programmes that made people less sensitive to the world around them. The majority said that they might have programmes like that on in the background.

[...] Four respondents (the single mothers and the media student) felt that there were more black people in children's programmes, but, being so few, their presence was tokenistic. *Sesame Street, Different Strokes, Open Air* and *Grange Hill* were mentioned as being exceptions because they did have a 'mixture'. The criticisms voiced about the portrayal of black people on British television, including adverts, concentrated on how far such representations were from their own experience. The scarcity of black people on television was another area of concern. It was as if the Cosby family had to represent all black families because it is the only regular programme about a black family:

> The way they do TV over here, they can't portray black people properly because they don't understand them. They don't know how to portray them. Whereas in the States they've been there longer and they've got a lot more

freedom. Black people have been in America longer and they get a lot more chances.

– student, aged 21

It is evident from the survey that age, education and gender as well as race influenced television viewing practice. Black adolescents, like their white counterparts, were less inclined to watch television, and more likely to pursue other interests – listening to music, doing homework, going out with friends. Their viewing habits were, to some extent, constrained by those of their parents. However, the decision to view particular pop programmes and documentaries was often influenced on grounds of race. Education, rather than just age, was an important factor in determining viewing. The more highly educated young women were more selective, watched a wider selection of programmes and were less likely to be influenced on programme choice by race. Race, however, *was* a factor in wishing to retain programmes like *Ebony* and to have black people better represented in mainstream programming. The most popular programmes were soap operas. Here, gender and class considerations were as influential as those of race – though one respondent said of the *Cosby Show*: 'When you watch it, you don't think of them as a black family; you think they're like you.'

In her research on soap opera, Dorothy Hobson found that working class women were less inclined to watch documentaries and current affairs programmes because they had: 'content which has little or no intrinsic interest for these women, and the way they are presented means that they exclude these women from "participation" at the point of identification with the items included.'[2] The black women in the survey differed in this context because, for them, news and current affairs about *black* people were a high priority – though other news and current affairs programmes were not.

John Fiske and John Hartley in 1978 state that one of television's functions as a social ritual is to draw into its orbit both the audience with which it communicates and the world to which it refers: 'Implicate the individual members of the culture into its dominant value-systems, by exchanging a status-enhancing message for the endorsement of that message's underlying ideology [as articulated in its mythology].'[3]

From the findings of this survey, it is evident that the value system and ideology of television messages about black people are not regarded as 'status-enhancing'. The following responses were typical:

> If I see a black person on television I would watch although I wasn't too interested in the programme before. The mere fact that I see a black person intrigues me as to how they are using them. And then I'm going to be forever critical, and that to my mind makes it very uneasy for black people to exist and to live in this country because we are always critical. It's not our fault that we are always critical because we are so used to seeing ourselves so badly represented, and we're always going to be analysing and picking, and it makes you angry because you're having to do that. They seem to problematise the existence of black people.

– media student, aged 21

Notes

1. John Fiske and John Hartley, *Reading Television* (London, Methuen, 1978), p. 103.
2. Dorothy Hobson, 'Housewives and the Mass Media', in *Culture, Media, Language* (London, Centre for Contemporary Cultural Studies/Hutchinson), p 112.
3. John Fiske and John Hartley, op. cit., p. 88.

Section IV

Interventions: industry, organisation, working practices

This section looks at some of the different ways in which feminist theory and practice, both inside and outside the academy, have intervened to challenge existing media representations of women and the working practices involved in their production. The extent to which a feminist critique can be used to negotiate alternative representations in the media opens up the question of whether women have a distinctive and different contribution to make to media content, and why it is so difficult for women to create change.

One form of feminist challenge to the mass media's portrayal of women has been the formation of independent media, what Marilyn Crafton Smith calls 'women's movement media' (see Creedon, 1993, Chapter 4). These have evolved to oppose the mass media and offer alternatives to women's movement supporters. Examples of this practice include the formation of feminist publishing groups and the work of independent feminist film-makers who have developed channels of independent distribution and exhibition for their films (see Citron, 1988).

A very different approach argues that female professionals can, and should, change employment policies and content from *inside* the mainstream media. This position has led to a number of initiatives to increase women's participation in the media workforce. Research indicates that there is still plenty of room for improvement. Both in terms of overall numbers and of distribution across and within specific occupations, women media workers are at a distinct disadvantage compared with their male counterparts (Stone, 1988; Baxter, 1990; Part II in Creedon, 1993; Gallagher, 1995).

Many early studies on representation put forward the view that the employment of more women in positions of greater authority in the media would lead to a change in media content (King and Stott, 1977; Tuchman *et al.*, 1978; Epstein, 1978). Recent accounts have charted the history of women's professional progress in the field of print and broadcast journalism (Hosley and Yamada, 1987; Sanders and Rock, 1988; Robertson, 1992; Sebba, 1994). However, the assumption that there is a direct correspondence between women working in the media and the representations produced has proved over-simplistic. It fails on two major counts. Firstly, it does not take account of the institutional and professional constraints on women working in a male-dominated media industry. Secondly, it fails to recognise a more complex concern with the language of representation and the need to identify: 'a specific women's perspective or aesthetic which could radically transform – rather than simply adapt to – discriminatory structures and practices in the media industries (Gallagher, 1992).

The extent to which any engagement with the mainstream can produce new representations of women continues to be questioned by some critics, who argue that this kind of intervention only results in: 'a modest allotment of institutional legitimation ... bought at the price of reducing the contradictory complexity (of feminism) for simpler and more acceptable ideas already existing in the dominant culture' (de Lauretis, 1987).

In 'Identity in feminist television criticism', **Charlotte Brunsdon** examines the intervention made by feminist academics studying television. She observes that in the past two decades feminist television criticism has moved from outside to inside the academic disciplines of communication, media and cultural studies. She suggests that academic feminist cultural criticism is becoming increasingly 'professionalised' and producing a set of identities and positions for the feminist television critic and the female viewer. Feminist critical discourse is doing more than simply analysing television programmes. It is in the process of constructing a distinct 'identity and difference' between the 'ordinary woman viewer' and the 'feminist critic'.

The call for the inclusion of a body of thought concerning black feminist theory is addressed in 'Black feminism and media criticism...' Recent research studies raise important questions about black women's relationship to the mass media (Manuel, 1985; Cummings, 1988), but **Jacqueline Bobo** and **Ellen Seiter** point out the problematic relationship that continues to exist between the feminism of middle-class white women and issues affecting women of colour in the study of the media. They insist that black women be included in empirical work in reader/audience research and in the study of popular films and television programmes.

'Firing a broadside: a feminist intervention into mainstream TV' is a case-study of *Broadside*, a feminist television production company set up to produce a weekly current affairs series for Channel Four. Given the organisational practices and structure of UK television, the opportunities open to women to make feminist television programmes are extremely limited (Baehr and Dyer, 1987). **Helen Baehr** and **Angela Spindler-Brown** describe how just such an opportunity arose in 1982 with the advent of Channel Four. It examines how the pressures to do a 'professional' job collided with the feminist objectives which the programme-makers set themselves.

One major 'interventionist' success story has been the television adaptation of Jeannette Winterson's novel *Oranges Are Not The Only Fruit*. This was first broadcast by the BBC in a peak-time drama slot in January 1990. It was immediately well received, not only within a lesbian subcultural context, but also by mainstream critics and audiences. In 'Fruitful investigations: the case of the successful lesbian text', **Hilary Hinds** analyses some of the ways in which this TV drama achieved such popular success and the discourses which shaped its media reception. She investigates why, in her view, a generally homophobic press reacted so positively to the representation of lesbianism in a mainstream TV drama.

The pressure on broadcasting organisations to employ more women has resulted in them becoming more visible on the screen. In the early 1980s, the biggest proportionate gains for any job category was recorded by women newscasters, with television's commitment exceeding that of radio (Eddings, 1980; von Zoonen, 1991). Yet, while women have been making gains on the air, surveys show that their absence in the real decision-making, producer and executive level jobs continues (Baehr and Dyer, 1987; Stilson, 1990; Gallagher, 1995). **Patricia Holland** in 'When a woman reads the news' examines why, even though women have become established as newsreaders, the image of a woman reading the news is still caught within the conflicting definitions of femininity and 'the news'.

Radio is a much less expensive medium than television and feminist groups have been making use of radio broadcasting as an avenue for involvement in the public sphere since the mid-1970s. **Birgitte Jallov** in 'Women on the air: community radio as a tool for feminist messages' describes how feminists in several European countries have made use of radio as a political tool. **Rosalind Gill**'s 'Ideology, gender and popular radio: a discourse analytic approach' uses radio as a case study to show that sexism – as a particular ideological discursive practice – remains a pervasive force, shaping British commercial radio both on and off the air.

References and further reading

BAEHR, H. 1981: Women's employment in British television: programming the future? *Media, Culture and Society* 3, 125–34.
BAEHR, H. and DYER, G. 1987: *Boxed in: women and television*. London: Pandora.
BAXTER, M. 1990: *Women in advertising*. London: London Institute of Practitioners in Advertising.
BRUNSDON, D. 1987: Feminism and Soap Opera. In Davies, K., Dickey, J. and Stratford, T. (eds.), *Out of focus: writings on women and the media*. London: The Women's Press, 147–50.
CITRON, M. 1988: Women's film production: going mainstream. In Pribham, D. (ed.), *Female spectators: looking at film and television*. London/New York: Verso, 45–63.
CUMMINGS, M. 1988: The changing image of the black family on television. *Journal of Popular Culture* 22, 75–87.
CREEDON, P. 1993: *Women in mass communication*. London: Sage.
DE LAURETIS, T. 1987: *Technologies of gender: essays on theory, film and fiction*. Bloomington: Indiana University Press.
EDDINGS, B. Murray 1980: Women in broadcasting (US) *de jure, de facto*. In Baehr, H. (ed.), *Women and media*, pp. 1–13.
EPSTEIN, L. (ed.) 1978: *Women and the news*. New York: Hastings House.
GALLAGHER, M. 1992: Women and men in the media. *Communication Research Trends* 12 (1).
— 1995: *Employment patterns in European broadcasting: prospects for equality in the 1990s*. Brussels: European Commission.
HOSLEY, D. and YAMADA, G. 1987: *Hard news: women in broadcast journalism*. Westport, Connecticut: Greenwood Press.
KING, J. and STOTT, M. 1977: *Is this your life? Images of women in the media*. London: Virago.
MANUEL, P. 1985: Blacks in British television drama: the underlying tensions. *Media Development* 4, 41–43.

ROBERTSON, N. 1992: *The girls in the balcony: women, men and the New York Times*. New York: Random House.

SANDERS, M. and ROCK, M. 1988: *Waiting for prime time: the women of television news*. Urbana/Chicago: University of Illinois Press.

SEBBA, A. 1994: *Battling for news: the rise of the woman reporter*. London: Hodder and Stoughton.

STILSON, J. 1990: Stuck on the ground floor. *Channels*, September 24.

STONE, V.A. 1988: Trends in the status of minorities and women in broadcast news. *Journalism Quarterly* 65, 288–93.

TUCHMAN, G., DANIELS, A. and BENET, J. (eds.) 1978: *Hearth and home: images of women in the mass media*. New York: Oxford University Press, 3–38.

VAN ZOONEN, L. 1991: A tyranny of intimacy? Women, femininity and television news. In Dahlgren, P. and Sparks, C. (eds.), *Communication and citizenship: journalism and the public sphere in the new media age*. London: Routledge, 217–35.

19

Identity in feminist television criticism

Charlotte Brunsdon

From *Media, Culture and Society* 15, 309–20 (1993)

It is about fifteen years since the first feminist television criticism began to appear in Britain and the US, and it is now possible to begin to construct a history of this criticism, and particularly, a history of its personae, of the characters who are specific to feminist television criticism: the feminist television critic and the female viewer. This pair, and the drama of their identity and difference, seem one of the most interesting productions of feminist television criticism, and in the contours of their relationships I think we can see patterns of feminist intellectual work which are not specific to the criticism of television.

My argument is briefly, that the formative stage of feminist television criticism extends from about 1976 to the mid-1980s, and that the key feature of this formative stage is the move from outside to inside the academy. While in 1976 the feminist critic writes with a primary address to her movement sisters, in a tone quite hostile to the 'mass media', yet concerned to justify her attention to television, by the mid-1980s she inhabits a more academic position, tends to address other scholars and is beginning to be anthologized in books used on both Communications and Women's Studies courses [...].

[...] I want to construct a typology which is based on the conceptualization of the relationship between *feminism* and *women*, or the feminist and other women as inscribed within the critical text. I offer this categorization most immediately as an heuristic, rather than an historical typology. That is, I am not suggesting that feminist criticism has moved from stage one to stage three, although I would argue that there are discernible historical shifts in the type of paradigms that are dominant at any one moment. My three categories would be the following:

(a) Transparent – no others;
(b) Hegemonic – non-feminist women others;
(c) Fragmented – everyone an other.

Each of these categories is defined through the relationship between the feminist and her other, the ordinary woman, the non-feminist woman, the housewife, the television viewer. It is this relationship, the way in which feminism constructs and has constructed itself in relation to the category 'woman', rather than the way in which women's subordination is theorized, which is essential to an understanding of feminist cultural criticism. That is, I am suggesting that feminist critical discourse itself constructs and produces, rather than simply analyses, a series of positions for 'women'.

Transparent

The positing of a transparent relationship between feminism and women is characteristic of the utopian, activist – and I think we could properly say formative – phase of post-1960s feminism. Although very rarely found without some articulation with the second 'hegemonic' relation, this utopian moment posits a shared sisterhood between all women, a consciousness of women as a gender group who are subject to a global patriarchal subordination and who thus have gender specific experiences in common. The dream, and the frequently asserted reality, of this moment is that all women are sisters, there is no 'otherness' between feminism and women, and that the appropriate pronoun of criticism is 'we'.

It is this consciousness that dominates media reviews in, for example, early British movement magazines like *Spare Rib* in the 1970s, and it is this consciousness, this 'we', which has been most vulnerable to attack for its political exclusions (which women?) and its epistemological assumptions (do women know differently?).

It is also, however, this notion of a shared gender experience which underpins part of the challenge that feminist work has offered to sociological and ethnographic research. Thus Dorothy Hobson's early research – which was scrupulous in its understanding of the complexity of the relationship between interviewer and interviewee, and which was consistently cautious about the class assumptions of the feminist 'we' – was not initially about the media, but about the experience of *being* a young working-class housewife/mother, and she insists on the way in which reference to shared experience increased the richness of her interviews (Hobson, 1978). Similarly, the work of the distinguished sociologist, Ann Oakley, offers some of its most radical challenges to existing social science methodologies in her consistent refusal to occupy conventional positions of neutrality in response to the questions of her 'interviewee mothers' (Oakley, 1981). She adopts this strategy as a specific response to what she calls 'the dilemma of a feminist interviewer interviewing women' (Oakley, 1981: 47), when the topic of the interviews is the frightening, but eagerly anticipated experience of a first baby.

Ironically, given that it has partly been the political attacks on the unthinking exclusions of this feminist 'we' that have marginalized it as an enunciative position, it is currently in response to the writing of women of colour that we most often find the assumption of transparency. Thus we find Jacqueline Bobo's work often characterized as 'what black women think' and as the site for the investigation of ethnicity – as if all those white audiences were without ethnic identity – and as if the articulation of ethnicity and gender here is not also historical, contradictory and sometimes provisional (Bobo, 1988). Indeed, in less academic feminism, it could be argued that the acceptance of the political critique of the transparency of the straight white Western feminist 'we' has led to a multiplication of special category, transparent, representative identities – older lesbians, working-class women, etc. – who are perhaps enabled to speak as a 'we', but also imprisoned by the inflexible demands of this identity fixing. This tendency is clearly represented by the British collection on women in the media, *Out of Focus* (Davies *et al.*, 1987).

Hegemonic

What I am calling the hegemonic relationship between the feminist and the woman has been the most common position within feminist television criticism. It would also be possible to call this structure of relationship 'recruitist' to use Angela McRobbie's term (McRobbie, 1982), the impulse to transform the feminine identifications of women to feminist ones. The construction of feminist identity through this relation involves the differentiation of the feminist from her other, the ordinary woman, the housewife, the woman she might have become, but at the same time, a compulsive engagement with this figure. The position is often profoundly contradictory, involving both the repudiation and defence of traditional femininity. In psychoanalytic terms, we could hypothesize that the encounter between the feminist and the housewife – a very clear arena for early and proto-feminist work from the 1960s on (Friedan, 1963; Gavron, 1966; Oakley, 1974; Hall, 1980; Lowry, 1980) – involves not just the construction of an identity 'independent woman' against another possible one 'dependent woman', but, specifically, an engagement with the mother. In terms of feminist television criticism, this usually meant the television viewer, in relation to whom much of the early writing is profoundly ambivalent.

A key rhetorical device here, one with which we are familiar from other traditions of anthropological and sociological work, is the introduction of a guide or intermediary, who gives instruction to the researcher about the pleasures and procedures of television viewing. These figures are often to be found in acknowledgements – for example, Carol Lopate, in one of the first feminist discussions of soap opera: 'I should like to thank Irena Kleinbort, whose insights were invaluable in helping me develop some of the ideas in this paper, and who furnished me with examples from her more extensive soap opera watching' (1977: 51). This disclaimer about soap expertise was anticipated by her earlier comment about learning how to watch, 'Until I got to know the stories, the afternoon felt like one long, complicated saga...' (1977: 41). It is almost as if the researcher must prove herself not too competent within the sphere of popular culture to retain credibility within the sphere of analysis.

Tania Modleski's influential essay, 'The Search for Tomorrow in Today's Soap Operas', is marked by a similar ambivalence, particularly in its early version. For example:

Clearly women find soap operas eminently entertaining, and an analysis of the pleasure that soaps afford can provide clues not only about how feminists can challenge this pleasure, but also how they can incorporate it. For, outrageous as this assertion may at first appear, I would suggest that soap operas are not altogether at odds with a possible feminist aesthetics. (1979: 18)

This passage displays a clear separation between the author and 'women', with the author explicitly addressing herself to 'feminists', a category in some ways opposed to 'women'. The key words are 'clues' and 'outrageous'. 'Clues' reveals that this is an evangelical enterprise of detection, the analysis of soap opera will render information about other pleasures – pleasures that must be challenged. So the justification of the academic enterprise to other feminists is through its gathering of politically useful knowledge. However within this address to an imagined sceptical feminist audience, Modleski is also making a polemical point: 'outrageous as this assertion may at first appear'. This 'outrageous' marks the other element in what I am calling the hegemonic relationship, the defence of 'women's culture'. In 1979, this insistence is made against the grain of feminist attitudes to popular television, insisting that there is something here to be taken seriously. Both 'clues' and 'outrageous' disappear from the rewritten book version of the essay, where the two sentences are split.

Clearly, women find soap operas eminently entertaining, and an analysis of the pleasure these programs afford can provide feminists with ways not only to challenge this pleasure but to incorporate it into their own artistic practices. (Modleski, 1982: 104)

and a page later

Indeed, I would like to argue that soap operas are not altogether at odds with an already developing, though still embryonic, feminist aesthetics. (Modleski, 1982: 105)

These rewritten versions, smoother, more confident, less embattled, also give much less sense of that author as caught between the positions of 'woman', 'feminist' and 'intellectual'.

What we find, over and over again, in early feminist television criticism, is the complicated negotiation of the position from which the author writes. There is a fleeting and fluctuating identification with a gender group (the residue of 'we women') which is at the same time a disavowal of many of the attributes of conventional femininity, crossed with the contradictory demands of intellectual credibility, which is of course conventionally ungendered. The identity of the feminist intellectual, which strains to combine these identities, is – necessarily – at this stage, profoundly unstable. What I have called the hegemonic impulse within feminist criticism, apart from its straightforward desire for a political mobilization around the inequities of gender, is also I think, an attempt to make the femininity/feminism relationship less contradictory by recruiting the one to the other.

Fragmented

The third way of thinking about the relationship between feminism and women I am calling 'fragmented' because it is founded on the possibility that there is no necessary relationship between these two categories. This moment is constituted by the force of the critiques directed at what I have called the 'transparent' moment both politically and theoretically as the implications of what is normally called the 'essentialism' debate percolate through the academy. 'Woman' becomes a profoundly problematic category – and arguably and ironically – 'feminist' becomes rather more stable (Riley, 1988; Haraway, 1985; Spivak, 1987). [...] I want to sketch briefly two distinct directions in current research work which share a radical particularism. One is towards 'historical autobiography', the other towards a stress on the contingency of gender identifications, and the significance of the articulation of these identifications with the whole range of other formative identifications. Valerie Walkerdine's work (1990) on the video-viewing of the *Rocky* films in the home of a working-class family can be understood in the context of a growing body of very sophisticated feminist autobiography (Heron, 1985; Steedman, 1986; Trinh, 1989; Kuhn, 1991; Lury, 1991; Wallace, 1990; Ware, 1992), all of which can be understood as contributing to, or commenting on, the fragmentation of the 'transparent' relationship between feminism and women in their exploration of the constitutive dynamics of class, ethnicity, migration and gender in the story of each self. All of these accounts suggest the impossibility of telling stories in which individuals are 'just' gendered. The other thread, best exemplified by Ang and Hermes's radical review of the use of gender as an explanatory category in recent ethnographic projects, argues for the radical contingency of gender identifications, and against a research agenda which concentrates on 'women's culture' to the neglect of an articulation with ethnicity and class. The logic of Ang and Hermes's position is to jettison 'some fixed figure of "women"', and to argue that 'any feminist standpoint will necessarily have to present itself as partial, based upon the knowledge that while some women sometimes share some common interests and face some common enemies, such commonalities are by no means universal' (Ang and Hermes, 1991: 324).

Conclusion

In summary, I have offered a typology of feminist television criticism in which the varying inscriptions of the relative identities 'feminist critic' and 'ordinary woman viewer' are seen as distinctive. [...] The period (1975–84) of the institutional acceptance and development of feminist television criticism in the white anglophone academy (Britain, USA, Australia) is a period in which we see the professionalization of the enunciative identity 'feminist critic'. I have tried to stress that I am offering an analytic, rather than an historical, typology, although Raymond Williams's distinction between residual, dominant and emergent modes of production might allow some mapping of these modes of feminist identity over both institutional changes in the academy and political changes in the feminist movements. I can offer here only the most blunt hypotheses. I could thus characterize the utopian, transparent moment, as dominant within the early days of second wave feminism. There are also at this stage no scholars appointed to teach 'Feminist Theory' or 'Gender Studies' in universities and colleges. The uncon-

scious class and ethnic identity of the 'we' of this moment has been exten-
sively documented elsewhere. I suggest that the dominant mode of feminist critique in the period of academic institutionalization is an
hegemonic/recruitist one, hegemonic in the sense that this feminism has
aspirations to dominate all accounts of the feminine. In this mode, the
feminist critic is distinguished from her other, the ordinary woman, and
the complicated defence and repudiation of conventional feminine
culture which characterizes much feminist criticism of popular culture
begins to be institutionalized. The pronouns here are 'we' and 'they', with
the shifting referent of the 'we' being both 'feminists' and 'women',
although the 'they' is always 'women'. The third moment is that in which
the epistemological grounding of the political category 'woman' is thrown
into crisis' – engulfed in a sea of what Dick Hebdige has called 'the Posts'
(Hebdige, 1988). Here we have the confluence of the political critique of the
1970s with post-structuralist thought and the theorization of the post-modern. Everyone here is an other – and there are no pronouns beyond the 'I'
– but there are, relatively, lots of women teaching and writing books about
these ideas.

It is customary, in typologies of this type, for the approach or position
being advocated to come at the end. However, I am not sure that this type
of theoretical clean get-away is either possible or desirable. Firstly, the logic
of my own argument so far compels me to observe that my theoretically
chic third category is itself dependent on its otherness from the first two
categories. It too involves a repudiation of earlier femininities – in this case,
feminisms. Indeed I would even venture that the fierce debate about essentialism which dominated feminist academic work in the later 1980s could
be understood symptomatically as the repudiation of the 'transparent' and
'hegemonic' moments (de Lauretis, 1990). Second – and this is a point which
I can only make most tentatively – I think the apparent intellectual autonomy of the third category would reward sociological scrutiny. That is, I am
interested by arguments made by feminist scholars such as Meaghan Morris that post-structuralism/postmodernism should partly be understood as
responses to the political and epistemological challenges of feminism – and,
one should add, post-colonial movements (Morris, 1988). However, I also
think this last position may be a much less conflictual one for *women* to
inhabit *as intellectuals,* and it is to this end that I would, very crudely, point
to the increasing dominance of this position as feminism becomes more aca-
demically visible outside the specialist enclaves of Women's Studies.

So if there are no theoretical clean get-aways, how can we reinterrogate
this typology? Perhaps with the humility and sense of history that Christine Geraghty shows in the following passage which comes at the end of
her book on soap opera:

> In marking a change in the experience of writing about *Coronation Street* in the
> mid-seventies and in writing about soap opera now, I am conscious of my
> own ambiguities about the project. What then was a desire to re-evaluate a
> cultural form which was denigrated, at least in part, because it was associated
> with women, now runs the risk of celebrating an illusion – the assertion of a
> common sensibility between women and a set of values sustaining us simply
> because we are women. In this context even to write 'we' rather than 'they'

becomes problematic in its assumption and smacks of a community of interest which needs to be constructed rather than asserted. (1990: 197)

Geraghty here gives an account of the historicity of identities and identifications, a micro-history of the identity 'woman' during the brief period of feminist work on television with which I have been concerned. She rejects the assumptions of shared interest – but she is still interested in sharing interests. The logic of her argument is a recognition of the difficulties of any move outside the potential solipsism of a 'fragmented' feminist identity – but not an abandonment of the project. She did finish the book.

References

ANG, I. and HERMES, J. 1991: Gender and/in media consumption. In Curran, J, and Gurevitch, M. (eds.), *Mass media and society*. Sevenoaks: Edward Arnold, 397–428.

BOBO. J. 1988: The color purple: black women as cultural readers. In E.D. Pribram (ed.), *Female spectators*. London: Verso, pp. 90–109.

DAVIES, K *et al.* (eds.) 1987: *Out of focus*. London: The Women's Press.

de LAURETIS, 1990: Upping the anti (sic) in feminist theory, pp. 255–70 in M. Hirsh and E. Fox Keller (eds.), *Conflicts in feminism*. New York: Routledge.

FRIEDAN, B. 1963: *The feminism mystique*. New York: Dell.

GAVRON, H. 1966: *The captive housewife*. London: Routledge and Kegan Paul.

GERAGHTY, C. 1990: *Women and soap opera*. Oxford: Polity.

HALL, C. 1980: The history of the housewife in Ellen Malos (ed.), *The politics of housework*. London: Allison and Busby, pp. 44–71.

HARAWAY, D. 1985: A manifesto for Cyborgs, *Socialist Review* 15(80): 65–107.

HEBDIGE, D. 1988: *Hiding in the light*. London: Comedia/Routledge.

HERON, L. 1985: *Truth, dare or promise*. London: Virago.

HOBSON, D. 1978: Housewives: Isolation as Oppression. In Women's Studies Group (ed.), *Women take issue*. London: Hutchinson, pp. 79–95.

KUHN, A. 1991: Remembrance. In Jo Spence and Patricia Holland (eds.), *Family snaps*. London: Virago, pp. 17–25.

LOPATE, C. 1977: Daytime television: you'll never want to leave home', *Feminist Studies* 4(6): 70–82.

LOWRY, S. 1980: *The guilt cage*. London: Elm Tree Books.

LURY, C. 1991: Reading the self: autobiography, gender and the institution of the literary. In S. Franklin *et al.* (eds.), *Off-centre*. London: Harper Collins, pp. 97–108.

McROBBIE, A. 1982: The politics of feminist research, *Feminist Review* 12: 46–57.

MODLESKI, T. 1979: The search for tomorrow in today's soap operas, *Film Quarterly* 33(1): 12–21.

MODLESKI, T. 1982: *Loving with a vengeance*. Hamden, CT: Shoestring Press.

MORRIS, M. 1988: *The pirate's fiancée*. London: Verso.

OAKLEY, A. 1974: *Housewife*. London: Allen Lane.

OAKLEY, A. 1981: Interviewing women: a contradiction in terms. In Helen Roberts (ed.), *Doing feminist research*. London: Routledge and Kegan Paul, pp. 30–61.

RILEY, D. 1988: *Am I that name? Feminism and the category of 'women' in history*. London: Macmillan.

SPIVAK, G. 1987: *In other worlds*. London: Methuen.

STEEDMAN, C. 1986: *Landscape for a good woman*. London: Virago.

TRINH, T. MINH-HA 1989: *Woman, native, other*. Bloomington: Indiana University Press.

WALKERDINE, V. 1990: *Schoolgirl fictions*. London: Verso.
WALLACE, M. 1990: *Invisibility blues*. London: Verso.
WARE, V. 1992: *Beyond the pale*. London: Verso.

20

Black feminism and media criticism

Jacqueline Bobo and Ellen Seiter

From *Screen* 32, 286–302 (1991)

That black women are writing and talking about their history, their politics and their socioeconomic status is not a recent occurrence, though it has sometimes been treated as if it is a 1980s phenomenon. Hazel Carby, in *Reconstructing Womanhood*, documents the fact that black women have long used the mechanisms available to them to attain a 'public voice'. Whether in writing, public speaking, or establishing national networks among a wide spectrum of black women, black feminists have worked diligently to comment upon and improve their social condition.[1] Other recent research by black women has recovered a wealth of literary and political work written by black women and used this as the basis for formalizing a body of thought concerning black feminist theory.[2] This archaeological work was necessary, notes Valerie Smith, because black women had been structured out of the writings of others.[3] The consequences of this neglect were that black women were misrepresented in the theoretical writings of others, if not omitted entirely. For cultural critics this was a particularly vexing problem, in that one of its consequences has been a limited access to works created by black women: now, however, the groundwork has been laid by literary scholars for an analysis of a range of cultural products. No longer can a text constructed by a black woman be considered in isolation from the context of its creation, from its connection with other works within the tradition of black women's creativity, and from its impact not just on cultural critics but on cultural consumers. As we witness the aggressive move towards adapting black women's literature for film and television, a similar effort directed at film and television criticism is now needed. Of course, different considerations must be brought to bear on a work of literature and on its media transformation; which suggests that some theoretical work needs to be done. Film studies has in large part shunned the study of adaptations as too literary, too traditional, and too uninformed by developments in film theory. But, in the case of black women's fiction, adaptations to film and television are the primary, if not the only, source of black feminist thought available to a large audience.[4] Works such as *The Color Purple* (Steven Spielberg, Warner Bros, 1985) and *The Women of Brewster Place* (Donna Deitch, ABC, 1989) represent a particularly vital area of popular narrative film and television today, and have the potential to challenge existing conventions of representation and characterization of women in ways that can also attract a broad, mass audience.

[...] The problematic relationship between the feminism of middle-class white women and issues affecting other women, in particular women of colour, has been documented in several well-known works which examine differences between women from historical and social perspectives.[5] For example, Hazel Carby, a black feminist cultural critic, has looked at the historical, social and economic conditions governing the lives of black and white women, emphasizing that oppression manifests itself differently in black and white women's lives. A crucial difference arose from women's roles during the slavocracy: white women were used (in part) to produce heirs to an oppressive system; black women functioned as breeders to produce property that added to the capital accumulation of the plantation system. The continuing divergent material circumstances would later affect the production of black and white women's texts about the status of their various oppressions.[6]

Aïda Hurtado, writing about the different ways patriarchy has affected white women and women of colour, notes that white women in the US have responded with the notion that the personal is political. Hurtado stresses that the political consciousness of women of colour 'stems from an awareness that the public is *personally* political'.[7] Her conclusion that the public sphere contains the elements of political thought and activity for women of colour is especially important for white feminist critics to recognize:

> the public/private distinction is relevant only for the white middle and upper classes since historically the American state has intervened constantly in the private lives and domestic arrangements of the working class. Women of Color have not had the benefit of the economic conditions that underlie the public/private distinction. White feminists' concerns about the unhealthy consequences of standards for feminine beauty, their focus on the unequal division of household labor, and their attention to childhood identity formation stem from a political consciousness that seeks to project private sphere issues into the public arena. Feminists of Color focus instead on public issues such as affirmative action, racism, school desegregation, prison reform and voter registration – issues that cultivate an awareness of the distinction between public policy and private choice.[8]

White feminist film and video critics can learn from the writings and experiences that have characterized fiction and literary criticism by women of colour. However, greater effort needs to be devoted to making this work available. Michele Wallace – a black feminist cultural critic who has taken some difficult stands against impediments to black women's progress – addresses a significant aspect of the problem. Her book *Black Macho and the Myth of the Superwoman* (1979), along with Ntozake Shange's choreopoem *for colored girls who have considered suicide when the rainbow is enuf* (1978), are considered pivotal works in contemporary debates about the racial 'correctness' of black women's cultural works. Wallace has criticized Adrienne Rich in her role as an intermediary between black women's writing and the public dissemination of their work. In her review of Rich's *Blood, Bread, and*

Poetry (1986) for the *New York Times Book Review*, she chronicles Rich's political evolution, noting that when Rich won the National Book Award for poetry in 1974, she insisted that the honour be shared between herself and the black women who were also nominated, Alice Walker and Audre Lorde.[9] Wallace writes that even though Rich might have the best of intentions, she 'pretends to sponsor that which is not in her power to sponsor, that which she can only silence: a Black feminist voice and/or theory'. Wallace explains that Rich exercises control over the works of black women and other women of colour in that she is a gatekeeper for those works that will appear on the 'essential reading list'. She adds: 'When I say reading list, that's a euphemistic way of referring to book contracts, book sales, teaching jobs, tenure, publication in anthologies and journals, without which it is now impossible to be a writer, much less a black feminist writer.'[10]

The gatekeeping function of certain strains of white feminist thought extends beyond being a filter through which designated works are sifted: it limits the kinds of issues that can be written or thought about. Because much of the creative and theoretical work written by black women is available only through alternative outlets, some mainstream critics remain ignorant of, and uneducated in, black feminist thought. Wallace writes that the problem at present represents

> a critical juncture at the crossroads of a white mainstream academic feminism, which is well paid, abundantly sponsored and self-consciously articulate, and a marginalised, activist-oriented Black feminism, which is not well-paid, virtually unsubsidized and generally inarticulate, unwritten, unpublished and unread.[11]

In the face of these shortcomings, feminists working within cultural studies need to rethink their writing. Jane Gaines, a white feminist cultural critic, has assessed the inadequacies of contemporary feminist criticism (Lacanian psychoanalysis and Marxist feminism) in its practice of examining creative works only for their significance to white, middle-class heterosexual women. Gaines chastises mainstream feminists for their token gestures towards the inclusion of different perspectives, stating 'our political etiquette is correct, but our theory is not so perfect'.[12]

In a similar critique, Coco Fusco details the political expediency within the current 'crisis of conscience'. Fusco criticizes avant-garde art institutions and the individuals who operate them for their selective inclusion of works by people of colour and for the assumption that a 'single event' series can serve as a corrective to decades of racism and sexism. Since these serve as mediators between works by people of colour and public knowledge of their existence, Fusco feels that the avant garde needs to look to its own practices and reexamine its perspective on 'the other'.[13]

A survey of the opinions of many feminist media analysts in the recent special issues of *Camera Obscura* on 'the spectatrix' makes clear the lack of substantial theorizing about issues around class or race and cinema. After summarizing the terrain of female spectatorship, the editors admit that there is a difficulty in redressing this omission: it is easier, they say, to recognize that spectator positions involving race, class, age, and so on need to be taken into account than it is 'to arrive at satisfactory methods for doing so, or even more simply, to understand what it is that we want to know, and why'.[14]

What we want to know and why we as cultural commentators need to know it is exemplified in the problem of sampling currently confronting researchers in cultural studies, audience studies and ethnographic work. Recently there has been a surge in empirical work in reader/audience studies, especially relating to women's genres such as romance, melodrama and soap opera. In cultural studies work on audiences (as in much of the mass communications research it seeks to oppose), samples have tended overwhelmingly to be white. This fact deserves a closer look: it is too frequent an occurrence to be shunted aside or excused by the brief apologies which attribute white samples to limited funding or scope. It is not something that 'just happens', not simply a case of sampling error, nor of the failure of individual researchers to be sufficiently diligent in making contacts, although these are certainly factors that contribute to the problem.

This situation has partly to do with the demographics of the academy in the United States: who the researchers are (predominantly white), where they live (in segregated white neighbourhoods), and where they work. Occupational segregation has been durably established in US universities: whites filling professorial ranks and senior positions, and people of colour relegated to service and clerical positions, or assuming faculty positions in small numbers and at untenured, junior levels. This structure remains in place even as many institutions pay fashionable lip service to their efforts towards diversity in faculty and student population. It also, and less obviously, has to do with the trend towards interviewing respondents in their homes. Women of colour will probably be less likely to welcome white researchers into their homes than will white women. As long as the state so often interferes in their private sphere under the guise of a range of seemingly innocuous ventures, women of colour will be wary of intrusions into their domestic space by white middle-class professionals. Thus, while theoretically sound, the increased emphasis of late on the crucial role of the domestic sphere in shaping media consumption must be scrutinized in terms of the limitations it may set on the kinds of participants available for studies involving the home as both site and object of research.[15]

James Clifford, among others, has called attention to the unequal power relations inherent in the ethnographic enterprise and to the 'objectification' of the subject in ethnographic discourse.[16] While many white social scientists are only now considering these issues, people of colour have long been aware of the possibilities of being ripped off by researchers, and of the ways in which academic studies are often used in the long run to legitimate various forms of oppression. While it would be wrong to dismiss ethnography as a valuable method, it has to be recognized that it produces knowledge which circulates in influential ways within the disciplines in which it is used. Thus, for example, many of the notions of gender difference deriving from ethnographic work with all-white samples in current circulation are reified and ethnocentric: the experiences of women of colour with the media remain unheard, unstudied, untheorized.

Nevertheless, some recently published research by women of colour promises to change the way researchers consider media audiences. Jacqueline Bobo's work with black women's responses to the film *The Color Purple* has demonstrated how black women, because of their low expectations of the media (and their expectations of encountering racism) can read around and through a Hollywood text.[17] Minu Lee and Chong Heup Cho's work with middle-class Korean soap opera fans in the United States similarly points to a much wider range of reactions and uses than has been imagined in theorizing the (white) spectator.[18] It can be predicted with certainty that other work by women of colour will not only alter the pool of empirical findings in cultural studies, but also challenge, redefine, and renovate the theoretical agenda in ways white academics cannot at present imagine. White researchers must work harder to consider the problems of racial and ethnic difference, scrutinize their research designs and their methods of contacting respondents, and bring to their work a high degree of selfconsciousness about racism and the power relations inherent in research.

Ultimately, however, substantial improvement in the situation awaits bringing more women of colour into the field of cultural studies and its descriptions of media audiences. There is an unfortunate tendency to consider as a separate agenda – one set apart from theoretical work – issues of affirmative action, diversification of academic faculties, recruitment of students, and equitable entrance requirements. Experience also demonstrates that far too often graduate students of colour lack academic advisors who are strong advocates for them or for their course of study. It is no accident that there are few black, latino, native-born Asian and native American doctoral students or PhDs in the United States – and with numbers especially small in media studies. Problems range from a curriculum and canon which are overwhelmingly white to a lack of precedent for students to do research relating to their experience – and a lack of encouragement from advisors.[19] A rewriting of the canon and the curriculum must take into account popular films and television programmes, as well as independent and experimental work by black filmmakers. White feminists must recognize that, as an area of academic interest, feminist cultural studies is likely to appear trivial to women of colour until white academics connect more strongly with the politics of the public sphere and the university.[...]

Notes

1. Hazel Carby, *Reconstructing Womanhood: The Emergence of the Afro American Woman Novelist* (New York, Oxford University Press, 1987).
2. Examples are Barbara Christian, *Black Women Novelists, The Development of a Tradition 1892–1976* (Westport, Conn., Greenwood Press, 1980); Mary Helen Washington, *Invented Lives: Narratives of Black Women 1860–1960* (New York, Anchor Press, 1987); and more recent essays about black feminist theory in Cheryl Wall (ed.), *Changing Our Own Words: Essays on Criticism, Theory, and Writing by Black Women* (New Brunswick, NJ, Rutgers University Press, 1989); and Joanne Braxton and Andree Nicola McLaughlin (eds.), *Wild Women in the Whirlwind: Afra-American Culture and the Contemporary Literary Renaissance* (New Brunswick, NJ: Rutgers University Press, 1990).
3. Valerie Smith, 'Black feminist theory and the representation of the "Other"', in Cheryl A. Wall (ed.), *Changing Our Own Words*, pp. 38–57: 'Gender and Afro-

Americanist literary theory and criticism', in Elaine Showalter (ed.), *Speaking of Gender* (New York, Routledge, Chapman and Hall, 1989), pp. 56–70.

4. This point is made by Barbara Christian in 'The race for theory', *Feminist Studies*, vol. 14. no. 1 (1988), pp. 67–79. This is a revision and update of an article first published in *Cultural Critique*, no. 6 (1987), pp. 51–63.

5. See, for instance, bell hooks. *Ain't I a Woman? Black Women and Feminism* (Boston, South End Press, 1981); Gloria I. Joseph and Jill Lewis (eds.), *Common Differences: Conflict in Black and White Feminists' Perspectives* (New York, Anchor, 1981).

6. See Carby's *Reconstructing Womanhood*, and also her earlier assessment of the relationship of white feminism to the actual lives of women of colour in 'White woman listen: black feminism and the boundaries of sisterhood', in Centre for Contemporary Cultural Studies, *The Empire Strikes Back: Race and Racism in Seventies Britain* (London, Hutchinson, 1982), pp. 212–35.

7. Aïda Hurtado, 'Relating to privilege, seduction and rejection in the subordination of white women and women of color', *Signs: Journal of Women in Culture and Society*, vol. 14, no. 4 (1989), p. 849.

8. Ibid. p. 850.

9. Michele Wallace, 'Sexism is the least of it', *New York Times Book Review*, 17 March 1987, p. 18.

10. Michele Wallace, 'The politics of location: cinema/theory/literature/ethnicity/sexuality/me', *Framework*, no. 36 (1989), pp. 42–55.

11. Ibid. p. 48.

12. Jane Gaines, 'White privilege and looking relations: race and gender in feminist film theory', *Screen*, vol. 29, no. 4 (1988), pp. 12–26. Gaines succinctly assesses the difficulties of theorizing about 'the other' using traditional feminist analysis.

13. Coco Fusco, 'Fantasies of oppositionality: reflections on recent conferences in Boston and New York', *Screen*, vol. 29, no 4 (1988), pp. 80–93. A rebuttal to Fusco's article was presented in a later issue of *Screen*: Berenice Reynaud and Yvonne Rainer, 'Responses to Coco Fusco's "Fantasies of oppositionality"', with reply from Coco Fusco, *Screen*, vol. 30, no. 3 (1989), pp. 79–100.

14. Janet Bergstrom and Mary Ann Doane, 'The female spectator: contexts and directions', *Camera Obscura*, nos. 20–21 (1989), pp. 5–27.

15. See, for example, David Morley, *Family Television: Cultural Power and Domestic Media* (London, Comedia, 1986); Janice Radway, *Reading the Romance: Women, Patriarchy and Popular Literature* (Chapel Hill, University of North Carolina Press, 1984); and studies such as those by Rogge, Tulloch, and Seiter, in Ellen Seiter *et al.* (eds.), *Remote Control: Television Audiences and Cultural Power* (London, Routledge, 1989).

16. An early influential article on this topic is James Clifford, 'On ethnographic authority', *Representations*, vol. 1, no. 2 (1983), pp. 118–46.

17. Jacqueline Bobo, '*The Color Purple*: black women as cultural readers', in E. Deidre Pribram (ed.), *Female Spectators: Looking at Film and Television* (London, Verso, 1988), pp. 90–109.

18. Minu Lee and Chong Heup Cho, 'Women watching together: ethnographic study of Korean soap opera fans in the US', *Cultural Studies*, vol. 4, no. 1 (1990), pp. 30–44.

19. For specific examples of this problem for students of colour in graduate programmes, see Yolanda T. Moses, *Black Women in Academe: Issues and Strategies* (Washington DC, Project on the Status and Education of Women/Association of American Colleges, 1989). An especially frank and insightful look at the issue is given by Karen J. Winkler, 'Minority students, professors tell of isolation, anger in graduate school', *The Chronicle of Higher Education*, 9 November 1988, pp. A15, A17.

21

Firing a broadside: a feminist intervention into mainstream TV

Helen Baehr and Angela Spindler-Brown

From H. Baehr and G. Dyer (eds.), *Boxed in: women and television* (Pandora 1987)

In April 1982, Channel 4 announced that its weekly half-hour current affairs series would be produced by women. Liz Forgan, Senior Commissioning Editor for Actuality at the time, said this decision to hand over its current affairs to women had 'nothing to do with positive discrimination or social justice, it is a journalistic experiment' (Channel 4 press release, April 1982). In fact the Women's Broadcasting and Film Lobby (WBFL) had come up with the idea for the series two years earlier in 1980.[1] That was the year that women first made it onto the agenda of the Edinburgh International Television Festival, prompted by WBFL. Mary Holland addressed the EITF participants on the lack of a women's perspective in television news and current affairs.

> As for what one might call women's news – violence against women, blatant cases of sex discrimination, the condition of women prisoners – these do not get covered in the main news programmes unless there is some particularly sensational angle to them. Even in the comparative freedom of the ghetto areas we have yet to see a TV equivalent of *Spare Rib*. (EITF official programme, 1980, p. 41)

In December 1980, Jeremy Isaacs, Chief Executive of Channel 4, publicly accepted the proposal of a women's current affairs series. In a *Guardian* interview with Liz Forgan (then editor of the women's page), he argued that women would show 'an interestingly different view of the world...I intend to give them the opportunity to demonstrate that' (1 December 1980). In those heady pre-transmission days the emphasis was on innovation. Isaacs was keen to include people from outside television, with a fresh outlook and new arguments, in his team. Indeed, twelve months later, after a different kind of interview with Liz Forgan, he appointed her Senior Commissioning Editor in charge of news and current affairs.

In the spring of 1982, Channel 4's weekly current affairs series was given to two new production companies: Gambles Milne, whose series *20/20 Vision* was headed by Claudia Milne and Lyn Gambles, and *Broadside*. Milne and Gambles were both experienced in television production but had never worked together before. *Broadside* had twelve members (shareholders) who had been working together as a television discussion and lobby group since

1979. When it became incorporated as a company in 1981, each member held one share, leaving the remaining eighty-eight shares unallocated. The group included experienced producers, directors, researchers and a camera operator as well as journalists and academics. All had played an active role in WBFL and in getting the idea of a women's current affairs slot accepted.[2] Unlike Gambles Milne, *Broadside* presented itself as a feminist production company. From the start these two very different companies – united only by the fact that they were women – were under enormous pressure. Like other television programmes produced by women, their slot came to stand for, and be judged as, representative of all women's work. *20/20 Vision* went on air in November 1982 and *Broadside*'s first programme, *Taking on the Bomb*, was transmitted in January 1983. By November 1983 the 'experiment' was over. Channel 4's weekly current affairs coverage was handed back to men's editorial control. [...]

[...] The twelve founding members of *Broadside* shared a basic feminist viewpoint. This ideological position and determination to make certain types of programmes necessitated a questioning of traditional ways of working in the industry. Television appeared as an impenetrable citadel. We had seen feminist enterprise flourish in the world of publishing, bringing with it ideologically new products and new ways of working. Women film-makers were attempting to create an alternative film language within a reconstructed context of distribution and exhibition. But for those women working within established broadcasting institutions, the possibilities of introducing alternative modes of production, distribution and consumption were severely limited. (That is not to underestimate the considerable diffi-culties involved in funding and exhibition of independent film projects.) In this sense, we felt we were engaging not so much in an 'experiment', as the channel had labelled us, but in a project to expand the frontiers of televi-sion coverage. The Broadcasting Act 1981 requires Channel 4 to transmit a suitable proportion of matter calculated to appeal to tastes and interests not generally catered for by ITV. This statutory obligation, in conjunction with Isaacs's and Forgan's earlier statements, were interpreted by the *Broadside* production team as a public admission that there was a lack of women and women's issues within television current affairs. The same Act encourages the channel to 'innovate and experiment' in the form and content of its pro-gramming. Together with many other independent producers, *Broadside* programme-makers saw this brief as an opportunity to shift – if not totally remove – conventional notions of 'balance' and 'impartiality'. We wanted to organize ourselves and make programmes informed by our feminism.

Most of us tried to make these kinds of programmes within mainstream television. We were well versed in the stock responses from male colleagues in powerful positions who challenged 'women's interest' ideas as being 'minority' or – worse – of 'no interest' to a general audience. Our experi-ence told us that only by holding editorial control might we collectively suc-ceed where, as individuals, we had previously failed. Those who were experienced television researchers brought with them a history of many years stuck at researcher grade with little prospect of promotion. All the evidence points to the fact that the number of women employed in the television industry decreases as you move up the production ladder (ACTT, 1975; Gallagher, 1979; Baehr, 1981; Sims, 1985). In one survey of six BBC departments, including current affairs, general features and light entertainment, out of 79 researchers, 56 were women. At the next level – junior and senior director – the proportion of women took a sudden dive: 38 women compared to 64 men. Out of a total of 157 producers only 25 were women (Baehr, 1981). Those in *Broadside* who had reached producer/director level, or were camera operators, were keen to work with other women and share editorial control over the kinds of issues covered. We were all tired of the constraints imposed on us by the tried and tested ways of television. To use Mary Holland's phrase, we knew we were not victims of 'any particular wickedness of men within television' (Holland, 1980). We recognised that broadcasting is a practice carried on 'not by individual broadcasters, but by institutions' (Garnham, 1973). Our insistence on making programmes which reflected women's position in society, their interests and views, was a reaction to a set of professional 'values' enshrined in the institutions of mainstream broadcasting rather than in its personnel. The only way to succeed in making the programmes we wanted to see would involve the construction and application of an alternative set of 'professional' values. It was in this context that the *Broadside* team was labelled by Diana Simmonds as 'feminist professionals' rather than 'professional feminists' (*Sunday Times*, 23 February 1983). At the same time, our aim was to make pleasurable and interesting programmes accessible to mainstream television audiences, not just to the feminist cognoscenti and metropolitan avant-garde.

In the run-up to *Broadside*'s commission in April 1982, we held close to a hundred meetings in the evenings and at weekends. We endlessly rehearsed our editorial strategy and our production structure. We devised ways of reaching a consensus and paid enormous attention to the need to establish an atmosphere of support and collective effort which so many of us had found lacking in the working practices of the industry. We recognised a responsibility to employ women technicians and wanted to do our best to include them in the very early stages of production planning. We agreed that the practice within the BBC and ITV companies of putting a crew together at short notice might be cost effective, but did not necessarily make the best programmes or provide job satisfaction. Our discussions over *Broadside*'s structure were hotly debated. All twelve founding members wanted to be involved and participate in the company's future. At the same time we recognised the need to delegate responsibility within the group. Discussions revolved around how, and whether, this could be achieved in a non-hierarchical but accountable way. The formal demands of union practices had to be considered in conjunction with our own need to provide opportunities within which we could develop new skills to take us higher up the production ladder. The question was: how to ensure all this within the context of a tight production schedule and fixed budget?

In the end, Channel 4 settled this issue for us. It demanded a traditional editorial structure with one editor at the top who would make all editorial decisions and liaise with the channel. It transpired, in our negotiations with the Commissioning Editor for Actuality, that this structure was to be the condition under which the commission for the series would be granted. We were asked to recruit a woman 'with top current affairs editorial experience' to act as our series editor, although both Liz Forgan and Jeremy Isaacs readily admitted that part of the reason for launching the series was precisely because of the dearth of experienced women in this field. If we were to have a conventional editorial structure imposed on us, we decided to elect one of the original *Broadside* members rather than appoint an outsider. We felt that since we had won the commission, we wanted to be in control of how and what we produced. Our feelings throughout this period was that, in comparison with other newly established companies, *Broadside*'s structure was being scrutinised and interfered with as if it were 'a special case'.

On balance, however, when we embarked on the first series we were pleased to be making the programmes of our choice, albeit with a chain of command that felt like an unnecessary intervention along the lines of the production practices we had been retreating from. Early on, the editor issued her own job description as follows: 'The editor should have final decision-making power on matters of staffing, editorial policy and budgets' (memo, 8 April 1982). Thus the debate around what would constitute non-traditional, new working practices and structures was cut short.

[...] By the time we started on our second series of eight in May 1983, with no indication of any future commission, we felt anxious about jobs and future prospects for the series and the company. As well as the current affairs series, we had other ideas in the pipeline, including film scripts and 'one-off' documentaries (several of which were subsequently produced by *Broadside* shareholders for different companies). By now, a struggle for control of the company was causing a split between ten of the original *Broadside* members and the editor. Her attempt to take control of the company failed. But, as editor of the series, she succeeded in effectively marginalising the majority of the company's shareholders, over half of whom were working as part of the current affairs production team. *Broadside* was only one of a number of companies kept uninformed right up to the last minute as to whether it would get a contract for another series. We were told in writing that no further series was to be commissioned from us only two weeks after our last transmission. The channel has since had to modify its terms of trade to include procedures for terminating long-standing series. In July 1983 a union dispute arose over alleged non-payment of monthly cheques. In reality, what was at issue was the future control and ownership of the company and its remaining shares.

We started our production schedule in the full glare of publicity and expectation. Liz Forgan readily admitted that the task ahead was to make 'this current affairs series a triumphant success in what we know will be the teeth of every kind of criticism, ridicule and carping from the world at large' (Blanchard and Morley, 1982). Economic considerations guided our productions very quickly into the tried and tested way of doing things: development, pre-production, perfectly planned shoots and fast post-production. Given the constraints on budget people were employed for only as long as was absolutely necessary. Gone were all our ideas for pre-production meetings involving our technicians. Economic pressures produced an atmosphere in which we were reproducing established working practices.

At all costs we wanted to do a 'professional' job and prevent carping from the world at large. This resulted in an economic and psychological lack of space for experiment.

If we were hampered in challenging the existing forms and practices of production, we were much more successful in breaking new ground in the kinds of topics we chose and perspectives we adopted. With only sixteen programmes, we had to pick our subjects carefully. We launched the series with a film about women and the peace movement and followed this with a 'scoop' about the incidence of cancer resulting from British and Australian atom bomb tests in South Australia in the 1950s. Out of the sixteen programmes *Broadside* made, a surprisingly high number (four) dealt with the war and its aftermath. We were trying to get away from the *Boy's Own* approach to war, but by choosing to shoot conflict overseas we were also tackling the kind of story from which we, as women, had previously been barred. All our stories were thoroughly discussed at editorial meetings and subsequently within smaller production teams. As time went on, questions of resources and who got what job sometimes interfered with editorial judgment, but, on the whole, there was always agreement on which subjects should be included on our agenda. There were no arguments about 'women's interests' being of 'no interest'.

[...] *Broadside* was formed out of a core of women who had initially come together to lobby for more opportunities for women in the industry. It subsequently changed from a campaigning group into a television production company. This unique history set it apart from other independent companies producing for Channel 4, which had been set up simply to produce programmes. These companies are run on the principle that 'small is beautiful' – at least in terms of their ownership structures. As it turned out, *Broadside*'s size meant that not all of its members could be accommodated and satisfied within the limited number of opportunities available. In the two years that *Broadside* existed as a discussion and lobbying group, it had established an informal structure which made the difficulties it later faced as a production company very hard to manage. We had been used to meeting in each other's homes in our own time. We had become friends, exchanging stories about the industry's treatment of women and supporting each other in our careers and personal lives. Our individual experiences and professional aspirations, as well as the way we organised ourselves as a group, were informed by the women's movement. In this sense, we had combined the traditionally separate worlds of the 'public' and the 'private'. But our sense of 'solidarity' stood in direct contradiction to the professional values we had acquired through working in television. That world is notoriously competitive and does nothing to encourage a sense of co-operation over and above the line of duty (see Kumar, 1977; Alvarado and Buscombe, 1978; Hood, 1980).

The 'political unity' of *Broadside* was mixed up with individual and collective professional objectives which were in turn bound up with friendships. Once *Broadside* was operating as a fully fledged production company, sisterly intentions became undermined by highly charged personal ambitions and fears about job security. When conflicts arose they became bitter and, inevitably, highly personalised. The fight for the right to a job and the maintenance of friendships became irreconcilable. The imposed editorial structure did nothing to encourage collective effort. The editor's power to 'hire and fire' led to a classic situation of always trying to please the boss. As often happens in these situations, this was frequently given higher priority than programme production. There were clear structural reasons for dissent and dissatisfaction within the company. The lingering uncertainty about whether Channel 4 would commission another series produced feelings of anxiety and job insecurity for everyone. The fact that *Broadside* had been set up as a collective response to a set of individual frustrations faced by women working in the television industry increased the strain. *Broadside* appeared to offer the chance to show our skills unimpeded by male colleagues, many of whom have allergies to women and/or women's interests. However, the understandable ambitions of experienced researchers for promotion to producer/director level created a highly competitive working environment. We may not have had disagreements about programme content but it was difficult to contain the frustration and bitterness when people's professional ambitions were curbed – this time seemingly by 'sisters'.

Broadside was amongst the first batch of companies commissioned to produce a series for Channel 4. Since those early days new procedures have had to be introduced by the channel for re-commissioning and terminating series. Delays in re-commissioning and industrial disputes have been reported within other independent companies working for Channel 4. [...] Nor are boardroom struggles an uncommon feature in the television industry. Witness the battles at London Weekend Television in the late 1960s and the near collapse of TV-am in 1983 (Tinker, 1980; Leapman, 1984). Put in this context, what happened to *Broadside* is hardly atypical or worthy of comment. But because it happened to a women's production company it refused to be hidden by history. What *Broadside* did was to challenge the conventions of an industry which had hampered women's progress yet, by working in that industry, it internalised many of its professional practices and aspirations. Mary Howell, in her study of women and professionalism, offers this cautionary note: 'I believe that *none* of us survives socialisation as professionals without a profound compromise in the way we live out our feminism' (Howell, 1979). Within television, it seems, the contradiction that exists between professionalism and feminism remains unsolved and, possibly, insoluble.

Notes

1. The Women's Broadcasting and Film Lobby (WBFL) was set up in 1979 to improve the employment and training opportunities for women in the industry and challenge sexist images of women.
2. A more detailed history of this period (1982) is to be found in Blanchard and Morley (1982), Chapter 7, and Lambert (1982).

References

ASSOCIATION OF CINEMATOGRAPH AND TELEVISION TECHNICIANS (ACTT) 1975: *Patterns of discrimination against women in the film and television industries*.

ALVARADO, M and BUSCOMBE, E. 1978: *Hazell – the making of a TV series*. London: British Film Institute.

BAEHR, H. 1981: Women's employment in British television: programming the future? *Media, culture and society* 3, 125–34.

BLANCHARD, S. and MORLEY, D. (eds.) 1982: *What's this Channel Fo(u)r? An alternative report*. London: Comedia.

GALLAGHER, M. 1979: *The portrayal and participation of women in the media*. Paris, UNESCO.

GARNHAM, N. 1973: *Structures of television*, Television Monograph 1, London, British Film Institute.

HOLLAND, M. 1980: 'Out of the bedroom and onto the board?', *Edinburgh International Television Festival Official Programme*, London, Broadcast.

HOOD, S. 1980: *On Television*. London, Pluto Press.

HOWELL, M. 1979: 'Can we be feminists and professionals?', *Women's Studies International Quarterly*, vol. 2, pp. 1–7.

KUMAR, K. 1977: 'Holding the middle ground: the BBC, the public and the professional broadcaster', in J. Curran, *et al.* (eds.), *Mass communication and society*. London, Open University Press.

LAMBERT, S. 1982: *Channel Four, television with a difference?*, London, British Film Institute.

LEAPMAN, M. 1984: *Treachery? The power struggle at TV-am*. London, George Allen and Unwin.

SIMS, M. 1985: *Women in BBC management*, BBC Report.

TINKER, J. 1980: *The television barons*. London, Quartet.

22

Fruitful investigations: the case of the successful lesbian text

Hilary Hinds

From her *Women: a cultural review*, vol. 2 (Oxford University Press 1991)[1]

[...] Jeannette Winterson's adaptation for television of her novel *Oranges Are Not The Only Fruit* was first broadcast in January 1990. Particularly significant for the reception of the text at this time were the repercussions from arguments that had circulated in relation to two events of 1988 and 1989 respectively: the passing of Section 28 of the Local Government Act, which aimed to ban the 'promotion of homosexuality' by any bodies funded by local authorities, and the death threat made against Salman Rushdie on the publication of his novel *The Satanic Verses*. These two events had elements in common, most significantly in the responses and opposition that they elicited: the liberal arts establishment saw each as undermining the principle of free speech. One of the most successful counter-arguments made in opposition to Section 28 was that posed by the arts lobby, who saw 'great works', either by lesbian and gay writers or concerning lesbian and gay issues, as being under threat from this legislation.[2] This argument carried the implication that lesbianism and homosexuality were to be understood differently in this context: they necessitated a response in keeping with their status as art, rather than in relation to their sexual/political status. Concerning Rushdie, the arguments were similar: the novel may be offensive to Islam, but this was no justification for trying to stop the mouth of an artist, who should be allowed to function free from outside political or religious constraints. In both instances, then, the issue of 'art' was seen to be paramount: a text's status as art should protect it from the crudities of political critique. As became the case with *Oranges*, the concerns of art were to take precedence over values and beliefs that might hold sway in other contexts. Thus *Oranges* was read in a cultural context where high-cultural 'art' had been established as having a meaning separable from questions of politics, sexual or otherwise.

Significant, too, in relation to Rushdie and to *Oranges* is the way that religious fundamentalism was represented in the media: not only was freedom of speech being threatened, but it was being threatened by religious extremists, who were characterised as repressive, violent and alien to the traditions of their 'host' country.[3] Although this related specifically to the Muslim faith, it fed into and fortified a pre-existing climate of opinion regarding so-called fundamentalism fuelled by news stories from the USA exposing financial corruption and sexual intrigues within the ranks of high-profile evangelical groups. 'Fundamentalism', then, came to be characterised as being, on the one hand, a violent threat (viz. Rushdie) and, on the other, an object for our superior laughter, as its essential hypocrisy was exposed (viz. US groups). Both these elements can be seen to have played their part in the TV representation and media reception of the evangelical group so central to Jess's childhood in *Oranges*.

In addition to these historically very specific phenomena was the question of the status of *Oranges* as a 'quality' television drama – an example of 'art television'.[4] Mandy Merck has argued that there is a particular relationship between art cinema and the representation of lesbianism;[5] and this argument offers an important perspective on the critics' reception of the lesbianism in *Oranges*. Merck aphoristically suggests that 'if lesbianism hadn't existed, art cinema might have invented it' (p. 166): by this, she means that the representation of lesbianism in art cinema is sufficiently 'different' from dominant (more popular) cinematic representations of sex and sexuality to be seen as courageous and challenging, and yet, in fact, it simply offers more of the same: that is, it works with the familiar equation: 'women = sexuality'. (p. 166) Merck concludes that 'it is the legitimisation of the female spectacle which makes lesbianism such a gift to art cinema'. (p. 173) Thus what is at stake is not only *what* is represented, but *where* it is represented: the underlying equation of women with sexuality may be the same in all kinds of representation, but none the less lesbianism is read as 'meaning' something different in art cinema from in other contexts; similarly, it was read as meaning something different in 'art television' than it would have done elsewhere in television.

Oranges was read in a tradition of other 'quality' dramas that had occupied the Wednesday night 'controversy' slot',[6] the controversy being seen to arise primarily from the explicit representation of sex in these previous productions. Certain of these acted as sexual reference points for *Oranges*:

> A lesbian love scene between two adolescent girls on BBC2 next week could mark a new stage in the passage of television from the kitchen sink to the boudoir.
>
> This new challenge to viewers comes after the explicit straight sex of David Lodge's *Nice Work* and Dennis Potter's *Blackeyes*.[7]

The representation of sex in *Oranges*, then, was seen as an advance on the work of Potter and Lodge because it shows lesbian rather than 'straight sex', which of necessity represents something more challenging, risky and 'adult'. This seems to confirm that for 'art television', as for art cinema, there is a strong association with and expectation of 'adult' and 'realistic' representations of sex. The scheduling of *Oranges* in the 'controversy slot', with its dual associations of sex and high quality, then, was of significance for its reception. The representation of sex here could be seen as risky and challenging, rather than merely titillating; its 'quality' acted as a guard against 'those dreary public outbursts of British prudishness'.[8] Together, these two elements contributed to the production of a context in which lesbianism could be read as something positive.

A second possible reason for the acceptability of the lesbianism in *Oranges* follows from Merck's claim that another of the features of art cinema is that it 'characteristically solicits essential humanist readings' (p. 170); it has some kind of universal human relevance with which we can all identify. In relation to *Oranges*, then, this would imply that the adaptation's success rested on the critics' ability to read it as being essentially about something other than its lesbianism. If this is the case, it is working against Winterson's own assertion that her text was framed as a challenge:

> I know that *Oranges* challenges the virtues of the home, the power of the church and the supposed normality of heterosexuality. I was always clear that it would do. I would rather not have embarked on the project than see it toned down in any way. That all this should be the case and that it should still have been so overwhelmingly well received cheers me up.[9]

Did the critics, in the mainstream press at least, pick up the gauntlet that she had thrown down, or did they read around this challenge, read it, as Merck suggests, as having above all else an allegorical, essentially humanist, meaning?

Overwhelmingly, the latter seems to have been the case: the lesbianism is decentred and the critics present us with a drama 'about' all sorts of other things. The three-part series, we are told, 'is fundamentally about a young person looking for love';[10] it is 'a wonderfully witty, bitter-sweet celebration of the miracle that more children do not murder their parents';[11] it 'follows Jess in a voyage of self-discovery from her intense religious background, via a friendship with another girl';[12] it is 'a vengeful satire on Protestant fundamentalism'.[13] Most critics find the universality that they perceive, the opportunity to sympathise with the heroine despite her peculiar circumstances, to be in the programme's favour. *Time Out* (18 January 1990), it is true, complains about 'the author's own use of that hoary liberal cop-out about *Oranges* being about "two people in love" – who wants to see that tedious story again?' Most, however, welcome the opportunity to read *Oranges* as essentially about all (or other) human relationships, rather than about the specificities of lesbian ones.

The decentring of the lesbianism, however, does not involve its denial: in most reviews it is mentioned, but nearly always in relation to something else, generally the ensuing rejection and exorcism of Jess by members of the evangelical group. In this context, lesbianism is seen either as comic come-uppance for her mother's repressive childrearing methods – 'Warned off boys by this hell-fire freak, Jess turns instead to girls'[14] – or as a source of pathos: 'a bitter-sweet tragedy, the tale of how a young woman tries and fails to reconcile her religion with her lesbianism'.[15] Lesbianism, then, is always seen in relation to other issues, be they religion, the family, or simply 'growing up'.

However, as well as being read from a broadly humanist perspective, as a story about young love, there is another element of this decentring of lesbianism that is significant: the emphasis that is placed on the representation of religion. This is important not only as an example of this decentring, but also because, contrary to what most previewers predicted, it was this, rather than the representation of lesbianism, that became the focus for viewers' and reviewers' anger. So, as well as the evangelical group being seen as one of the main sources of the humour of the series, its members are written about as ridiculous ('prattling, eye-rolling, God-fearing women'[16]), and as potentially violent ('each and every one ... looked as though she could kill with a blow of her nose'[17]). Moreover, the Christian fundamentalism of *Oranges* is explicitly linked to Muslim fundamentalism, overwhelmingly associated with repression and violence in the press reviews: we are told that Jess is brought up 'in a provincial family whose fundamentalist religious beliefs make the Ayatollah Khomeini, by contrast, seem a model of polite tolerance'.[18] This association of the two fundamentalisms, Christian and Muslim, with repression, is further reinforced when *Television Today* (18 January 1990) expresses the hope that the 'small, if vocal, number of objectors' to the serial will not 'turn writer Jeannette Winterson into the nineties Salman Rushdie'.

Subject to the most anger, however, was the exorcism of Jess carried out by the pastor and assorted members of the congregation when Jess is found to have been having a sexual relationship with Melanie. Critics commented on the 'brutal' nature of this scene, noted that it is 'sexually-charged', and suggested that:

> if anybody was disturbed by the scene in which the pastor – armed with rope, gag and pulsating neck – straddled the young Jess to exorcise the demon of illicit love, then so they should have been.[19]

Hilary Kingsley in the *Mirror* (15 January 1990) concurred: the headline announced that the scene was 'Brutal, Shocking, Horrifying. But You Mustn't Miss It'. Anger and disgust are not only legitimate – they are to be actively sought as the 'correct' response; thus emotions that many expected to be directed towards the lesbian scenes are actually located instead with the representation of this repressive religious group. Perhaps it was possible for so much sympathy to be shown to the plight of Jess and Melanie not only because of the way their relationship was interpreted, but also because we witness – and abhor – the punishment that they undergo. Their persecutors have already been established as outmoded, repressive and anti-sex, and it is a small step to add violence to this list. This, indeed, is facilitated by the pre-existing links between fundamentalism and violence that I have outlined above. Christopher Dunkley writes:

> Jess ... is promptly subjected by her mother's fundamentalist sect to the sort of persecution and torture so dear to the hearts of religious fanatics throughout the ages.[20]

Here he clearly suggests that the punishment tells us more about religious fundamentalists than it does about the status of lesbianism in our society. The liberal viewer, then, can feel distanced from the punishment meted out to Jess because these people are not 'normal' members of our society. This sympathy, then, can be seen to rest on two mutually reinforcing bases: first, it is a response to the punitive, anti-sex attitudes of the evangelical group – and even gay and lesbian sexual rights have increasingly become the objects of liberal championing since the passing of Section 28; and secondly, it is responding to the representation of fundamentalism, which has become so prominent a liberal target in the wake of the Rushdie affair. Thus, it appears that the yoking of the lesbianism with the fundamentalism was itself crucial for the favourable mainstream liberal response: lesbianism became an 'otherness' preferable to the unacceptable otherness of fundamentalism.

Notes

1. The full version of this article [was] published in 1992 in a collection of lesbian literary criticism edited by Sally Munt, *Being there: new lesbian criticism* (Harvester Wheatsheaf).
2. See Jackie Stacey, 'Promoting Normality: Section 28 and the Regulation of Sexuality', in Sarah Franklin, Celia Lury and Jackie Stacey, eds., *Off centre: feminism and cultural studies* (London, Harper Collins Academic, 1991).
3. This article was written before the Gulf War; since then these associations have developed and intensified. See Kevin Robbins, 'The mirror of unreason', *Marxism Today*, March 1991, pp. 42–4.
4. 'Art television' remains a tentative concept within critical work; see John Caughie, 'Rhetoric, Pleasure and "Art Television" – Dreams of Leaving', *Screen* 22, no. 4, pp. 9–31. On 'quality' television, see Paul Kerr, 'Classic Serials – To Be Continued', *Screen* 23, no. 1, pp. 6–19, and Charlotte Brunsdon, 'Problems with Quality', *Screen* 31, no. 1, pp. 67–90.
5. Mandy Merck, '*Lianna* and the Lesbians of Art Cinema', in Charlotte Brunsdon, ed., *Films for Women* (London, BFI Publishing, 1986), pp. 166–75.
6. For example, David Lodge's *Nice Work* and Dennis Potter's *Blackeyes*.
7. *The Sunday Times*, 7 January 1990.
8. *Birmingham Post*, 18 January 1990.
9. Jeanette Winterson, *Oranges Are Not The Only Fruit – The Script* (London, Pandora, 1990), p. xvii.
10. *Today*, 10 January 1990.
11. *The Observer*, 14 January 1990.
12. *Todmorden News*, 18 August 1989.
13. *The Listener*, 18 January 1990.
14. *The Financial Times*, 10 January 1990.
15. Uncredited review 4, 11 January 1990.
16. *Daily Express*, 11 January, 1990.
17. *The Times*, 11 January, 1990.
18. *Evening Standard*, 22 January 1990.
19. *The Sunday Times*, 21 January, 1990.
20. *The Financial Times*, 10 January, 1990.

23

When a woman reads the news

Patricia Holland

From H. Baehr and G. Dyer (eds.), *Boxed in: women and television* (Pandora 1987)

[...] The newsreaders' confidence derives partly from the fact that the way they look is less important than what they have to say. The image is subordinate to the speech. For men this is something we take for granted – it is only to be expected – but for women it is an unfamiliar situation. [...] Women's right to speak in public may easily be subverted by drawing attention to their visual appearance. The authoritative male newsreader is a well established presence on the screen. The image of a man, head and shoulders, in formal jacket and tie, is familiar across the media as a sign of assurance and power. It is used to introduce the company report, it appears on the business pages of the quality press, it presents politicians and statesmen. Characteristically it shows a middle-aged man of worldly experience and dignified presence, the lines on his face and his serious expression indicating the respect he commands. But it is an image which contains a problem. By refusing any hint of visual pleasure or sensuality, it attempts to deny its own image-presence. It suggests that this pictured man is not simply framed here to be looked at. His steady gaze, direct at the camera, appears to assert that he is the one doing the looking. He is the controller rather than the controlled, the active subject rather than the passive object. In its rigid formality his physical presence refuses to draw attention to itself, attempts to slide into invisibility. We take it for granted that, like the newsreader, what he has to say is more important than the way he looks. This paradoxical convention for men is in striking contrast to the familiar conventions for women, which contain a different set of problems and inconsistencies. We expect images of women to stress not head and shoulders, but faces and bodies. Women's faces, when they appear, are not normally poised for looking or for speech, but are painted, decorated, presented for beauty and the pleasure of the viewer (Berger, 1972). Laura Mulvey, and together with her a whole school of feminist critics, have argued that the very construction of sexual difference through the Oedipus and castration complexes makes women the objects of male scrutiny, their visual presence itself a symbol of sexuality standing in for male fears and losses (Mulvey, 1975 and 1984; Cook and Johnston, 1974; Cowie, 1978). Images of women are not images of *women* at all but images of men's impossible desires, of their fears for the full masculinity they can never achieve. The most striking examples of such fetishised imagery are among the most familiar ways in which women are shown as pin-ups, as the fragmented bodies of hundreds of advertisements, as the polished and streamlined limbs linked to the imagery of sado-masochism popularised in the work of Allen Jones (Mulvey, 1973). If this argument is accepted, it is not surprising that women have rarely been presented as Alastair Burnett, Robin Day and Leonard Parkin have long been seen, controlling and competent, grey-haired and unruffled.

On television the visual presentation of a head and shoulders image is always inadequate by itself. Something is missing; the image must be completed. In the case of a man it is unproblematically completed by what he has to say. In the case of a woman the commentators point to an absence of a different sort. For them what is missing is the woman's body. [. . .]

Women's speech, too, is beset by difficult problems, problems which, like those around the imagery of women, are linked to the very construction of femininity itself. Traditionally, women's speech has been downgraded as mere gossip or babble (Spender, 1980). Some feminists want to reject this devaluation and lay claim to the 'neutral' language now appropriated by men. Others have embraced and celebrated a special 'women's language', a language that is more expressive and fluid, which is said to have sprung from a stage of development that was more creative, before the laying down of conventions and prohibitions (Daly, 1979). Yet the image of the woman newsreader has difficulty with both these options. Like the image of the man it claims to be completed not by [the body] but by speech – a speech which is forbidden to be specifically feminine and must be taken seriously in the public world of the news. The tension between an image which may not forget its femininity and a speech which may not embrace the feminine is central to the challenge posed by women newsreaders.

The spaces on television that we describe as 'the news' must be understood both in continuity with and in opposition to the rest of the daily output. The audience is expected to understand and respond to 'news' in a way that is different from, say, sitcom, chat shows, or even its close relation 'current affairs' (Schlesinger, *et al.* 1983). One of the most striking characteristics of the news remains its dramatic under-representation of women. This absence – amounting, in the words of Gaye Tuchman, to a 'symbolic annihilation' – has been pointed out with increasing impatience by feminists in this country and elsewhere over the past fifteen years (Butcher *et al.*, 1974; Tuchman *et al.*, 1978; Eddings, 1980; Jensen, 1982). In news bulletins women still appear on the screen in smaller numbers and more limited roles than men, while opportunities for them to speak are even more restricted. A glance at almost any randomly selected news programme will confirm that women tend to be seen in the background rather than as the main subjects of a news item. They are passing in the street, shopping, working in a canteen or hospital. Certain well-known women, like Princess Diana and other Royals, actresses and performers, make regular non-speaking appearances as part of the public spectacle, but women rarely appear in their own right as actors in those fields which are the central concern of the news and they are rarely selected as experts to comment on or interpret the news. When they are invited to speak it tends to be either as an anonymous example of uninformed public opinion, as housewife, consumer, neighbour, or as mother, sister, wife of the man in the news, or as victim – of crime, disaster, political policy. Thus not only do they speak less frequently, but they tend to speak as passive reactors and witnesses to public events rather than as participants in those events (compare Goulden *et al.*, 1982, p. 81). The use of women as regular newsreaders and to a lesser extent as reporters, has made a dramatic difference to the gender balance of news programmes.

The expulsion of women from the news can only be fully understood when it is seen in the context of the whole of the television output. John Ellis has argued that the television flow is typically divided not into programmes, but into 'segments' of around two to five minutes in length – an advertisement, a news item, a single scene in a soap opera (Ellis, 1982). Faced with this irregular sequence, members of the audience do not turn on for discrete uninterrupted cultural events as in the cinema or theatre, but they compose their viewing from fragments, dropping in and out, catching the end of one programme or the opening titles of another, perhaps turning their backs or watching with only half their attention. Recent studies of the television audience have shown that it is actually made up of many audiences, each reacting differently to different parts of the programme output. Women and men, in particular, tend to have radically different tastes. Thus the experience of watching together becomes itself a re-enactment of the relations of power between them. The man of the house tends to be in charge of the programme selector. It is left to the woman to react to the imposition of programmes she dislikes by leaving the room, busying herself with other tasks or mentally switching off ([. . .] Collett, 1986; Morley, 1986). When we look at the way women are represented in the news it is not surprising that this is one area of television that women in the audience feel is not for them; they pay little attention to it even though it is frequently on in their presence.

However, the news is only part of a stream of material. It flows inexorably out of and in to the quiz shows, the sports reports, the American cops series that surround it and the advertisements which, on ITV, interrupt it. This is the mass of material from which the disparate audiences can select their imagery and construct their impressions. The reduced visibility of women in the news is more emphatic, carries more significance, precisely because of its routine juxtaposition with their heightened visibility in the rest of the output. Those qualities that are absent from the news are inescapably present elsewhere. When we watch the serious face of the newsreader we are reminded that women's faces on television normally display emotion (in soaps, feature films, dramas), that women's bodies are part of the spectacle of television (in the ads, in game shows, as entertainers), that women are characteristically placed in a domestic setting (in sitcoms, family dramas) and that their sexuality is never forgotten. Standing in sharp opposition to the rest of this output the news is presented as a space where emotion is inappropriate, where domestic issues are defined as private and as subordinate to public conflict and the world of hard politics, and where women's sexuality is trivialising and a distraction.

[...] This area of seriousness and responsibility excludes women in its own way. Women are vastly outnumbered by men in positions of social and political power, by those whose views are most likely to be reported on or whose opinions sought. They include prominent politicians, police chiefs, union leaders, judges and bishops. Stuart Hall and his colleagues describe them as 'primary definers' of the issues of the day (Hall *et al.*, 1978). They are individuals who are likely to have built up relationships with those who make the news through both formal and informal channels. Women are not prominent among them. Women are expelled from the imagery of the news just as they are expelled from those areas of public life from which the news is derived.

Here I must add the reminder that I am discussing the main national news programmes and not the local and regional programmes. Local news deals in a completely different range of topics and imagery and includes many items on social problems and everyday life. Indeed, where the national news discusses policy and interviews policymakers, the local news of necessity looks at the effects of policies and speaks to those who must carry them out and those who suffer them, often predominantly women.

In the national news, the area where women now play an increasingly visible part is that of presentation – as reporters who speak over and appear in the actuality footage and as newsreaders in the studio. It is in the studio, where they have become part of the narrative continuity of the news, that their presence has made the most noticeable change. Is there some quality expected of newsreaders which, despite the apparent contradictions, is turning this into a suitable role for women to play? The readers sit between the audience and the news, not quite belonging to either, but offering themselves as a point of identification through which the news can be understood. They mediate between the audience and the rawness of the actuality items, distancing viewers from potential involvement, placing them as willing observers, as people who are eager to be informed but never to be involved, as witnesses rather than participants in the reported events. [. . .]

[...] Women have become established as newsreaders, but they have not moved alongside men in the same way as those prestigious professional broadcasters, like Robin Day or David Dimbleby, whose popular presence is balanced by the political respect they command. Instead they are caught within the conflicting definitions of femininity and of 'the news' – themselves trivialised, they can be blamed for trivialising. Women represent the antithesis of news values. They are the very sign of dissent and disruption. Yet the job of the newsreader is to smooth over dissent, to provide the studio calm which receives and moderates the chaos from outside. Women newsreaders are called on to speak from a carefully constructed position, with the mythical neutrality of the universal voice, and yet, as women, they are defined as outside both the political consensus and the masculine structure of language. They cannot escape their femininity, yet the possibility of making a contribution that is specifically on behalf of women is ruled out. They may not speak as women or for women. Women newsreaders must search for a visual style that stresses their femininity yet defers to the seriousness of the news, that complements that of the man, yet takes care not to impinge on the male preserve. Hair that has not been 'done', lack of make-up, the less studied appearance associated with feminism, must be avoided. They must embrace the 'post-feminist' worked-on appearance of the young businesswoman of the 1980s, a style made current in advertisements and magazines directed at women executives. Their self-presentation must stress a rigid and unbridgeable *difference* between men and women, while distracting from the continuing process of *differentiation*.

However, it is not an eternal and unchangeable difference but the process of differentiation itself which works to secure and re-secure the relations of domination and subordination between men and women. It is a process which is flexible, able to change its ground, to adapt to circumstances, to re-establish new forms of relations of power. The invitation to speak with the voice of authority may be nothing but an invitation, yet again, to be a decorative performer. Women have become accustomed to being asked to identify with men and to express themselves through men. Any attempt to speak with a universal voice within a system grounded in deep divisions of domination and subordination is doomed to failure. The question may not be, 'Can women speak from this position?' but 'Do they want to?' The feminine position in which we have been placed is surely one we would wish to recover and make use of rather than to deny. If the cost of being offered a public voice involves giving up the right to speak specifically as a woman, is it a price worth paying? Should we not argue that the voice of those who are subordinated can reach for an expression of truth to experience that is denied to an authority grounded in domination? Theirs is 'the sound mind whose soundness is what ails it' (Adorno, 1973).

The appearance of women newsreaders is not necessarily a step towards women's liberation. In the contemporary style of news presentation where the reader may be recognised as a front, a mask, a performer, a transmitter rather than an originator of news, it is not difficult to imagine news reading becoming a 'women's job'. After all women are easy on the eye, speak clearly and still add that element of spice that the press found so exciting in Anna, Angela and the rest. If we are not watchful we will find that once more, with the infinite flexibility of effortless power, women will have been put in their place yet again.

References

ADORNO, T. 1973: *Negative dialectics* (trans. E.B. Ashton). London: Routledge & Kegan Paul.

BERGER, J. 1972: *Ways of seeing*. Harmondsworth: Penguin.

BUTCHER, H. *et al.* 1974: *Images of women in the media*. Duplicated paper. Birmingham: Centre for Contemporary Cultural Studies.

COLLETT, P. 1986: Watching the TV audience. Paper presented to the International Television Studies Conference, London.

COOK, P. and JOHNSTON, C. 1974: The place of women in the cinema of Raoul Walsh. In P. Hardy (ed.), *Raoul Walsh*. Edinburgh: Edinburgh Film Festival.

COWIE, E. 1978: Women as sign. In *M/F*, no. 1.

DALY, M. 1979: *Gyn-ecology*. Boston: Beacon Press.

EDDINGS, B.M. 1980: Women in broadcasting (US) de jure, de facto. In H. Baehr (ed.): *Women and media*. Oxford: Pergamon Press.

ELLIS, J. 1982: *Visible fictions*. London: Routledge & Kegan Paul.

GOULDEN, H. *et al.* 1982: Consciousness razing. In S. Blanchard and D. Morley (eds): *What's this channel fo(u)r? An Alternative Report*. London: Comedia.

HALL, S. *et al.* 1978: *Policing the Crisis*. London: Macmillan.

JENSEN, E. 1982: Television newscasts in a womans perspective. Typescript from the E. Jensen and M. Kleberg report *Kvinders rolle i TV-nyheder og underholdning-sprogrammer*. Stockholm: Nord-publikation.

MORLEY, D. 1986: Family television: cultural power and domestic leisure. Paper presented to International Television Studies Conference, London.

MULVEY, L. 1973: You don't know what is happening, do you, Mr Jones? *Spare Rib*, no. 8.

MULVEY, L. 1975: Visual pleasure and narrative cinema. *Screen*, vol. 16, no. 3.

MULVEY, L. 1984: The image and desire. In L. Appignanesi (ed.): *Desire*, London: ICA.

SCHLESINGER, P. *et al.* 1983: *Television Terrorism*. London: Comedia.

SPENDER, D. 1980: *Manmade language*. London: Routledge & Kegan Paul.

TUCHMAN, G. *et al.* 1978: *Hearth and Home*. New York: Oxford University Press.

24

Women on the air: community radio as a tool for feminist messages

Birgitte Jallov

From Jankowski, Prehn and Stappers, *The people's voice: local radio and television in Europe*, Academic Research Monograph 6 (John Libbey 1992)

One of the basic aims of the new feminist movements in Western Europe is to encourage the visibility of women. In the course of the past decades women have come to take a more dominant role on 'public stages', in cultural, political and artistic life. And, as part of this struggle, feminist groups in several European countries became forerunners in the development of 'free radio'. Women began making use of radio broadcasting as yet another avenue for involvement in the public sphere.[1]

Radio Donna in Rome, *Les Nanas Radioteuses* in Paris and *Radio Pleine Lune* in Ferney-Voltaire in France along the Swiss border, were some of the groups which began experimenting with local radio, often as pirates, since the mid-1970s. Radio programmes were made on a variety of issues seldom considered in conventional radio programming. Abortion, for example, then virtually a taboo topic, was raised by these female radio pirates.

During this period, in 1978, a group of British women formed *Women's Airwaves* a collective of women who produced radio programming and lobbied for community radio. After a time in which women were mainly involved in pirate radio stations – as in France, Belgium and Italy – a second phase of pirating began to develop simultaneously in several countries. In the Netherlands *Vrouwenradio* went on the air in 1981, and the lesbian collective in Barcelona, *Onda Verde*, began producing programming in 1982.

In the Scandinavian countries developments proceeded differently in that there was no strong grassroots movement pushing for community or free radio stations. Instead, government-initiated experiments with community radio were launched: in 1979 in Sweden, in 1982 in Norway and in 1983 in Denmark. In spite of this more regulated start of the community radio movement in these countries, many women's groups reacted positively to the opportunity and created or took part in stations.

Women's programming on national broadcasting companies

The national broadcasting companies in most West European countries tend to stress traditional notions of balance and impartiality in their programming, and the women's programmes produced by these institutions reflect such conventions as well as the historical traditions and roles assigned to women in the respective countries. These programmes, in other words, have traditionally been directed towards the housewife and have dealt with topics such as homemaking, childcare, beauty and fashion. In most instances these programmes portray women in the roles of housewives and mothers, and as such cannot be considered serious efforts for strengthening women's own interpretations of and expectations in society.

In some places these traditional women's programmes have been transformed into programmes dealing with the lives of present-day women. The focus here is on the limitations and potential for conflict between traditional and new roles for women, rather than merely conservation of the status quo. Such programmes have been produced, for example, in Berlin, where *Frauenfunk* ('Women's Radio') presently broadcasts for two hours a day, five days a week, on *Sender Freies Berlin*. This programme receives among the highest audience ratings for programming on the station.

In spite of a few excellent examples demonstrating the transformation of women's programmes produced by national broadcasting companies, women in the new feminist movement knew all too well how easily progressive voices can be muted in such settings, how effective self-censorship takes hold, and how little possibility there is in actuality to attain a position of significant influence and role in decision making. For a time such initiatives may be tolerated, but after a while the (often male) editors believe that women's concerns have been adequately covered and that it is time to consider another theme or topic. Such a mind-set is difficult to combine with a more radical feminist perspective. At *Frauenfunk* this difficulty has been the source of frequent attempts to modify or eliminate the programming, and only strong listener support for *Frauenfunk* programming has prevented its demise.

Recognizing that there was little chance to rapidly transform attitudes within and accessibility to the national broadcasting companies, some European feminists decided to develop their own communication channels. The 'free' radio stations, either in an illegal pirate environment or in a state regulated experimental setting, provided opportunity for addressing the issues and concerns of feminists.

Most of the women's radio stations surfacing in Europe in this period, generally the early 1980s, were collectives which produced programming during scheduled time slots on community or movement oriented radio stations. The autonomy of these collectives and the possibility of producing and airing regularly scheduled programmes were major attractions of these stations for feminists. The geographical restrictions of low-power transmitters used by the stations were considered less important than the above mentioned advantages. Community radio stations have mainly been of interest by feminists to reach their own community-of-interest, members of the wider feminist movement. The ideal and sometimes intended audience, however, was all women, independent of their position on feminist issues.

The awareness and spirit of these groups is reflected in the names given to the programming initiatives. And, whether a women's group might have its own radio station, be an autonomous collective within a station serving many groups, or be a collective among other collectives in operating the station, they would refer to the enterprise as 'their station', 'the women's radio' or 'the collective' indiscriminately. These labels all describe the same phenomenon: a collective of women producing regularly scheduled radio programmes broadcast on a community oriented station.

Based on the assumption that senders and receivers have the same interests and concerns due to their common background, feminists have considered community radio a tool for organising the experiences and needs of the movement. As such, radio has been seen as a valuable channel for consciousness raising among both producers and listeners.

One of the top priorities of women's radio stations has been to increase the visibility of women and of women's experiences through use of the medium. Realizing women generally are not free to make crucial decisions in their lives, the women working in the stations attempt to organize the experiences of individual women into a collective unit of experience. By letting women speak for themselves, the individual experiences are transformed into a collective understanding of their life situation. Such understanding can contribute to further choice and action.

Rooted in the women's movement with a tradition of attaching equal value to tasks performed, hierarchical structures are seldom implemented. Managerial, journalistic and technical tasks are shared by all members of the collective. In some cases the technical quality of the programming has suffered, but this aspect is generally considered secondary to the opportunities created for self-expression and self-realization of the women involved.

In addition to this shared theoretical framework, there are differences among the women's radio stations. Some of the differences are a consequence of regional and national variations, but there are also differences based on the structure of the particular stations. These differences are illustrated in the examples below found in stations in France, Holland, Great Britain, Norway and Denmark.

Paris: Les Nanas Radioteuses

Originally part of the unregulated 'free' pirate French community radio stations, *les Nanas* and *les Radioteuses* joined forces in 1981 to become the major women's station in Paris. The following year it was granted an official broadcasting license by the government. A voice of the women's movement in Paris, *Les Nanas Radioteuses* moved from a women's center after theft of the studio equipment and shared premises with a grassroots station, *Canaille FM*. The women's group made use of the studio and other facilities, but maintained autonomy regarding programming policy and content.

A central objective of this station was to create a women's information channel and a forum for pluralistic, feminist discourse. They attempted to attain this objective by involving women from all walks of life in the programming. One programme was produced weekly. This programme, lasting six hours, was composed of items devoted to specific topics. There were items on employment, female chanson traditions, news from the women's movement, and portraits of known and unknown women. There were special programmes on women's culture and informational programmes on a wide range of themes: abortion, housework, childcare, legal matters and themes related to international solidarity among women.

Programme production was carried out by a core group of 10 women assisted by additional free-lancers. Production expenses were met through membership dues and self financing. The group was organized as a collective in which all members performed both the technical and journalist tasks. Programme planning and evaluation were also equally shared by group members.

Les Nanas Radioteuses was among the most productive of the women's community radio collectives in France. A change in legislation for community radio stations in the country, however, brought an end to this effort. *Canaille FM*, the station which had provided airtime to *Les Nanas Radioteuses*, decided to finance its own programming by selling airtime and cancelled the contract with the women's station. After a period of sporadic transmission on other frequencies, *Les Nanas Radioteuses* stopped production entirely in 1985.

Nijmegen: Vrouwenzender

While the Parisien feminists decided to abandon pirate radio activity and participate in the legalized community radio stations, Dutch feminists generally chose to avoid the legal stations and to instead maintain their own pirate stations. During the mid-1980s very few women were active in the 100-odd legal community radio stations then in operation [...]. This was in spite of special training courses and other initiatives undertaken to attract women to the stations.

On the pirate stations, however, Dutch women have been a prominent element since around 1980, emerging from the squatter movement then active in the country. Nijmegen, a university dominated city, has been one of the more active centres of this development.

In the period between 1981 and 1987 seven women's collectives took part in the programming schedule of *Rataplan*, a pirate station whose programmes reached most parts of the city. These collectives concentrated on several facets of the women's movement: radical feminism, lesbianism, working class women, young girls, and a more general group which focused on in-depth features on women's lives and culture. Of these collectives only the last one continued producing programming as part of *Rataplan* by the end of the decade.

Much earlier, in 1984, two of the women's collectives left *Rataplan* to form an all women's radio station called *Vrouwenzender* (see Wiersma, 1988). The basic idea of this station was to fill one of the gaps of traditional media coverage and provide news and informational programming about women. The programming included in-depth interviews with prominent women and attention to cultural and musical programming involving women. The station, as in many other places, was primarily funded by the producers themselves and occasional grants.

Vrouwenzender began transmitting in late 1986, producing around 5 hours of programming, aired one day each month. Later, the group attempted to produce a weekly programme, but in the course of the following year the collective was forced to close down. Economic problems and attrition among collective members proved too great for the initiative.

London: Women's Airwaves

British women, in contrast to French and Dutch feminists who chose the alternative of pirate broadcasting, decided to engage in political battle with the government in order to create a legal community radio alternative within the British broadcasting system. While engaged in this enterprise, the women involved also began training themselves and other women in the production of quality radio programmes.

Women's Airwaves was one of the collectives involved in these undertakings. The group originated during a feminist conference held in London in 1979. Its basic objective was to make the lives and perspectives of women more visible. The group felt it important to create a sphere of openness and confidence when approaching a new, technically oriented profession such as radio programming, and decided the best manner to achieve this was by restricting their activities to women only.

Because of the absence of legislation for community stations at that time, the collective chose to work on three fronts simultaneously: lobbying for new legislation, providing training in radio production, and producing audio cassettes which could be used by women's groups. The collective also wanted to develop more open and less hierarchical programming formats, such as modifying the conventional roles of interviewer and interviewee and letting, for example, the interviewee participate in the editing process after a taped discussion along with the interviewer.

Inasmuch as legislation for community radio stations was slow in coming, *Women's Airwaves* came to concentrate less on programming production and more on training activities. Demand for such training has been increasing, particularly among teachers and women advisors of youth clubs. The training activities are used to help young city girls formulate employment options and to consider other lifestyle alternatives than those offered by traditional role models.

Initially, *Women's Airwaves* was a large group composed entirely of volunteers. As the demand for training increased, the collective hired a full-time staff member and considered a second paid position. Additional forms of professionalism in the activities of the group were also implemented.

With no opportunity to broadcast programmes, then, *Women's Airwaves* was unable to achieve its primary goal: making women more visible through community radio But through the training activities, the collective has been able to achieve extensive contact with groups in and around London. It is unlikely that as many groups could have been trained had there also been demands on *Women's Airwaves* to produce regular radio programmes.

Oslo: RadiOrakel

RadiOrakel began broadcasting in 1982 from studios situated in a women's cultural centre in Oslo. From the beginning *RadiOrakel* was distinct from most other women's radio collectives in Europe. They considered themselves less a movement radio station than one in competition with other stations for listeners. Committed to reflecting women's lives and activities, the choice of this station was to produce high quality professional programming. In this manner *RadiOrakel* hoped to attract listeners as well as provide information and awareness regarding women's issues.

During the mid-1980s *RadiOrakel* was the fifth most popular radio station in Oslo; the other four stations were all economically secure music oriented stations. The original seven hours of programming per week was increased to 26 hours per week by 1988.

RadiOrakel was at that time the only known women's radio station in Europe which allowed men to participate in station activities. The number, however, was limited to no more than a third of the entire group. Initially, there were five men and 80 women. Five years later, in 1987, the ratio was 8 men and 27 women.

RadiOrakel is financed through a diversity of sources: membership fees, listener donations, city subsidies, benefit concerts, studio rental fees, and sale of airtime to non-profit organizations. Indications were, should advertising become legalized for community radio stations, that *RadiOrakel* would expand its economic base through broadcast of selected commercials.

Although *RadiOrakel* considers its organizational structure non-hierarchical, some 'functional hierarchies' have been established in order to produce programming of high technical quality in an efficient manner. The programme editors plan and evaluate in closed weekly meetings; decisions are then passed on to the rest of the staff. Three positions – chief editor, station manager and one journalist – are salaried. In addition, a special governmentally funded unemployment scheme provides salaries for five technicians.

Training consists of 'learning by doing'. Experienced producers work together with new volunteers in order to maintain a high level of professionalism. In addition, production courses are established as needed and discussion evenings are organized with representatives from other media. These discussions are intended to help re-examine and renew perspectives within the collective.

Copenhagen: Kvindeboelgerne

In the early 1980s, about half of all community radio producers in the larger cities in Denmark were women, and women played a very active role in the government initiated experiment with community radio and television launched in 1983 [...]. A number of women's collectives were also formed and special women's programmes were launched in many places around the country.

One of the first of these initiatives to go on the air was *Kvindeboelgerne*, ('Woman Waves') in Copenhagen. *Kvindeboelgerne* is part of a Copenhagen grassroots radio station, *Sokkelund Radio*, the latter being an initiative of some 15 groups and organizations. Three of these were women's groups: 'The Redstockings' (part of the new feminist movement), 'The Lesbians' and 'Women over 40'. These three groups composed *Kvindeboelgerne* and one day a week was reserved on the station for women's programming, with a 1.5 hour-long broadcast each evening, a transmission repeated the following morning.

The original 25 women active in the station formed three groups responsible for the programming in alternating weeks. This created the time and space necessary for learning to use the equipment and for the volunteers, most of whom were new to radio production, to produce programmes. The collective was also organized with a horizontal organizational structure, with no editors or divisions between technical and journalistic positions. Since 1986 the number of women active in the station has decreased by about half, and some of the production groups have reduced their programming frequency.

The intention of *Kvindeboelgerne* was to reflect the lives and concerns of different groups of women in the Copenhagen area. During the first two years of programming about two-thirds of the programming concentrated on activities in and around the feminist movement: actions, cultural manifestations, women's role in society, women's politics, and health issues. Whether the group's objective was achieved with these programmes is uncertain. The volunteer producers, affiliated with the women's movement, produced meaningful programmes about issues that interested them. Whether these programmes reached a wider audience, however, is uncertain.

Part of the ideology of most of the women's collectives was to develop an open, horizontal organizational structure which would reflect the ideas and concerns of the active participants at any given time. One of the few rules of *Les Nanas Radioteuses* was, that only the women currently active in the radio collective could have a say in the planning and evaluation sessions. This notion was also practiced in most other collectives. This means, that the amount of enthusiasm and energy in the group of producers at any given moment in time would determine expansion or termination of a particular programme.

This organizational structure of women's radio groups stems from the history and ideas of the feminist movement, with all its strengths and weaknesses. The feminists in the collectives did not intend to create institutions which would last any longer than needed. Involvement in a radio station was, for them, not for the sake of the radio, but for creation of a communication channel able to convey messages important to women in general. This conviction certainly holds for women's radio groups during the process of development and when they were active in broadcasting programming. But when a station is faced with closure, does this ideology remain intact? Would, for example, the French *Nanas Radioteuses* or the Dutch *Vrouwenzender* stations have wanted to cease programming if they had not been forced to do so by circumstances?

The silence and invisibility of women within society – the eradication of which was the motivating force behind women becoming involved in community radio – are not aspects which can be changed overnight. When overt physical repression or severe financial problems are present, along with the continuous threat of attrition caused by personnel burn-out, it may be relevant to question the suitability of the organizational structure chosen. It is not at all clear whether a non-authoritarian structure is the best organizational form for confronting and changing imbalances and injustices in the society at large.

In an institutional setting very different from that of community radio, *Frauenfunk* in Berlin has for a number of years been producing two hours of women's radio on a daily basis as part of the state sponsored *Sender Freies Berlin*. The staff is paid, the technical quality of the equipment is high, and the programme has many listeners. Still, the women involved in *Frauenfunk* talk about forms of self-censorship which occur, where topics and programming angles are chosen which they feel will not jeopardize the other activities of *Frauenfunk*.

In choosing community radio as a medium for expression, European feminists found what they were initially looking for: autonomy and the absence of censorship. This was a choice taken, knowing there was little opportunity for creating a suitable platform within the established media, at least in the short run. In the present situation, however, none of the available choices seems to adequately provide a communication medium able to satisfy both the objective and subjective needs of listeners. Whether community radio, by providing opportunity for working in the margins of the media, has contributed towards increasing the visibility of women, or whether real changes can only be brought about by securing space in the established media is uncertain. What has emerged from these experiences, however, is that women need and want structures which can more directly be used to address their concerns and within which they can operate more effectively than is now possible.

One of the women's radio stations discussed earlier, *RadiOrakel*, seems to contain important elements for solving some of the above problems. By combining elements from grassroots radio stations as well as from professional media traditions, this women's station seems to be able to combine the 'best of both worlds'. The formal structure is that of a community station: a 'free' radio station with no obligations towards 'balanced and impartial programming' and with no decision makers elsewhere in the organization who determine the fate of a particular programme. *RadiOrakel* is an independent station which shares a single frequency with other groups. The station is run in a collective spirit, but with aspects of a hierarchical structure: there are some paid staff members and there are editors responsible for certain programming areas. This structure ensures a stable daily routine. *RadiOrakel* is the only collective examined in this chapter which has during the past years been able to expand its transmission hours.

RadiOrakel is defined as a women's radio station, but has discarded one of the fundamental principles in the feminist movement: the importance of women working together without the influence of men. *RadiOrakel* women argue that they are perfectly able to work together in a respectful and productive atmosphere with the kind of men wanting to work inside a women's radio station. The editors are, incidently, women and the point-of-view taken on topics discussed is that of women.

In another area *RadiOrakel* deviates from the conventions of the women's radio movement. The original collectives were concerned about producing programming significant to the producers as well as the listeners, and where the process was as important as the final result. *RadiOrakel*, however, aspires to high professional standards, and wants to compete with popular disc jockey programmes in terms of content and of technical quality. A horizontal structure in which everyone may perform all tasks is not a feature of the *RadiOrakel* station.

In a sense, community radio has provided an ideal opportunity for women to get on the air and contribute women's voices and perspectives to public debate. Channels became available and, given the audience was local and initially interested in content rather than form, there was less difficulty for women without experience to begin producing programming.

In terms of programming content, however, most women's collectives have not been locally oriented. The programming themes could just as easily have been the basis of national radio programming. Realistically, though, the programmes produced on these themes would not have been broadcast by national stations. In this sense, then, community radio has very much been a tool, rather than an end in itself, for the women's collectives.

Movement radio can best be seen as reflections of activity and discussion in the movement and the society in which the station is based. These radio stations are the bearers of the original ideas of free community radio with open access and maximum participation for everyone in all areas of activity.

These 'carriers of messages' exist as long as there are messages, or until external pressures forces a collective to abandon operation. This type of radio station comes and goes as the need for communication arises.

The free and professionalised women's radio, as in the case of *RadiOrakel*, demonstrates a trend in the opposite direction. Here, a choice has been made to professionalise and compete with commercial radio stations for space on the airwaves. Although they continue to operate from within the women's movement, they do so with a professional approach and structure.

These different approaches to women's radio are well defined, each in its own world, following its own regularities. In this respect the developments and discussions within the women's radio movement are similar to those in the community radio movement generally. A central issue remains that of determining the proper balance between public access and democratization of the airwaves on the one hand, and the desire to reach a wider audience with women's programming on the other.

One approach to securing such balance can be found in strategies employed by American women active in community radio stations. The production of messages remains central; volunteers are involved in radio production, but with assistance from professional staff. Such an approach maintains the freedom of community media while complementing it with programming continuity and quality found on the more traditional and established media.

Visibility of women seems, in this manner, to be insured. What is uncertain is whether such a structure will permit radio programming, grounded in enthusiasm and desire to communicate significant societal messages, to survive. Removed from its movement basis, such radio activity may have nothing to serve as a tool. The challenge for women's radio groups today, then, is to maintain both affinity with that basis and to perfect the communicative tool at their disposal.

Note

1. This chapter is based on a comparative study of women's radio groups located around Europe (Jallov, 1983) and has been updated with personal correspondence and interviews with women involved. Documentation was also compiled during an international forum on women in community radio, held in Berlin in 1985. Additional resources include Baehr and Ryan (1984) and Gallagher's (1981) study of women and the media.

References

BAEHR, H. and RYAN, M. 1984: *Shut up and listen! Women and local radio; a view from the inside.* London: Comedia.
GALLAGHER, M. 1981: *Unequal opportunities: the case of women and the media.* Paris: UNESCO.
JALLOV, B. 1983: *Women on the air; women in (community) radio in Europe.* Roskilde, Denmark: Roskilde University Centre.
WIERSMA, A. 1988: *Dan liever de lucht in! Nijmeegse vrouwenradio's en hun feministiese ideologie.* Nijmegen: Institute of Mass Communication, University of Nijmegen.

25

Ideology, gender and popular radio: a discourse analytic approach

Rosalind Gill

From *Innovation* 6, 323–39 (1993)

Radio, as a medium, has been ignored by cultural and communication studies. Research has been dominated by analyses of the visual media – film, video and television – and to a lesser extent by a focus on newspapers and magazines. In contrast, radio has received hardly any attention, since the pioneering studies by Lazarsfeld and his co-workers in the 1940s (Lazarsfeld and Stanton, 1944). The impression given by many texts aimed at media studies students is that radio began a period of cultural demise in the 1950s, when it was replaced or superseded by television (e.g. Curran and Seaton, 1981). Indeed, in several state-of-the-art textbooks radio is not mentioned at all – or is referred to merely as an historical phenomenon. It is, as Paddy Scannell has argued 'the cinderella of media studies' (Scannell, 1988a).

This paper represents an attempt to take radio seriously. It is time – to stay with the Cinderella analogy – that radio went to the ball. If media studies truly reflected the use, pervasiveness and popularity of various media and programme types then there would be a wealth of research on radio, and especially on DJ programmes, for listening figures suggest that many people spend more time with radio than with any other medium (Karpf, 1980; Laurance, 1991). [...] Studying radio presents us with opportunities for developing new approaches to the study of the media more generally. Specifically, bringing radio onto the research agenda highlights the need for a thorough and principled approach to analysing *talk*. It is such an approach – discourse analysis – which I draw on in this paper.

[...] Developing from work in the sociology of scientific knowledge and social psychology, [discourse analysis] has now produced analyses in fields as diverse as gender studies, social policy, labour market analysis and media studies, and constitutes a theoretically coherent approach to the analysis of talk and texts. It has four central ideas. First, it takes *discourse itself* as its topic; that is, it is concerned with discourse in its own right – with its content and organization – rather than seeing it as a pathway to some underlying reality, whether psychological or material.

Second, it treats talk and texts as *constructive*. Rather than viewing language as a neutral transparent medium which simply reflects reality, discourse analysts are concerned with the way discourse is used to constitute or construct particular versions of reality. To say this is to highlight the fact that we deal with the world through discursive constructions or versions, and to draw attention to the key role which language plays in our understanding of the issues and events that make up everyday life.

Third, discourse analysis sees all discourse as *social practice*. That is, it sees all talk and texts as being oriented to action; people use discourse to perform social actions – to offer blame, to make excuses, to present themselves as wonderful human beings, etc. But discourse is not used only to perform interpersonal goals; it is also centrally implicated in accomplishing particular versions of events, issues or phenomena – which may have profound social and political implications.

This brings us to our fourth point: discourse analysis treats talk and texts as *organized rhetorically*. Unlike conversation analysis, discourse analysis sees social life as being characterized by conflict of various kinds. As such much discourse is involved in establishing one version of the world in the face of competing versions. This directs our attention to the ways in which all discourse is organized to make it persuasive. [...]

Case study: flexible sexism

The case study I want to discuss comes from an analysis of interviews with five male DJs and Programme Controllers PCs from two commercial radio stations in the UK. The interviews covered a variety of topics, including how the broadcasters saw their role and responsibilities, how much autonomy each felt he had, what he talked about on air and how he saw his listeners. Here, though, I will simply discuss the broadcasters' responses to a question about the lack of female DJs. This question is a highly pertinent one in the UK context, where male DJs dominate the airwaves, outnumbering female presenters by more than ten to one, and presenting almost all prime time shows (Gill, 1991b). The two stations surveyed were not atypical in this respect: one had one female presenter, whose phone-in show was broadcast between 23.00 hours and 01.00 hours; the other had no female DJs at all. I have discussed the analysis of this material at length elsewhere; the aim here is merely to indicate some of the potential of discourse analysis for examining this kind of material.

A traditional approach to investigating the lack of women DJs might take the form of an attitude survey of broadcasters, a questionnaire, or a series of structured interviews with those responsible for appointment decisions. What all these approaches have in common is the desire to pinpoint the definitive answer to the question of why there are so few female DJs. The assumption that there is one single answer would be built into the very design of the research (the questionnaire or the interview schedule), to be reinforced by the coding practices of the researcher. Thus a questionnaire may have different options for broadcasters to tick, suggesting why women are not employed, but if respondents tick more than one option then the researcher will have to make a decision as to how this should be coded. As such, most research becomes involved – in various ways – in the suppression of variability (Potter and Wetherell, 1987).

Discourse analysis, in contrast, takes variability seriously, as something interesting in its own right. Both the methods used for collecting data (in this case the informal interview) and the manner in which it is analysed facilitate this. Rather than trying to force broadcasters' responses into pre-constructed categories, what this research was interested in were the practical ideologies (Wetherell *et al.*, 1987) through which gender inequalities in the employment of DJs are understood. All the broadcasters were asked the same question – 'why do you think there are so few female DJs?' – which was followed up by probes specific to their response. What was found was that far from there being just one answer, DJs and PCs seemed to have available to them a *whole range* of ways of accounting for the lack of women in radio. The initial stage of analysis identified six different broad types of account, each organized around a different theme. These are set out below.

1. Women do not apply to become DJs.
2. Audience objections: listeners prefer male presenters.
3. Women lack the skills necessary for radio presentation.
4. Women interested in broadcasting become journalists rather than DJs.
5. Women's voices are not suited to radio presentation.
6. Male DJs are necessary to serve the predominantly female ('house-wife') audience.

It is important to note that these were not *alternative* accounts. In fact, each was drawn on by all or most of the broadcasters at different points in the interviews. They moved between different accounts in order to do different discursive work.

The aim of the research, however, was not simply to identify the different accounts selectively drawn on, but to examine how they were constructed and made persuasive. One of the major discursive problems or 'ideological dilemmas' (Billig *et al.*, 1988) facing the broadcasters was how to account for the lack of women DJs at their station whilst attending to the fact that they may be heard as sexist or blameworthy. This, of course, was particularly significant for the PCs who were responsible for the stations appointments. It seems likely that this dilemma was heightened by the fact that the interviews were conducted by a young, almost-certainly-feminist from the broadcasters' perspective woman. Had the interviewer been male, it may be that they would not have gone to such lengths to disclaim a sexist identity. There are several ways in which the broadcasters dealt with this dilemma.

Constructing the problem as lying in women themselves

One method involved constructing the reasons for women's non-employment as lying in women themselves. One of the most interesting features of the interviews is that for each of the broad explanations put forward to explain the lack of female DJs, broadcasters spontaneously offered further accounts, often constructed around little narratives, or stories. These can be understood as ways of *warranting* their explanations to make them more persuasive. One of the 'stories' put forward to warrant the claim that 'no women apply' to become DJs was organized around the idea that radio presentation is 'not something which women are interested in doing'. This claim serves to deny that there is any real or genuine motivation on women's part to become DJs. It would be interesting to discover how common this pattern of accounting is. I would suggest that the idea that subordinated groups do not 'really' want to change their position is one which is frequently drawn on by members of dominant groups in order to justify their action or inaction.

The assertion also serves to deflect charges of sexism from the radio stations concerned: it gives the impression that radio stations would be happy to take on female presenters, but are faced with a wall of disinterest from women themselves. The responsibility is placed firmly on women's shoulders. This style of argument is given a number of different inflections by various broadcasters. Another example is the following:

> DJ: 'I am sure there is a helluva lot of them out there that would be really good communicators but have never even given a thought of doing it. Maybe they are doing a job that either pays more money or is more interesting to them.'

This argument (resting upon an implicit view of society as characterized by social mobility) suggests that women could become DJs but have *chosen* to do other work. The salary and satisfaction of radio presentation are downgraded, and, in fact, women's putative non-application is made to appear eminently sensible when contrasted with the likelihood that they are doing better-paid or more interesting jobs. Again, this serves to undermine the idea that women really wish to become radio presenters.

Constructing particular versions of women

A second way in which broadcasters deal with the ideological dilemma raised earlier is by constructing particular versions of what it is to be a woman which make women's non-employment in radio seem natural and self-evident. One such construction is the idea (mentioned earlier) that women lack the skills and personalities necessary for radio presentation. Many broadcasters deployed this construction, suggesting that women lacked the 'technical abilities', the 'manual skills' and the 'communicative sensitivity' which good radio presenters require. The problem with this construction, however, is that it does not necessarily avoid the possibility that the broadcasters will be heard as sexist, as somehow blaming women. They oriented to this problem by *warranting* such versions of women with some kind of explanatory narrative which presented women as victims of forces beyond their and the radio stations' control. That is, the broadcasters provided *mitigations* for women's apparent failure to make the grade. One of the PCs, for example, invoked 'education and social process' as explanations, arguing that women had been disadvantaged from developing the skills necessary for radio presentation. He went on to elaborate about 'the background' and 'kinds of environments' in which boys and girls are raised. In offering mitigations for women's putative failure, these lay sociological explanations reduce the likelihood that the broadcaster will be heard as sexist. Paradoxically, however, they also serve to reinforce the 'outthereness', the appearance of factualness, of his characterization of women.

The versions of womanhood which the broadcasters employ in order to account for women's absence from radio do not have to be negative to function ideologically. In fact there are many examples of overwhelmingly positive sounding constructions of 'woman' which are nevertheless drawn upon to justify the radio stations' decision to appoint no (or just one) female DJs. A good illustration can be found in broadcasters' praise for female journalists. As we indicated earlier, the idea that women interested in broadcasting become journalists was one of the broad accounts put forward for the absence of women, drawn on by four out of five of the broadcasters.

> DJ: 'Now if you look at journalism for instance ... the past ... five journalists we have appointed have all been women. We have a woman news editor ... we have more women in the newsroom. Oh all the sales staff at the station are predominantly women and ... in those areas great strides have been made. Women are better than men at a journalist's job.'

The tone of this extract is overwhelmingly positive: 'the past five journalists we appointed have all been women'; 'great strides have been made'; 'women are better than men at a journalist's job'. Yet the wider interpretative context in which these claims are made concerns the station's non-employment of women as DJs. The extract above is part of a justification for this, and serves to defend the speaker against the potential charge of sex discrimination. By emphasizing the station's positive attitude towards the employment of women and its progressive stance in taking 'great strides' forward, the extract makes available the idea that if the radio station is not employing women as DJs it must be because women are either not up to it or are not interested in it. But it does this without making such a claim explicit.

Ironically, then, these positive sounding assertions about female journalists actually contribute to the justification for *not employing* women as DJs. It is worth noting that precisely the reverse argument was used in the 1970s against employing women as senior journalists and newsreaders. Broadcasters argued that women lacked the authority, gravity and seriousness necessary to such posts – the implication was that they would have been entirely suited to the more lighthearted, 'chatty' DJ programmes (Ross, 1977). This contrast highlights the flexibility of the cultural resources available for 'doing sexism', and the value of examining the broadcasters' arguments as practical ideologies, tuned to particular discursive goals, rather than as definitive expressions of their own personal beliefs or attitudes towards women.

It also underlines a very important point about ideology. It draws attention to the fact that ideology is best seen not as a set of propositions or a style of language, but as a form of accounting which cannot be identified *a priori*, but always emerges from analysis. It is perfectly possible to imagine claims about women's strengths as journalists being used to challenge the *status quo* of male dominance, but, as we have seen, it is also possible for the 'same' claims to be used to justify the exclusion of women from particular employment opportunities. The point is that the ideological force of the proposition does not come 'inscribed on its back' but derives from the way that it is used in a specific interpretative context.

Constructing the audience as responsible

A third way in which the broadcasters dealt with the particular discursive problem – and the final one to be discussed here – involved constructing the needs of the radio audience as directly responsible for the lack of women DJs. This style of accounting was used repeatedly by all the broadcasters interviewed.

> PC: 'Research has proven ... and this is not mine but it's echoed by many surveys throughout the years ... that people prefer to listen to a man's voice on the radio rather than a woman's voice. Women like to hear men on the radio because they're used to it ... and it's a bit strange to have a woman talking to you. And men like hearing men on the radio ... perhaps because they're just chauvinistic. Whatever the reasons research has borne out this fact you know that people like to have men on the radio ... and we just go along with the consensus of opinion. We do have women – Marie does an admirable job on the phone-in. We've got a lot of women newscasters so you know there's certainly no prejudice.'

The argument presented in this extract again serves to present radio stations as blameless in relation to female DJs. The PC claims that the radio station is simply serving its audience by giving listeners the presenters they want. The emphasis on 'research' and 'surveys' and what has been 'proven' does considerable work here in establishing the facticity of the PC's claims about the audience. The audience's preferences are presented as indisputable, 'out there' and are distanced from the PC's own beliefs. His own role, as someone responsible for the recruitment and appointment of staff to the station, in mediating between research findings and appointment policy is completely glossed over in his talk. The research findings which 'prove' that listeners prefer male presenters, and the lack of female DJs, are presented as linked together in a way which is totally independent of human action.

As I have argued elsewhere (Gill, 1993), this style of accounting has considerable similarities with what has become known as 'new racist' discourse (Barker, 1981; Reeves, 1983; Van Dijk, 1984; Billig, 1988). The most obvious similarity is in the disclaimer: 'there's certainly no prejudice' (preceding something which could easily be heard as such). In this extract it is reinforced by the contrasts which are established between women who demand male presenters from force of habit (plus the fact that 'it's a bit strange to have a woman talking to you!'), men who do so because they are 'chauvinist' and the radio station 'where there is certainly no prejudice'. A further similarity is found in the claim that 'we just go along with the consensus' where the PC presents himself as a mere victim of *other people*'s prejudice. Taken together, they suggest the importance of investigating a new or more flexible sexism.

Overall, then, the broadcasters had available to them a whole range of different ways of accounting for the lack of women DJs, which they drew on selectively during the interviews. The accounts constructed were flexible, inconsistent and sometimes contradictory. The claim by all the broadcasters that no women apply, within moments of explanations by those same men about why those who do apply are not suitable, is simply the most dramatic example of this. It would be overlooked or suppressed by more·traditional approaches which work with a simple realist view of language. Rather than seeing such assertions as statements of fact, discourse analysis argues that they are best understood in terms of their discursive functions.

By looking in detail at how accounts are organized, discourse analysis can show that they were oriented to a particular discursive problem or ideological dilemma: namely, how to account for the absence of women DJs without being heard as sexist. Here we examined three different ways in which this was done. Specifically, all the accounts put forward to explain the lack of female presenters constructed the reason as lying in women themselves or in the particular wants of the audience. The role of the radio station was made invisible, and discussions of employment practices and institutionalized sexism were conspicuous by their absence. In this way broadcasters were able to present themselves as non-sexist whilst they simultaneously justified the lack of women DJs at their radio stations. In sum, sexism and ideology more generally were shown to be far more flexible and dynamic than is usually imagined. [...]

References

BARKER, M. 1981: *The new racism*. London: Junction Books.

BILLIG, M. 1988: Methodology and scholarship in understanding ideological explanation. In Antaki, C. (ed.), *Analysing everyday explanation: a casebook of methods*. London: Sage.

CURRAN, J. and SEATON J. 1981: *Power without responsibility: the press and broadcasting in Britain*. London: Fontana.

GILL, R. 1991b: Jockeying for position. *The Guardian*, August 28th.

— 1993: Justifying injustice: Broadcasters' accounts of inequality in a radio station. In Burman, E. and Parker, I. (eds.), *Discourse analytic research: readings and repertoires of texts in action*. London: Routledge.

KARPF, A. 1980: Women and radio. *Women's Studies International Quarterly*, 3, pp. 41–54.

LAURANCE, B. 1991: Commercial radio struggles to get on advertisers' wavelength. *The Guardian*, 5 January.

LAZARSFELD, P. and STANTON, F. 1994: *Radio research 1942–3*. New York: Duelli Klein.

POTTER, J. and WETHERELL, M. 1987: *Discourse and social psychology: beyond attitudes and behaviour*. London: Sage.

REEVES, F. 1983: *British racial discourse*. Cambridge: Cambridge University Press.

ROSS, M. 1977: Radio. In Stott, M. and King, J. (eds.), *Is this your life? Images of women in the media*. London: Virago.

SCANNELL, P. 1988a: Review of 'Sounds Real: radio in everyday life' by Higgins, P. and Moss, C., *Media, culture and society*.

VAN DIJK, T. 1984: *Prejudice in discourse: an analysis of ethnic prejudices in cognition and conversation*. Amsterdam: John Benjamins.

WETHERELL, M., STIVEN, H. and POTTER, J. 1987: Unequal egalitarianism: a preliminary study of discourses concerning gender and employment opportunities. *British Journal of Social Psychology*, 26, pp. 59–67.

Index

Printed in the United States
46710LVS00005B/228